FAREWELL
TO TRAINS

FAREWELL TO TRAINS

A LIFETIME'S JOURNEY ALONG
BRITAIN'S CHANGING RAILWAYS

DAVID ST JOHN THOMAS

FRANCES LINCOLN LIMITED

PUBLISHERS

Farewell to Trains

Frances Lincoln Ltd
74–77 White Lion Street, London N1 9PF
www.franceslincoln.com

First Frances Lincoln edition 2013

ISBN: 978-0-7112-3407-9

Printed and bound in China

9 8 7 6 5 4 3 2 1

AUTHOR'S NOTE

This is a personal tribute to railways and how I have
enjoyed them (and made much of my living by writing
about them) in words and pictures. Although there are
some cross references, it is really two books in one: words
and pictures. The pictures are spread through the text, but
they are their own ingredient rather than 'illustrating' it.
In making my choices, I have selected what has special
appeal and meaning for me, so with a few exceptions (such
as Chapter 7 on my photographic railway gallery) text
and photographs run parallel with each other rather than
being connected.

PAGE 1 *The entrance through the Doric
Arch to Euston. This photograph was
taken in pre-motor days, but later my
taxi followed many others through
the arch. Though Euston station was
something of a muddle (at Christmas
carols were sung in the Great Hall,
from which finding something like
a train was a puzzle) it transpired
that, frustratingly, the arch could well
have been retained and that a great
London architectural feature had been
destroyed for 'fashion'.*

PAGE 2 *This painting by George Heiron
poses a question. On the flyover, a
Cunard boat special from Southampton
passes over the Atlantic Coast
Express. Soon the two tracks will run
into one, so which will be delayed: the
Southern's crack train, or the Cunarder
normally given high priority? We can
only guess.*

CONTENTS

THE RAILWAY TIMES.

OPENING of the SOUTHAMPTON and DORCHESTER RAILWAY.—The RAILWAY from SOUTHAMPTON to DORCHESTER, in connection with the London and South-Western, will be OPENED for PUBLIC TRAFFIC on TUESDAY next, the 1st of June, when the trains will run as follows :—

DOWN TRAINS.

Class.	Leave Nine Elms.	Arrive at Southampton.	Leave Southampton.	Arrive at Dorchester.
1st and 2nd ..	..	..	7.50 a.m.	11. 5 a.m.
1st, 2nd, & 3rd	7.30 a.m.	11.30 am	12.15 —	3.30 p.m.
1st and 2nd ..	9. 0 a.m.	12. noon		
1st and 2nd ..	11. 0 a.m.	1.50 pm	2.30 p.m.	5.30 p.m.
Express 1st and 2nd..	12.30 —	2.15 pm		
1st and 2nd, and 3rd c. between Southampton and Dorchester ..	3. 0 p.m.	5.50 p.m.	6. 0 p.m.	9.15 p.m.
Mail 1st & 2nd	8.50 p.m.	12.17 nt.	12.30 nt.	3.30 a.m.

ON SUNDAYS.

Class.	Leave Nine Elms.	Arrive at Southampton.	Leave Southampton.	Arrive at Dorchester.
1st and 2nd ..	..	..	7.50 a.m.	11.50 a.m.
1st, 2nd, & 3rd	7.30 a.m.	11.30 am	1.15 p.m.	4.30 p.m.
1st and 2nd ..	10. 0 a.m.	1. 0 pm	6. 0 p.m.	9.15 p.m.
1st, 2nd, & 3rd	..	..		
Mail 1st & 2nd	8.50 p.m.	12.17 nt.	12.30 nt.	3.30 p.m.

CHAPTER I
INTRODUCTION

THE QUESTION HAS OFTEN BEEN ASKED: what is so special about trains and railways? How is that ministers of different denominations and supporters of rival political parties happily get together and argue only about which of two pre-Grouping railways was the better? Why does enthusiasm for railways spread across the whole male spectrum but rarely affect women? And when yesteryear's railways seem so much more interesting than today's, how is it possible that, more than ever, boys of all ages still find great fascination?

Many trains also ran non-stop for far greater distances than is normal today. Before laptops and mobile phones, the train was a place of rest as it hurtled through the countryside non-stop for hours. Yet, curiously, there were then physical connections between trains and land that have all been abandoned. Steam trains picked up water at speed from the troughs that have long been taken up. The Great Western's automatic signalling system involved physical contact between a shoe on the locomotive and a ramp in the track. (Today's system is purely electronic.) On single lines on which many express trains ran with restaurant cars, tokens were exchanged automatically between lineside apparatus and an arm stretched out from the loco, as indeed mail was exchanged at speed with the travelling post offices. There were slip coaches, expresses shedding their tails to serve places through which they ran non-stop. And that is not to mention the fact that dozens of times on a long non-stop train the engine crew would exchange greetings with signalmen, who might occasionally receive a message thrown out wrapped in a piece of coal, perhaps requesting banker or replacement loco. Now we all keep in touch with mobile phones.

Broad-gauge locomotives waiting their fate after conversion. A few were built to be convertible to standard gauge. Note the temporary track.

The first full-length manuscript of my publishing career was John Thomas's *The Springburn Story*. Like most English enthusiasts, I had made a couple of forays into Scotland, taking tea in the ex-Caledonian wooden-panelled converted Pullman and alighting when we crossed trains at Loch Awe on route to Oban, wondering at the marvels of the West Highland, utterly unprepared for the Hell-hole of Glasgow Queen Street Low Level in steam days. But I knew nothing about the world John so lovingly portrayed as the world's locomotive capital.

The book, of a kind then almost unknown, was an immediate local bestseller, most copies going through the linen department of Springburn Co-operative Society since, great though the industrial complex was, it was without bookshop. And then began a unique relationship, John for example writing the Regional Railway History volume on *Scotland: The Lowlands and Borders* (and beginning the North of Scotland one before his untimely death) while I had started the series with the West Country one. Many thought we were one and the same person and we were forever getting each other's mail.

By any standard John was not only the doyen of Scottish railway historians but a major performer on the national British scene, few titles, for example, rivalling *The West Highland Railway* in its sheer narrative excitement, people and events ever brought to life by examples and short quotations. Living in one of Springburn's tower blocks (the address 240 Gourlay Street ever remembered by many of his friends), John was a door-to-door insurance salesman and must have cheered the lives of thousands of customers with his ready banter.

Persuading him to become full-time writer took courage but paid off handsomely, his work always being of the best possible quality, based on much original research. Scottish railway historians were lucky that their records were stored in Edinburgh, while wherever you lived in England you had expensively to go to London to consult yours. Without that, John (and the world) would have lost a lot.

Quite a few of John's books are kept in print as a tribute to a great author and friend as well as for a genuine continuing demand from the younger generation. During his lifetime I paid a different kind of tribute: John was given a literary lunch on board a restaurant car shunted the length of Springburn's platform while we had our sherry.

The Romance of Scotland's Railways, 1993

Fishing is said to attract the largest number of people in an outdoor activity, but railway enthusiasm is a close runner-up. While access to the larger stations is now more difficult for those not travelling, linesides attract record numbers of onlookers including photographers. The dozens of preserved lines (which if placed end-to-end would stretch from London to the Scottish Highlands) are very largely supported by volunteers, including an army of those too young to remember the days of everyday working steam but aspire to be engine drivers. Mainline steam specials also retain their appeal and are increasingly driven by those with little or no experience of everyday steam.

I am one of millions of people who railways have served well in all kinds of ways. Remember the time when many railwaymen dreaded the day they'd retire? One of the chapters that follows is devoted to railwaymen and their extraordinary loyalty in the days when their children were expected to do better at school than most. When she was in old age, a woman related to me how the mistress of the school at Halwill Junction (one of several villages named after their one-time station) chided her for not doing better . . . 'and you the daughter of a railwayman'.

The love of railways is many-faceted. Typically, those talking over light refreshments after an operating session of my model railway fiercely debate the merits of different locomotives and the scenery and operating methods of rival lines, but unite in the glory of the whole. Personally, I'm inspired by the passing of a train, perhaps of hundreds of tons carrying hundreds of people at up to twice the British maximum motorway speed limit, knowing that even in an emergency it cannot stop in much less than half a mile yet is far safer than travelling by car which can be stopped in much less space. But I'm also fascinated by how many people are travelling, why and on what journeys. In youth my happiest days were spent helping work signalboxes, especially at South Molton, ever waiting for the next train and its engine but, just as interesting, talking to passengers and looking at their collected tickets, studying the timetable and seeing how our station and line fitted into the general scheme.

OPPOSITE ABOVE *An early broad-gauge mail train.*

OPPOSITE BELOW *Even lesser broad-gauge engines had a presence, such as the Bristol & Exeter's No. 44, later GWR No. 2044, Rothwell seen at Watchet Harbour.*

Is it any wonder that people mourned the abolition of the broad gauge, which offered spacious and smooth journeys? There was also the satisfaction of watching layouts of mixed-gauge track such as this.

Another source of interest is of course the great history and the ever-changing current position. The first thirty years of the Railway Age not only witnessed great technical innovations on the system itself but brought about the greatest turning point in peacetime Britain since the Norman Conquest. Directly or indirectly it revolutionised every aspect of society and economic activity and created new outlooks of expectancy.

As mentioned again later, three great waves of development have swept across the land in modern times and the railway was at the heart of each. Though the Industrial Revolution started earlier, it was fulfilled by the railway. The second wave, suburbanisation, was almost wholly railway led. And railways were certainly heavily involved in the third wave, leisurisation to coin a word. Ironically, while railways play a decreasing role even within the much-reduced industrial sector, they serve the suburban and leisure ones in diametrically different ways. The cost of suburban season tickets have gone through the roof, while advance leisure or off-peak ones offer far greater bargains than perhaps have ever been available before on a regular as opposed to one-off excursion basis.

So again what is so fascinating about railways? It is perhaps telling that two things go through my mind when facing pain such as in hospital. One is the image of a lower quadrant signal being dropped as a narrow-gauge train comes round a curve to join a lake or an arm of the sea. That might be inspired by the West Coast of Ireland or North Wales. The other is a large junction station where, the platform I see in vivid imagination, is deserted apart from one or two people making their way to the station restaurant and a couple of train-spotting youngsters putting two old pennies into a machine to obtain a piece of Rowntree's chocolate. Steadily things come to life. A branch train comes into a bay platform, some of its passengers joining those arriving over the bridge to wait for the expected express. An official selects the pointer board for that, and places it in a slot with its finger pointing to the platform. Porters carry the luggage of more arriving passengers, check their seat reservations and take them to the appropriate point. Soon passengers several deep line the whole length of the platform, a whistle is heard and the express comes in rapidly, halting at just the right point. Seeming mayhem follows as crowds alight and others pour in. Gas in the restaurant car is replenished from a trolley on the platform, a red flag sticking out meanwhile. Station inspector and guards blow whistles, those seeing off family and friends make their final farewell and, as the train restarts, the last of the alighting passengers disappear while luggage is still being loaded onto the branch train in the bay platform where another engine has backed on ready to start its journey.

In other words, I love the particular and the general organisation. That is a combination that seems particularly to attract lovers of organ music and indeed church organists: creative organisation bringing together many strands of sound.

At the top of the pyramid is the general organisation, the usual maintenance of order. On a long journey I note the expected trains we pass or overtake. And while I may regret that with the vast increase in services, few of today's trains have personal individuality, and that there are many fewer one-off trains – without change you can only reach a fraction of the places one could in yesteryear – one can discover a new thrill in seeing the up mainline platform at say Reading steadily refill with passengers, scores being picked up there by a High Speed Train every few minutes throughout most of the day.

Much though we might regret that everything including the kitchen sink no longer goes by train, it is marvellous that today there are more passengers than ever, though over a system much reduced in size. And while I'd love to board at Paddington having collected a meal ticket from the restaurant car attendant on the platform knowing that the next stop will be Taunton, Exeter or even Plymouth, again it is great that stations such as Pewsey and Castle Cary once ignored by expresses now have burgeoning traffic and extensive car parks. As time moves on, we cannot have our cake and eat it.

Each year brings its own joys and, especially in a Quiet Coach, you can still be at peace, lose yet find your true self meditating on an express.

Only a few things perennially cause grief. While there is well-deserved nostalgia for the pre-privatisation British Railways renamed British Rail, in the days of the slogans 'We're getting there' and 'Let the train take the strain', we continue to pay a heavy price for the nationalised system ineptly throwing money away on ill-conceived modernisation, especially failing to make savings that, many of us shouted, were crying out to be made on secondary routes and branch lines. Thus it was that with mounting losses there was a desperate wholesale hacking of the system. Great inconvenience and hardship could so easily have been avoided by a more orderly contraction, especially in staff numbers from the immediate post-war years on. The network could and should have remained larger. Whenever, against great obstacles, a line or station is reopened, passenger usage is almost always far greater than forecast. Scotland and Wales have a better record for reopenings than does England.

The worst of British Railways was their dedication to ceaseless internal reorganisation and occasional highly questionable policies. A little of this emerges later in the book. Thus in the early days, while some Regions made the most of unstaffed halts, the largest had an edict that staff had to meet every train where there was still a station. It was ridiculous that when Dr Beeching was appointed specifically to cut the system, a year passed in which there were no closures and no savings in operating methods. And so it went on with policy lurches and sometimes concentration on crazy issues, such as the need to cut mainline expresses even if they were well patronised, and a ridiculous campaign to eradicate toast from restaurant and buffet cars . . . because some crews had brought in bread to make their own sandwiches. 'There's been an outbreak of toast which must be stamped out,' said one circular. Later there was an attack on carrying sitting passengers on night trains, because a handful might occasionally be drunk. Travel by night had its unique aura. It especially attracted lonely people who discovered fellow loners when they slipped out to refreshment rooms for a drink, usually of coffee. Since British Rail refused to carry them, they are welcome in the sitting cars of the Scottish sleepers and usefully add to their viability.

I still look forward to my train journeys, but in my eighties know that most of my mileage is behind me, and that it is time to let go. Many have already gone through that stage, but as Britain's one-time bestselling railway author who built a formidable publishing empire first based mainly on railways, it is perhaps especially poignant for me. Moreover, as a strained, unhappy youth who could so easily have led a miserable life, my love of railways saved me and helped me develop wider interests, uniquely valuable in journalistic and broadcasting days. I hope you will share my progress in this unusual book.

Though all aspects of Britain's railways are covered, my especial love has always been the branch line or country railway going back to the days when, across large swathes of the country, the station was the largest trading place and employer. Some of the chapters including '24 Hours of Memory' and 'The Seaside Railway' have been specially written, while a few represent the best of former work, though much of it has never been readily available to a wide readership.

The book is about railways in the British Isles. I've always had a special affinity for those in Ireland, where new and reopened lines help its burgeoning passenger numbers, but standardisation has belatedly taken over. I've also enjoyed the railways of much of the English-speaking world and indeed the Continent over much of which one can still eat a decent cooked meal at speed, a pleasure all but denied in Britain.

Indeed, you can as it were put the clock back by taking one of the cross-country services (such as from Hamburg to Vienna and beyond) which offer many through journeys and numerous connections conveniently detailed in a brochure placed on seats. These trains may not be fast but are reliable and attract many older passengers with luggage who have deserted our railways except for mainline trips.

As railway writer, I've enjoyed dozens of footplate trips overseas as well as at home. But because trains do not travel between continents as do ships and planes, most interest is inevitably in our own systems and how mighty is the interest we have been offered in our lifetime, and how satisfying is it to know that it will continue in further generations.

I'd just reached this point when a visitor said her grandson, who travels to school by a unit train, had greatly enjoyed another showing of *The Railway Children*. 'Granny. I wish trains were like that today.' Told that some are, a visit has been promised to the Strathspey Railway. I hope it may be on one of our dining trains.

CHAPTER 2
DIFFERENT DAYS

T HEY WERE QUITE DIFFERENT DAYS. There were many more lines and stations, but fewer though more comfortable trains mainly carrying far fewer passengers. By today's standards services were sparce, but nearly all expresses had a restaurant car serving full meals and morning coffee perhaps in several sittings, but no bar or snacks. Food was not 'fast' but prepared and cooked on board by a qualified chef, many of whom had their own distinctive style.

In the bygone days to which many of us look back nostalgically, each express had its own character. There were many one-off ones including cross-country services such as the *Pines Express* from Manchester to Bournemouth, the Somerset & Dorset being one of several mainly single-track routes to host a daily restaurant car.

Another big difference was that infinitely more towns had two or more stations. Bath, Barnstaple and Bodmin were a few West Country Bs. In Scotland, Glasgow had four major termini, three with their grand railway hotels. Edinburgh had Princess Street in addition to Waverley which, as today, was partly a through station. Perth and Grantown-on-Spey had two stations between which people might travel by taxi.

There were also many more routes. Scotland has seen several mainlines wiped out. Whatever else now uses the Midland's 'picturesque' route to Glasgow, there are no expresses – south or north of Carlisle.

In times past, nearly all trains other than on the Southern's electrified system were locomotive hauled. Unit trains may be cheaper but they've come at a great cost to comfort. Because of their restricted space, seating is tightly packed, some against window pillars

Around 1890 passengers enjoying a view of the Exe estuary at high tide would enjoy the greater stability of the 7ft gauge, whose days were already numbered.

Beloved by parsons who were happy to consult it for their parishioners, *Bradshaw's Railway Guide and Hotel Directory* was published monthly from 1839 (when it was exceedingly thin) to 1961.

For most of its life it was a cramped affair. When I first published a reprint, radio and TV interviewers sought to make fun, but my including the one-line commercial – 'enlarged with black ink on white paper' – brought the punters in by the thousand.

Most railway companies – all but the Great Western in the Grouping era – used reprints straight from the appropriate pages of *Bradshaw* for their own timetable.

There would have been no point in reprinting later issues, since in its final years *Bradshaw* was a fine volume. Consulting the last issue in May 1961, it seems like only yesterday – both in presentation and actual train times: Table 81, for example, Paddington to Penzance. The GWR/ Western always came first in *Bradshaw*, followed by the Southern, London Midland, Eastern, North Eastern, North Eastern (with its peculiarity of stating which were Diesel trains), with Scottish Region last.

Why did *Bradshaw* cease? Profitability had obviously declined. The price went up from 7s 6d to 12s 6d a month when in 1958 the page size increased from 6½ x 5in to 9 x 6in. But I wonder why monthly publication continued when the Regions using it for their timetables only had a summer and winter issue?

It didn't save consulting those fat booklets listing changes, since *Bradshaw* also had a supplement of late alterations. Anyway, few ordinary people would have bothered to pay a monthly 12s 6d to avoid them. Was twice-yearly publication ever considered? Had it been, the Regions could have saved the cost of publishing their separate and often quite different timetables, and there would have been a national one, which BR didn't introduce until 1974.

Less known is that for many years there was a slimmer Manchester edition. Henry Blacklock & Co., who printed and owned it, were Manchester-based though had a London office. The last issue proudly boasted 'By Appointment, Publisher of Bradshaw's Guide to the late King George V.' George V had a keen interest in railways.

Among the curiosities of *Bradshaw* is its extraordinarily rich mix of typefaces, according to how much was to be compressed in a given space.

Most valuable for collectors are the large folding plans with table numbers alongside the routes. They were an expensive part of our reprints . . . reminding how much we miss the all-system map which BR included in their timetables until they ceased publication but are not in the Stationery Office's more expensive one of today.

West Country railway lovers of the day mourned the loss of the broad gauge as much as today's generation has been saddened by line closures. A line-up of casualties of the 1892 abolition wait their fate at Swindon.

even on the great scenic routes. It is pitiful to see how many passengers struggle to enjoy the majesty of the routes to Mallaig and Kyle of Lochalsh.

Today there is a train every half hour from Paddington to Bristol *via* Bath. Apart from the fact that some now lack a full buffet car, they're all of a kind, and all disgracefully slow. By an occasional train, such as the non-stop *Bristolian*, one could reach Bristol significantly faster in steam days. And whereas standard ticket prices used to be followed, at the time of writing the senior citizen's first-class fare to Bath now varies between £77 for peak time and £16.50 at off-peak. That huge difference usually means the day's busiest services are those just after or just before the expensive time. And while there is a great choice of trains, cheap tickets tie you to a particular one.

Another tremendous difference is the reduction in passengers changing trains. Many now drive to a mainline station to avoid a change. The closure of many branch lines was indeed aided by people driving from the junction, as did Jeremy Thorpe (once with Harold Wilson as passenger) from Taunton on his way home to his North Devon constituency rather than suffer the agony of the all-stations-and-halts slow train to Barnstaple. Time saving (or impatience) had much to do with the closure of country railways.

In *Double Headed*, the book we wrote jointly, my father describes how the annual journey from Leicester to Redbrook on Wye was a leisurely affair involving six changes. That kind of journey has long vanished into history – as have nearly all those that involved stringing branch lines together. Yet even in my time I recall an almost all single-line track trip from Winchester GWR to Tetley, changing stations in Cirencester and (in the 1950s) seldom having more than half a dozen passengers on board. Such journeys were a wonderful way of exploring the uniqueness of the British countryside and live in the memory of a declining number of those fortunate enough to have made them.

There were few regular-interval services in those days, forcing one to consult the timetable. But then the timetable was a veritable art form, timings and calling patterns evolving over the years to serve great mixes of passengers. Today most trains become emptier the further they are from London, but then most remained well used till the end. What a contrast there is between yesteryear's and today's arrival in Exeter St Davids. Once the platform was crowded with waiting passengers, as many getting on as alighting. Few join there on most of today's westbound trains.

Local business (which in Southern England largely meant anything not from London) was seen by BR as a fiddling nuisance, and was substantially killed by frequent timetable changes. Once hundreds went by train to work in Newton Abbot, including a dozen or so for David & Charles. If only in one timetable period, many local journeys became impossible. For example, there was once a gap of over four hours in trains between Newton Abbot and Plymouth. Once people need to make other arrangements, they seldom return. Today's franchised railways are far from perfect, but managers are too revenue conscious to avoid the revolving management fads of BR.

BRADSHAW – 2

The trains of the last days of *Bradshaw* are those we are most nostalgic about today. There were many fewer of them. Two Scottish examples are typical. Wick and Thurso had two daily trains instead of today's four. Though then served by two routes instead of today's single one, Nairn had seven in each direction instead of twelve. Frequencies have increased even on most of the minor lines that are still open.

On most routes today, trains are pretty standard. In 1958 there were infinitely more through train options, though many by a single all-the-year-round service, such as the *Pines Express* from Bradford *via* the Somerset & Dorset to Bournemouth. The *Atlantic Coast Express* was still a 'portmanteau' train with mainly single through coaches to a host of destinations: 'Restaurant car Waterloo to Exeter, through carriages to Padstow, Bude, Plymouth, Ilfracombe, Torrington, Exmouth and Sidmouth.'

Virtually all daytime expresses carried restaurant cars, serving even the Far North and Kyle of Lochalsh routes, offering an early service from Inverness and a later one back to it by switching trains. Another joy was that most expresses had their own character, for example the *Cornish*

Riviera Express being the only one to reach Plymouth in four hours, non-stop in summer. But most trains were slower: the 11.50pm to Penzance didn't arrive until 11.10am.

Serving many local needs, most expresses remained busy until their journey's end. With many trains carrying school children at convenient times, as well as the great holidaying public and people going about their ordinary workday lives (but people didn't get up so early in those days) it was felt that the timetable was almost God-cast. Had it to be started afresh, it would end up almost the same. Later 'improvements' saw local traffic largely ignored. The hundreds who commuted to Newton Abbot, some to David & Charles, had to make other arrangements since in at least one timetable period it was not possible to commute by train. So today, expresses which might leave Paddington and Reading full, steadily empty on their way west.

The last issue of *Bradshaw* actually catches things just as they were about to change, and BR's finances were about to go from bad to worse. The lengthy supplement of alterations spells out the agony ahead.

There was always great entertainment value in *Bradshaw*. For example, it showed one down train to Pembroke Dock calling at Beavers Hill Halt on Fridays only, while another stopped on Wednesdays and Saturdays only to set down, yet there was an up train that was called 'daily'. Mind you, Lydstep Halt was included in the list of stations but showed no trains stopping. Such oddities persisted for decades, as did the page showing a 'Sunday train' from Carmarthen to Aberystwyth by virtue of a connection from London starting on Sunday night. In all other cases that was covered by a footnote.

It was amusing, too, to see what remnants, useful or not, remained of services BR wished to axe but hadn't yet taken through the time-consuming closure process. Thus in 1961, only a single weekday service survived from Cheltenham to Southampton using the full length of the once-prosperous Midland & South Western Junction under Sam Fay.

Bradshaw died just as the voluntary railway movement was getting under way, and a few lines such as the Talyllyn are included, while the thin services of the last commercial days of the Isle of Man system, including the west coast line to Ramsey, are still shown.

The hotel advertisements were another source of entertainment. 'All rooms with radio', and 'standing in own grounds' were the boasts of the day. Private bathrooms were far from universal, but 'table tennis rooms' popular. 'Open year round' was another popular boast, 'separate tables' still merited some attention, as did 'interior sprung mattresses'.

Climate boasts were common. The Falmouth Hotel was 'coolest in summer, warmest in winter'. Who today would boast about anywhere being cool in summer?

Up broad-gauge track at Flax Bourton. Note the complication of the mixed-gauge pointwork.

Things have changed out of all recognition. For example, South Molton, the small North Devon country town about whose station I've written extensively, has long been trainless, yet a far greater proportion of its population now travel by train. They occasionally drive to Taunton to take the service to London or elsewhere. That is reproduced nationally and explains why record numbers of passengers are carried today though on a much-reduced system. When I was a boy, most children and a large proportion of their parents had never been on a train. Many trains then served specialised needs: servicemen coming home on leave, villagers such as those from Yeo Mill attending South Molton's monthly great market and traders the annual horse fair.

Though most of the five daily stopping trains in each direction carried fewer than twenty passengers, they made all kinds of things possible, such as attending distant Christenings and funerals – though that might include a long walk, even to and on from a train on another line. Fish reached South Molton for the first time, mail services were vastly improved and – above all – as in so much of rural Britain, coal, that domestic and business essential, came sharply down in price. Day-old chicks and calves carried in the guard's van

helped better breeding and – as I've said before – less human inter-breeding spelt the end of the village idiot.

I missed what were probably the greatest days of the country branch in the 1920s and 1930s. On the signalbox wall at South Molton there survived an old notice about a six-days-a-week summer express whose down and up services crossed and exchanged a restaurant car there. With run-away inflation, especially in wages, such luxuries were never to return after the 1939–45 hostilities. Barnstaple's triangular junction, with its three signalboxes, remained closed, through trains to Ilfracombe having to reverse before proceeding through Barnstaple Junction and Barnstaple Town. They carried their heaviest traffic shortly before final closure, for the spread of car ownership and motor coach services happened dramatically in the 1950s. The next generation went overseas to the sun and Ilfracombe struggles with far fewer visitors. Truly, our little systems have their day, they have their day, and cease to be.

VALUE FOR MONEY

Complaints about BR's prices in their diners are far from new. Take 1950, for example. There was an outcry over the increase from 3s 6d (17½p) to 4s (20p) for a full breakfast. Lunch and dinner went up from 4s (20p) to 5s (25p). Full afternoon tea was unchanged at 1s 6d (7½p) but for a shilling (5p) you could now get a 'simpler service' – tea, bread and butter *or* toasted teacake, sandwich, cakes *or* biscuits. As a sop, a plain breakfast was introduced at 2s 6d (12½p). Mind you, it was then possible to get a Friday night excursion from Glasgow Central to Euston and back the next night for £5 3s 6d (£5.17½). For this the excursioners got their return rail journey, breakfast, lunch and high tea in London, a sightseeing tour by coach and a seat either at the Hippodrome or Casino theatre.

Great Days of Express Trains, 1990

QUALITY HOTELS

People are not inclined to believe it today, but for a long time in the post-war years railway hotels were the best everywhere in Britain, apart possibly from London. Beds were luxurious and interior decorating in a class of its own. Nowhere could better food be found than at, say, Le Malmaison restaurant at the Central Hotel, Glasgow, or at the French restaurant at the Midland in Manchester.

Moreover, if you were going to take breakfast in the restaurant car, its cost would be deleted from the bed-and-breakfast rate.

That the hotels were so good partly resulted in directors touring the best on the Continent to ensure they incorporated the best features. Electric light and lifts first appeared in many cities in their railway hotels. Rival companies, such as three serving Glasgow and two in several places, competed to ensure their's was best.

Another great change has been the pattern of departures from the great termini. Sticking with the example of Paddington, a Pannier tank, or what my father described as a fat schoolboy, arrived with the stock of departing trains about twenty minutes before journey's start. A porter guided you to the seat you had reserved, or you leisurely found a window seat. Having put something on your seat you went onto the platform to collect your restaurant-car ticket, choosing between two or more 'sittings'. The chief steward passed through the train to ask you to take your seat for the appropriate one.

There was no disruptive intercom requesting you to check the safety card, warning what tickets were not valid, when the buffet is open and what is being served, and advising you that the train is 'arriving into' wherever, and to thank you for travelling by First Great Western or whoever. Also without mobile phones, travelling was much more peaceful. In the days of steam heating, you could feel relaxation coming through your pores. Prestige trains also ran much further without stopping, still in the case of Paddington, to Taunton, Exeter or even Plymouth, Bath or Bristol, Kemble or Leamington Spa. Reading was often passed at speed though, well into the post-war era, the day's first up train from the West Country, shed a slip coach there.

One loss after another has made the railways much less interesting. Slip coaches, mail and single-line tokens exchanged at speed, and water scooped up from troughs in the track – all have gone. So have compartments in which the facing corner passenger had control over the window in pre-air conditioned days. It is harder to shut yourself off from the world as you pass through it. What magic it was to have a compartment to oneself on say the morning Plymouth to Manchester express with its restaurant car serving late breakfast, lunch, afternoon tea and early dinner – the latter enjoyed before the days I could afford to stay at the railway's great Midland Hotel with a heavenly dinner in its French restaurant.

Yet what I miss most is sitting in the front third-class compartment of a stopping train with the window open, listening to the locomotive, peering through the smoke and steam, and hearing the chatter between staff and enginemen at stations. Our many heritage steam railways do their best but cannot recreate the workaday atmosphere of yesteryear when it was the routine ordinariness of it that made it so vital.

There were many other points of interest, including observing how much traffic was in the goods yard that nearly all stations once had, and how many passengers and how much luggage there was on the platform at which we stopped. How I loved it all – and now recall it especially when undergoing difficult dental or medical procedures.

Mind you, we knew we were in a time warp in the first decade and a half after the end of the Second World War. They were the days when third-class compartments, smartly finished in a variety of named woods, were so spacious and comfortable that many entitled to sit in them thought they must have made a mistake and instinctively backed out to return delightedly when realising they were in the right class.

SLEEPERS

GWR sleeping cars were an institution. For much of the Company's history, they were first class only. When lesser mortals were encouraged to spend the night horizontally they were directed into four-berth compartments where often the sexes were divided only by a central curtain. Only a pillow and rug were provided; you were not expected to undress, but nonetheless the Press were sharp in their criticism, especially after the Second World War.

There used indeed to be a rubber stamp at Paddington, Plymouth and Penzance stating (and imagine the thoughts of husbands sending their wives off an overnight journey by themselves): 'WARNING: whilst every endeavour is made to allot 3rd class sleeping berths to Ladies and Gentlemen separately, this is not always practicable and may not be possible in the case of this journey.'

The Great Days of the GWR, 1991

CHAPTER 3
THE ROMANCE OF
THE COUNTRY RAILWAY

The following was delivered as the annual Clinker Lecture of the Railway & Canal Historical Society (www.rchs.org.uk) at the Birmingham & Midland Institute on 17 September 2009.

TRAILS OF SMOKE AND STEAM LEFT BY LOCOMOTIVES panting up gradients – that's perhaps what first comes to many people's minds when the country railway is mentioned. And in a sense it's right to give steam engines priority. They were the first means that man had to travel faster than a horse – and they brought into the countryside the first trade union leaders, politicians campaigning nationally, cheaper coal and beer, Peterborough bricks, and (as we will see) much more.

The steam engine itself was a romantic machine: at least when new, the very latest in human technology, which made steam as it went and stored it so that extra power could be used when necessary and the reservoir replenished later. Moreover, steam engines needed skill to get the best out of them. In the remarkable relationship between man and machine, you could almost tell the very character of different drivers by how they performed. It's no wonder that drivers were the elite, something every boy aspired to becoming.

Yet those who concentrate on the steam engine to the exclusion of the broader picture miss much. There's the track, the permanent way – that pair of parallel rails tied to sleepers,

BETWEEN TRAINS

Many stations were akin to the *Marie Celeste* in long intervals between trains. Having prudently checked the weekly sheet to ensure there was not a special, the signalman, porter and stationmaster might all wander off, to fish, mend a bike or garden, sometimes for pleasure, sometimes to supplement their wages.

That meant that the country signalman often had a better standard of living than his mainline equivalents who might have fewer levers to control but had to remain on constant duty.

Before the South Devon Railway began building its own locomotives at Newton Abbot, in 1842 Stag was bought from Avonside.

RIGHT *Christow on the Teign Valley was one of the hundreds of stations where traffic from the quay accounted for the majority of income.*

OPPOSITE *South Molton and its signalbox where the author learnt signalling and (over the omnibus phone serving all stations on the GWR's Barnstaple branch) the facts of life.*

and kept in place by ballast, that ever disappeared into the distance, climbing and curving gently. Today we perhaps fail to realise just what an improvement even a single-track route was over the narrow, rutted roads whose sparse traffic they largely acquired and then greatly expanded. While roads went round obstacles such as hills and estuaries, the railway often went through them with tunnels, or over them by bridges and viaducts of unparalleled cost and engineering skill. Especially where the railway crosses an estuary and motorists still have to drive round it, even today some railway routes remain significantly shorter. Only in the north of Scotland were lines – notably the Far North route to Wick and Thurso – intentionally built indirect to tap as much population as possible.

There is, however, a still different aspect to the romance of the country railway, and that is the one I find most satisfying: it was a business, a commercial venture that often failed in narrow financial terms but proved of enormous benefit to the community. Nearly all country stations, at least those handling freight as well as passengers, were the most important trading posts for miles around. The business they handled revolutionised local life, and

SPECIAL OCCASIONS

There was scarcely a branch line that did not carry special traffic on a regular or occasional basis. Devon's Teign Valley might be thought of as the archetypal backwater, but regularly it carried heavy mineral traffic, and occasionally single-car auto trains were replaced by full-length trains including the *Cornish Riviera Express* diverted this way when the sea severed the mainline at Dawlish. The double-track Southern line around Dartmoor had too narrow a loading gauge.

Sunday School excursions, a visit by a 'City of . . .' express (those ran from large cities for a fortnight at the end of July and beginning of August visiting a different place each day) were perhaps the most numerous passenger specials, while parcels and goods ones included those for cattle fairs, and trains carrying seasonal harvests, in Somerset including teasels.

attitudes, and by just looking at the traffic you could tell whether they were times of boom or depression – and which trades and industries were doing better that others. Though from the time I first saw a country station I loved everything about branch line railways (and it is significant that there was no train during our visit), what especially grabbed me was how it served its community and how it became a vital and often decorative part of it. The station was Cadeleigh on the Exe Valley branch, a wonderful example of how the railway became an attractive part of the community it served.

As a teenager, signalmen trusted me to do most of their work, yet even in the signalbox the most fascinating thing of all was going through the tickets collected after the arrival of each train – and seeing the accounts. On quiet lines, it was usually left to the signalman to balance them at the month's and year's end. How fraught that was. Hours were taken patiently studying the figures to discover discrepancies, victory achieved often when only two or more were spotted and produced the correct balance. The figures themselves were extraordinarily interesting. By far the largest source of income at most country stations was from a single local quarry or other one-off industry. Over time those industries declined, some indeed rapidly seen off by competition, Burton-on-Trent for example killing the Oakhill Brewery on the Somerset & Dorset. Some remote county towns didn't recover for a century

WHEN WILL WE FINISH?

The running of the last express of a day with numerous branch line connections was a matter of interest often to several dozen signalmen.

If it were late, that meant they'd get home later . . . and earn good overtime too. A delay to, say, the 1.30pm, for many years the last train from Paddington to Penzance, could prove a very costly affair in wages.

Staff had to remain on duty until 'out of section' had been received from the next box down the line.

The ultimate in the country railway: Ireland's Fintona tram.

after their mills, unable to cope with cheap competition, were forced to close. North Tawton, near Okehampton, is an example of how local needs were now served from further afield. Passenger income was generally scant, even at tourist destinations, since visitors bought their tickets elsewhere. But then, when I was a boy, we all knew that freight was far more important than passengers to the railways. Only in our own time has passenger revenue dominated, resulting in railways, though carrying record passenger numbers, now needing hefty subsidy.

Except on special occasions and at peak times, most passenger trains earned less from passengers than what was carried in the guard's van. As in so much business, it was the bringing together of many sources of revenue that made it worthwhile. Almost everywhere the railway carried the mail, at most stations several daily trains being met by the postman who handed in the mail bags or collected them from the guard, porters never getting involved. The mixture of parcels reflected the nature, season and relative prosperity of each area, but usually included newspapers (if only the weekly ones, what newsagents insist on calling books, such as the *Radio Times*), catalogue shopping and perishables for local stores. When evacuated to South Molton in North Devon during the war, I was able to tell Mum exactly when to go to the grocers to enquire if they had any sausages, not then on ration. Except during the war years when it was banned, ice cream invariably arrived by passenger train, Lyons continuing to use the railways for its distribution until well into the 1960s.

Just being in the guard's van sometimes made one feel hungry, with cakes, chocolates and other delicacies mixed with private parcels wrapped up in all manner of ways and sometimes little separated from the day old chicks and even calves that helped keep the valley's stock healthy . . . in the same way that the railway encouraged greater mixing of people which meant less inter-breeding. Yes, the railway was largely responsible for eradicating the village idiot.

More bulky and less valuable parcels arrived once daily by the station truck which drew up outside the parcels office. The big question facing those sending off a parcel was 'Passenger or Goods?' The difference in price and risk of damage was substantial.

Between the two, far more money was generally taken through the parcels office than booking office window, though a large party or family setting off on a lengthy journey might bump up the passenger receipts on a particular day. Such happenings were relatively rare, one of the fascinations being that most people took only short journeys of a station or two. The train journey was sometimes the relaxing part of a longer one, on foot, possibly to attend a friend's wedding or funeral. Such journeys might involve walking to one station, between stations on different routes, and even on from the third station. At least the railway made it possible. Many country trains carried only a dozen or score of passengers and, when I found out why people were travelling, often each individual or family fell into a different category. Except on summer Saturdays, usually only on market days would a substantial group of people be making the same journey for the same purpose – though on some lines the busiest trains carried kids to and from school. That of course excludes special occasions which I'll return to later.

Normally two or three coaches, sometimes a single push-pull auto-car, sufficed. Mention of 'two or three' reminds one that, even at the height of the railway's popularity, trains raised controversy. Progress was slow, stopping trains frequently averaging little more than 20mph, while some branch lines were lengthy. Thus it took all but two full hours to cover the 46 miles from Taunton to Barnstaple, on which the Great Western traditionally used two non-corridor coaches. With no time to visit the toilet at intermediate stations, that caused a problem, especially for older men. It took a huge campaign to persuade the company to add an additional corridor coach – and a further one to ensure they did so reliably.

Emphasising how slow progress could be, even summer Saturday through trains to Ilfracombe with express headlamps took three hours to cover the 61 miles from Taunton. One recalls impatient youths and bored adults tightly packed four-a-side in corridor coaches. Before I reached the age of better discretion, when a mum told her young son 'We'll be in Ilfracombe in a quarter of an hour,' I caused upset by saying it would be another hour and a half. 'Then I want one of your prunes,' said the lad, to which the mum added: 'Give them him or he'll scream' – which he did even with a prune in his mouth.

There were irritating restrictions in past times, too. When through coaches for Ilfracombe were first introduced on the branch from Taunton, only those 'for whom they are intended' could use them. Passengers wishing to transfer to Barnstaple Junction, perhaps for the Bideford line, were still expected to cross the town independently even though the Ilfracombe carriages stopped there. But then North Devon was a rural backwater. Again showing that the railways were largely used for short journeys, in some summers in the 1920s, a full Sunday service ran from Barnstaple to Ilfracombe and Bideford and Torrington, but not a single train connected the area with the outside world.

There were restrictive agreements, too, an example of which is that when the Great Western began modernising its lengthy branch line to Barnstaple, among other things providing automatic token exchangers, it and the Southern agreed that neither would spend a penny further to speed things up. On the Southern that meant that long summer Saturday trains, even the *Atlantic Coast Express*, passing each other in station loops had to back their tails over hand-bolted points into refuge sidings.

Goods trains were naturally even slower, with inordinate time spent waiting to allow passenger trains to overtake, as well as cross those in the opposite direction. The daily sort out of goods yards again tied up trains and their crews. Two full hours were allowed for that at South Molton, the engine repeatedly puffing up the short headshunt and propelling trucks backward. As at most stations, there was a separate goods shed and a goods office, responsible for ensuring every truck was clearly labelled.

Another fascination of the country railway was that for generations it used mainline left-overs. So locomotives, and in some cases coaching stock, long banished from trunk routes, or in the Southern's case replaced by electrification, lingered on. The Southern's 'withered arm' west of Exeter was a veritable living museum, many old classes, notably the 4-4-0 T9s or Greyhounds sustaining yeoman service well into BR days. The same was especially true of the rural lines of the LNER, the poorest of the four in the Grouping era of 1923–47.

It was indeed the same throughout Britain and certainly in Ireland. Yet generally *esprit de corps* was high, staff on most branch lines enjoying a rich social life. Staff were always lending each other newspapers and magazines, trading eggs for beer or cider, willingly dispatched from stations near a pub to those without, bartered goods or cash coming back by the driver or guard on the next train. The telephone played a major part, too. I first learned the facts of life overhearing a conversation between a man about to be married who had asked for advice from an older gent up the line on what to do on his wedding night. That was on one of those omnibus circuits serving every signalbox on the route, each responding to a different bell code. Locomotive crews and guards reported on the state of the crops

Farm removal train from Llantarnam (between Newport and Pontypool) loading for its journey to West Grinstead.

along the line: the influence of the stopping train was far greater than it seemed from the relatively few people travelling by it. Above all, again, it changed attitudes and expectations.

The way the staff were managed was itself epoch making. Railwaymen, starting with signalmen who to this day are occasionally called bobbies, were the first civilians to wear uniform in the countryside – and to be promoted from the ranks. That made the stationmaster an oddball, often with a chip on his shoulder. He was in charge of the district's largest trading post, employing many staff and, in the eyes of most people, certainly ranking with the parson and schoolmaster. Unlike them, though, he wasn't born a gentleman and lacked their education and confidence.

In its own inimitable way, the country railway was generally both happy and efficient. Paid a pittance by today's standards (not much more than a basic £3 a week for a branch line signalman even in the Second World War), times were hard for staff, generally country ones were better off and certainly enjoyed far greater job security than other country folk. Father and son and grandson following each other as drivers led to particular stability. Though not as well paid as busier staff especially in mainline signalboxes, or enginemen on crack expresses, the country railwayman enjoyed a more leisurely lifestyle. Signalmen and other staff frequently had time for rabbiting, fishing or jobbing gardening, perhaps doing up bicycles or attending their lineside allotments, in long gaps between trains. Life on the branch was always punctuated by short periods of intense activity between lulls

The Southbound double-headed Pines Express *just emerging from Combe Down Tunnel, Bath, en route to Bournemouth.*

of lotus-eating stupor. But enginemen worked hard to make good time lost through late connections, though speed limits had to be observed strictly running downhill. Signalmen moved with alacrity when crossing trains and station staff jumped to it loading and unloading the guard's van and checking doors, especially if things were behind schedule.

So far having concentrated on the trains and stations, I'd now like to introduce greater perspective. Perspective. That's one of my favourite words. It was certainly one I used constantly when publishing transport titles in David & Charles. As Professor Simmons kindly pointed out, our Regional Railway History series (paralleled by Charles Hadfield's *Canals of the British Isles*) has been the only one to portray the role of railways in a region other than on a line-by-line basis. Even thematic railway books, such as on the country or seaside railway, are rare. That is perhaps because many so-called authors themselves lack perspective.

Especially lacking in perspective are many albums, collated rather than authored, thrown together often it would seem as though God had built branch lines so that the engines running up and down them could be glorified. Train services usually receive scant attention, and rarely is there any real attempt to explain the line's raison d'être, the railway as a business, who used it and what was carried by it . . . and what were its social and economic consequences. Except in technical locomotive matters, accuracy cannot always be relied upon. Just how little real research has been undertaken is sometimes revealed by a mistake in one book being repeated in a string of others.

At the other end of the spectrum, Clinker – Charles Clinker of this Clinker lecture – did much to inspire accuracy. He knew a great deal and we miss him. He correctly pointed out the shortcomings of some of the more famous and prodigious authors of 'scissors and paste' reputation – but alas was himself too nervous to go much into print and so added little to railway literature. Thus, though there may be few obvious 'gaps' in railway literature, much of it doesn't serve its subject well. Jack Simmons remains one of a very few authors who give a balanced picture.

A particular difficulty is that many authors are not interested in recent history . . . and by recent I mean anything from the end of the steam age, or nationalisation – or even earlier, such as 1923. At which point I'd like to add my own special comment on perspective – the length of human life in the Railway Age. The Railway Age started in 1830 with the opening of the first inter-city line, the Liverpool & Manchester. Yes, there'd been many earlier railways, nearly all for freight, mainly serving single industries (mostly the coal trade), but it took the Liverpool & Manchester to bring together the various technical strands into a new whole, engine power provided by George Stephenson, after his *Rocket* famously won the Rainhill Trials where there were also weird and wonderful contraptions that would never have sustained the pace. George Stephenson was needed.

I personally have lived through four ninths of the Railway Age, and anyone who has celebrated his ninetieth birthday will have lived through a full half of it. We think human life is short, but put that way either it really isn't – or it emphasises how recently trains as we know them were invented. When I was in my twenties I knew many who had clear memories of the GWR's broad gauge, abolished in 1892. As a boy my father would have mixed with those who were boys in 1830.

The truly astonishing thing is that by 1854, that's a mere twenty-four years after the Liverpool & Manchester, in England, Hereford, Yeovil and Weymouth were the only important towns not quite connected. By 1860, thirty years after the Liverpool & Manchester – what historians term a generation – the system as we know it today was virtually complete. In broad outline, what was built later has been closed.

When we consider how long it took for our post-war motorway system to develop, the pace of railway development is unbelievable. People of the day were giddy with change. I always feel that 1830–60 is the generation that really changed Britain, what's happened later just following on and filling in. Even the mobile phone follows on from the telegraph that came with the railway and for the first time allowed instant communication. The bus, lorry and car might be what we depend on today, yet the big revolution was the train, first allowing many of us to travel quicker than the speed of an animal.

Five-Day Runabouts, 1953

Monday, 179½ miles

Teignmouth dep 9.10

Taunton arr 10.14
dep 10.20

Bridgwater arr 10.41

Depart by bus to Glastonbury

Glastonbury dep 2.51

Templecombe arr 3.49
dep 4.15

Evercreech Junction arr 4.40
dep 4.48

Highbridge arr 5.46
dep 6.12

Taunton arr 6.40
dep 7.10

Teignmouth arr 8.20

Tuesday, 165 miles

Teignouth dep 10.00

Weston-super-Mare arr 11.52
dep 1.45

Yatton arr 2.02
dep 2.05

Clevedon arr 2.12
dep 3.48

Yatton arr 3.55
dep 4.00

Weston-super-Mare arr 4.15
dep 4.48

Teignmouth arr 6.40

Wednesday, 202¼ miles

Teignmouth dep 9.10

Bristol Temple Meads arr 11.21
dep 12.00

Bath Spa arr 12.17

Bath Green Park dep 2.58

Evercreech Junction arr 3.56

Walk to Castle Carey

Castle Cary dep 5.40

Taunton arr 6.37
dep 7.10

Teignmouth arr 8.20

Thursday, 155¼ miles

Teignmouth dep 9.10

Taunton arr 10.14
dep 11.05

Chard arr 11.45
dep 12.05

Chard Junction arr 12.13
dep 12.21

Yeovil Junction arr 12.49
dep 12.58

Yeovil Town arr 1.02

Yeovil Pen Mill dep 3.59

Taunton arr 5.07
dep 5.30

Teignmouth arr 6.40

Friday, 40¼ miles

Teignmouth dep 10.00

Newton Abbot arr 10.11
dep 10.32

Heathfield arr 10.42
dep 10.45

Exeter St David's arr 11.40
dep 12.05

Teignmouth arr 1.27

*Rail fares £2 16s 6d (£2.82½)
for 742¾ miles.*

*Great Days of the
Country Railway, 1986*

Wherever it went, roughly speaking, the railway halved the price of coal and doubled that of milk. Sending foodstuffs to more profitable distant markets led to food riots as prices increased in their country areas of production. Cheaper coal encouraged gas lighting, most cities and towns becoming well lit for the first time. I love the phrase 'creative destruction' to describe the railway's power. When the Napoleonic Wars were at last over, the climate was ripe for progress, the railway both being driven by and immensely driving forth the new age of enlightenment. The Reform Bill making fairer Parliamentary representation comes at the beginning of my generation. By the end of it, in 1860, newspapers (already widely distributed on their day of publication) had more in common with today's than those of 1830. Public libraries, education, health, with even sewerage schemes (encouraged by better lighting, making people more aware of how unhealthy streets had been) moved sharply forward. The extra demand for water stimulated reservoir building, often with temporary lines for the contractors. Cholera that had been rampant as railways reached places such as Exeter, was virtually eradicated.

Throughout Britain – though there was variable local opposition – clocks showed standard or 'railway' rather than local time. New agricultural skills and the opportunity to specialise to take advantage of local soil and climatic conditions, brought new wealth and – however slightly – a more even distribution across the country.

Machynlleth in the 1950s with an early Diesel unit alongside a steam train.

Hole, the ultimate rural byway, with two daily trains scarcely ever used on the North Devon & Cornwall Junction Light Railway. See snippet on page 27.

Many secondary and branch lines were successfully up and running by 1860, and even where they were still being built or planned, there was universal expectation of shortly participating in the revolution. Thus in England, eventually the furthest point from a station was Hartland near the Devon/Cornwall border. In Scotland with a tenth of the population spread over forty per cent of the land area, things naturally happened more slowly and haphazardly though in the end railways made just as important a contribution, especially to fishing, farming (for example, sheep moved from high lands to low ones for the winter) and tourism – led by Queen Victoria's love affair with the Highlands.

It didn't all happen smoothly. The Railway Mania saw speculation as ridiculous as that which recently laid our banking system low. Britain was bisected and dissected by schemes for country railways, of which only a small minority – and mainly the earlier and more obvious ones – were actually built. Perhaps the classic over-optimism was the Manchester & Milford, which in the end only succeeded in building a single line with stiff gradients and sharp curves between Aberystwyth and Carmarthen.

The easiest way to make a fortune in the nineteenth century was indeed through investment in railways, yet most who did so lost heavily. The reason? A railway was seen as a railway, expected to create traffic wherever it went. With rare exceptions, such as the Salisbury & Yeovil (which made a fortune for its shareholders by refusing to be other than part of a direct mainline), companies were too territorially ambitious and competitive. Those who supported locally sponsored rural lines generally saw their investment reduce by half, roughly what mainline companies paid for branches they later took over. However, remember that those rural investors were mainly landowners who benefited enormously through their running costs being cut and crops made more valuable.

Not merely were rural expectations of traffic generally over the top, but many secondary and branch lines were built to expensive mainline standards. Where single track was used, bridges and tunnels were often built for double. Everything was what we would today call Heavy Rail, stations with standard-height platforms, unnecessarily palatial, over-staffed with at first segregated specialities as justified by busy mainline ones. Though it is true that while early lines went through or over obstacles, later ones more usually went round them, yet most railways, main or rural, cost surprisingly similar sums, averaging about £40,000 a mile.

Moreover, sophisticated signalling cost much more per pound of revenue earned on country railways than trunk ones. Armies of signallers were employed, such as on the Penrith–Workington line with a pair of signalboxes at Keswick for example, while Workington Junction was just where the route to the goods yard diverged. On double track it was relatively cheap to enable intermediate signalboxes to be switched out at quiet times, while running an early or late train down a single line generally meant manning all boxes. In flatter eastern England, especially in Lincolnshire and eastern Yorkshire, three signalboxes controlling level crossings could often be seen at a time. Railways were built when the cost of capital was relatively expensive compared with that of labour. As wage costs shot up, the lack of funds to make even modest changes, such as building a bridge to save a level crossing, was a fearful price to pay.

The general lack of ability to distinguish between mainline and rural branch railways is something we still suffer from today. That led to quite unnecessary high losses, more closures than would otherwise have been necessary in the Beeching era, and generally served everyone from investors, operators and users badly, ultimately causing avoidable hardship.

Too late to make a real difference, Light or more rudimentary railways were authorised in 1896. They only filled-in truly remote gaps, as did the colourful narrow-gauge lines, especially in Ireland. Britons had become so used to a railway being a railway that open level crossings approached slowly with furious whistling and Emmett-like rolling stock emphasised the exotic, causing much humour but seldom attracting crowds. There were indeed a curious assortment of lines, a group of which came under the control of the most unusual of all railwaymen, peppery Col. Stephens, who practised make-do-and-mend while extolling passengers to patronise trains driven by British coal on smooth British steel. Though some did serve a real need, in retrospect their entertainment value seems to have been almost as great as their practical contribution to transport.

Then problems were compounded by the 1930 Road Traffic Act, an evil thing. It stopped railways running their – by then substantial – own bus services while leaving them as major shareholder. The result was that they could neither compete nor co-operate. Thus was born the practice of buses seldom connecting with trains. Since buses were generally cheaper, more frequent and stopped in town centres, after the First World War increasingly country trains lingered on with a declining and specialist patronage. The first of those specialist groups were people starting out on longer journeys – perhaps to London (or in Scotland, Edinburgh or Glasgow). Though only a handful connect at the junctions, they were journeys of supreme importance. Inadequate bus connections didn't suit them, and once in their own cars many were tempted to drive the whole way. Then there were people making journeys from or to villages with no bus, railwaymen with privileged tickets, mothers with prams . . . and in later times increasingly railway enthusiasts. That's about all that were left on many routes. I recall a train to Lossiemouth with just six passengers . . . all

CENSUS
··········

Judging by the figures that appeared on the annual traffic census returns taken at many country stations, it is surprising that branch lines were not gold mines. News of the census spread as rapidly as did that of an inspector from the Ministry of Food in the Second World War. People who travelled only occasionally but valued the local service made a point of taking a trip, and others encouraged friends to stop off – especially breaking their journey and so revealing a 'traffic' that revenue from ticket sales would not.

Even outside census periods, a few people drummed up business for the country station as though it were a charity. Two elderly ladies travelled every Monday to Friday for months trying to persuade the Western Region to stop the *Devonian* from Bradford at Kingskerswell during the summer as well as winter.

Agonising to the keen country railwayman were regulations that allowed the junction station to sell cheaper tickets, or to sell them earlier than he could. At some stations one man might bend the rules to ensure the revenue fell to him, while his colleague on the other turn would not.

Even less fortunate was the stationmaster keen to sell a long-distance ticket, but unable to do so because he 'didn't have the fare'. Fares to unusual destinations had to be requested from district office and usually took at least two days. 'I haven't a fare to Southampton or even Andover, but Mrs Hicks went to Marlborough last month, so *please* let me book you there', pleaded the stationmaster at Eckington on the Midland line between Worcester and Cheltenham. But the passenger who had to change at Cheltenham insisted he would rebook there. 'What a disappointment', said the stationmaster.

Great Days of the Country Railway, 1986

of us enthusiasts for railways or seeing Britain from a different perspective. Though it would have resulted in earlier closures which wouldn't have pleased such people, little hardship would have been caused had there been well-timed and reliable connections with mainline services for something like forty per cent of branch passenger trains from the early 1930s. Only the LNER seriously experimented with closing stations to passengers while keeping them open for parcels as well as freight, separate parcel trains being run.

The war temporarily put the clock back, imported oil being scarcer than indigenous coal. Ironically, many lines were at their busiest passenger-wise within years of closure. This is when I'd especially like time to say more about Ireland and its wartime shortage of coal and the use made of its narrow-gauge systems.

In the mass closures of the Beeching era, bus replacements were laughably inadequate and gave extremely poor value for money. As a television reporter, I recall talking beside subsidised buses that arrived empty at stations after the trains they were supposed to connect with had already left. Some buses replacing trains on a branch off a branch continued running down long approach roads to the junction stations that had themselves been closed.

Why is it that Britain still has a totally unintegrated transport system? It is sometimes hard not to be bitter, as I frequently was when researching the effects of branch line closures in different parts of the country from Devon's Teign Valley to deepest Northumberland. Such was the specialist nature of the remaining passenger traffic on many branches, that only a third switched to the replacement buses, and that rapidly eroded. There are a couple of connections that still work, but in most cases business, especially feeding mainline expresses, was thrown away causing quite unnecessary inconvenience and hardship.

At which point, let's leave the world of politics to return to the country railway itself. Finally, let me take you through the seasons to demonstrate what role it performed, how and in what style. This is how perhaps the romance can best be re-lived.

Except in Scotland and the extreme north of England, the year began slowly, most people being back at work before 1 January, which only became a holiday after most country railways closed. The great unpredictable was the weather. Again, most country stations closed long before global warming reduced snowfalls. Almost every year at some stage or other, routes were blocked, the Great North of Scotland/LNER once thriving Buchan system north-east of Aberdeen being a particular sufferer.

There were legendary tales of it taking days to dig out abandoned trains that had ploughed into an unexpected wind-driven drift and become stuck. Melted snow was used to keep the engine's boiler providing heat for as long as possible. However, generally snow and especially ice boosted passenger business. Trains kept going when buses and cars couldn't. Gentry used to being driven to the junction now bought their tickets from the branch line station and there were nostalgic scenes as commuters again huddled round waiting room fires.

The colder the weather, the heavier the coal traffic, the staple of all railways in the days when there was the equivalent of a coal truck for the smallest hamlet and at least one for every market town street. Coal merchants with their depots in the goods yard were among the most important country businesses.

The mileage of milk trains was at its greatest in mid-winter. When the grass was greener, supplies were adequate from nearer the points of demand and milk from further afield was turned into butter and cheese. The stirrings of spring brought queues of broccoli specials from West Cornwall and daffodils and early potatoes from the Isles of Scilly and, slightly later, the Channel Islands and Pembrokeshire. Early strawberries from the Tamar Valley at Calstock and the Cheddar area of Somerset, plums from the Vale of Evesham and raspberries from Fife were all big business necessitating careful planning.

An extra goods train sometimes ran down the branch to cope with the distribution of fertilisers, another vital traffic. And if farmers had a good previous year, new tractors and machinery arrived on wagons often unloaded sideways at a passenger platform. The season's first farm removal trains carried people and their personal belongings, livestock, hay and farm machinery.

Except in Ireland, where the pilgrimage business – always a special feature there – reached a peak, Easter made little impact on the country railway or Post Office. May was livelier, with fairs and markets and perhaps the first noticeable number of outsiders coming down the line. May has long been a month of clashes in people's diaries. June, on the other hand, was often quiet, though it might bring the first of those few who systematically set out to explore Britain by train. They could be found in hotels and boarding house lounges with timetable, paper and pen patiently working out what combination of trains would enable them to see the most next day.

If his station boasted one, the stationmaster prepared for the first camping coach visitors. That meant more in-coming passengers, since the price of a camping coach included the purchase of a minimum number of return tickets from the home station. Camping coaches were far more spacious and homely, if a trifle old-fashioned in their fittings, than the caravans of the day.

Though the railway was called the permanent way, and on branch lines rails might last half a century or more, spring meant repairing winter damage, inspecting culverts, dealing with landslips, replacing sleepers and sometimes replacing whole sections of track. Even where there was no normal service, the latter was usually Sunday work, with signalmen enjoying useful overtime just for the passage of the engineer's train down in the early morning and back up in the evening.

The first of the season's long-distance excursions ran, many country railways having connections if not through services to distant parts at a mere pittance. It wasn't unusual for the bus journey home from the station at the end of an 18-hour day to cost almost as much as the basic train fare to a distant place. Private buses – often glorified taxis also used to deliver parcels – linked many small towns and even large villages with their station. On the GWR, every station stocked *Holiday Haunts*, covering all resorts and their accommodation. Station gardens came into their own; on all lines there were competitions for the best kept.

Summer saw an extra train or two on many lines, especially those providing through connections. In some pre-war years there were three annual timetables, winter, spring and summer. The true holiday season was then a short affair, heavily concentrated in July and August, with nearly everyone travelling to or from their resorts on Saturdays. Many lines including branches had special timetables for those Saturdays, some trains marked as running only from early July to late August, when local firms also closed for their holidays. The peak fortnight, the weeks striding the old August Bank Holiday, the first Monday in August, saw a universal increase in passenger business, even normally quiet branch line trains disgorging crowds. Especially after the war, late running on peak Saturdays was endemic. The whole timetable might be an hour or more in arrears, crowded branch non-corridor line trains kept at a signal for an hour or more before being allowed into the junction in their 'correct' order.

Many Midland and North Country branches were used as relief routes for inevitably slow holiday services. The joint Midland & Great Northern and the Somerset & Dorset saw often-delayed heavy, overcrowded trains – successions of them – struggling on their largely single lines, only engineered like glorified branch lines. It was the same throughout Britain, though Scotland's peak holidays came earlier in July. Even into the 1960s, a small resort like Nairn was starting point for two summer Saturday trains, terminating at different stations in the Scottish capital. Elgin was a delightful place to watch the Saturday pressure, the single route from Inverness dividing into three through ones toward Aberdeen. And at Grantown-on-Spey, I record members of three families crowding into a taxi from the station on the Speyside line serving the distilleries (then on their summer break) to the former LMS station. Here a crowd waited, some returning visitors to catch an Edinburgh train (one of those starting at Nairn), others for the Glasgow one a few minutes later. Such was the pressure that on some lines that, for a few hours on summer Saturdays, no trains stopped at minor stations. Trains on several lines were prevented from using the mainline and terminated at the last station before the junction.

On Mondays to Fridays during the peak fortnight, the 'City of . . .' services (most cities had one) ran to a different place each day, passengers guaranteed the same seat, journeys often including a branch line or two. Sunday School specials saw many stations at their busiest. It was hard to believe that the end was nigh. The peak year for summer Saturdays was 1958. By then the railway's share of traffic was already declining, though the total increasing. Coach and car then expanded dramatically. Sadly, it was the railway's ability to cope with the crowds, albeit with less comfort and punctuality, that actually delayed the movement toward staggered holidays. When congestion was transferred to the roads, motorists took their own steps to avoid the worst – and, not realising how untypical it was – remembered the poor service the railways had given.

Come September and the country railway more truly reflected the land through which it ran. Hop-pickers specials in Kent, sugar beet ones in East Anglia and teasels in Somerset. September was also the month in which most villages held their 'do', often based on a huge cattle, sheep or horse fair. Livestock and passenger specials still ran long after ordinary trains had been withdrawn. I recall a busy one from Morpeth to Bellingham. It was the last such, the last time tickets were sold through the booking office windows at stations that still retained staff. Though a Diesel, we ran to steam times, arriving everywhere early, so had time to stretch our legs at some stations and see passengers still arriving in good time to buy their tickets. We reversed at Redesmouth, and were piped into Bellingham en fête.

September was also a month when many branches were finally closed, their funerals seeing greater passenger numbers than in whole months previously. Ironically, thereafter more country people often went by train than they had when their local station was alive. In the new age of mobility, London, especially for Smithfield, the Ideal Home Exhibition and Motor Show was an increasing draw. Farmers and others drove to the nearest main-line station. Farmers especially spent lavishly in the restaurant car.

Autumn was often a period of heavy rain and not infrequent floods, and as winter took over the fogs of yesteryear descended. Fog and heavy mail traffic delayed many services at the approach to Christmas, branch line trains sometimes having to set off before the arrival of the day's last connecting expresses, occasionally running six or even as much as twenty hours late.

So it wasn't always idyllic as when one could put one's legs up in an empty compartment at the train's front enjoying the countryside and able to listen in to conversations between crew and station staff. Yet happy memories will always dominate. I've always been glad I was able to participate and revel in so much of it. As I drive around rural Britain today and see abandoned embankments and strips of woodland that have invaded the 'permanent' way, I relive so many memories – including humorous ones, such as being handed an unwanted baby by a mother who jumped aboard just as the train started – and reading love letters to an illiterate horse trader for a welcome bob. 'Does she really say that? – Honest?'

The end of a busy summer's day on the Isle of Man Railway as a Port Erin train arrives at Douglas. Though traffic was heavy and speeds notorious for a 3ft gauge line, at this time there was no thought of the railway being rescued as a voluntary line, run only in summer. Allowed to walk freely as trains were marshalled and put to bed, I was rather pleased at the amount of steam I recorded. Note the semaphore. There was a busy signalbox.

PHOTOGRAPHY BY PETER W. GRAY

LEFT A classic view of the branch line terminus at Kingsbridge. This was the station I had in mind for the chapter on 'A Day in the Life of a Country Terminus' in my book, *Railway Season*. Except on summer Saturdays, when there were through coaches to and from Paddington, the number of passengers was seldom great, yet the station was very much key to the local economy. For many years, nearly all new agricultural equipment for the South Hams arrived by the daily goods train.

BELOW There was less goods traffic for Ashburton, sometimes reached by the wagons being propelled from Buckfastleigh. The picture almost looks like a photographic run on today's South Devon Railway, though alas this now terminates at Buckfastleigh since, having opposed the line's closure, the Devon County Council grabbed the land for a widened A38 and prevented reopening.

ABOVE In BR days, a single coach runs along one of the prettiest sections of the Dart, still much enjoyed by visitors to today's SDR, of which I am Patron. We like to be known as the Friendly Line.

RIGHT The train in the landscape. An auto-car at Pullabrook on the Moretonhampstead branch, still much missed.

LEFT A train of imported coal at Kingswear leaving for Torquay Gas Works. (See Chapter 8.)

BELOW Another day to remember, an enthusiasts' steam special hauled by a Drummond T9, a class nicknamed Greyhounds. We travelled at high speeds over the North Cornwall line since, till the end, track maintenance carried out from Halwill Junction, seen here, was of a very high order. Once shunting always seemed to be taking place where the routes to Bude and Padstow separated and the grandly named North Devon & North Cornwall Junction Light Railway from Torrington terminated.

RIGHT Rush hour at Thorverton on the Exe Valley branch with two auto-cars crossing …

BELOW … but there are many more passengers on board a summer Saturday express from Waterloo on the single line just having restarted after reversal at Sidmouth Junction. At Tipton St John the train will divide into Exmouth and Sidmouth portions.

With prominence given to the semaphore signals, Peter catches the old, long-lasting 7.30am Paddington to Kingswear, seen here accelerating having topped the summit at Whiteball Tunnel straddling the Somerset/Devon border.

LEFT *The year is 1959, the Royal Albert Bridge over the Tamar at Saltash is floodlit to celebrate the centenary of Brunel's last masterpiece.*

BELOW *And, before the road bridge across the river was opened, the familiar sight of a pannier tank sandwiched between two pairs of auto-cars on a suburban service to Plymouth. The first arch of the Royal Albert Bridge can just be seen on the far right. Five hundred or more passengers were carried by some such trains.*

The 'withered arm', the nickname for the
for the sprawling Southern system west
of Exeter.

ABOVE *Torrington, where through
carriages from Waterloo terminated, the
continuation being the little-used but long-
titled North Devon & Cornwall Junction
Light Railway to Halwill Junction.*

ABOVE *The single platform at Barnstaple Town, with a* West Country Pacific, *the first modern locomotive built for the withered arm.*

OVERLEAF *A pair of them storm Morthoe Bank with an Ilfracombe express.*

CHAPTER 4
65 YEARS OF RAILWAY WRITING
(1: 1946–63)

*Given prominence in 1946 when I was only sixteen, the publication of an article entitled
'Brunel was too Optimistic' kicked off my writing career. A schoolgirl telephoned to say her
father had seen it in the Plymouth evening paper. My parents weren't pleased; I should be sticking
to schoolwork. The schoolgirl gave me a copy of it between lessons the following day.*

*Published on 28 July 1952, what follows is the first of hundreds of reports on
summer Saturday rail traffic. The number of passengers doubled in the next six years
reaching a peak in 1958. Road traffic had been increasing even more rapidly.*

A SCHOOLBOY'S DREAM

VISITORS by train from London on a summer Saturday tell you: 'We raced most of the way, but we got stuck outside Taunton and took nearly as long to cover the last 60 miles as the rest of the journey.'

The wonder is that delays at Taunton are not greater for here the mainlines from Bristol, the North, South Wales and the Midlands, and from London converge.

The bulk of what has been carried on two independent routes now all has to go westward up steep Wellington Bank. Figures tell the story.

Up Wellington Bank an interval of five or six minutes must elapse between the passing of each down train. Yet leaving Taunton for Exeter as early as 3.00am on Saturday four express passenger trains went within a quarter of an hour.

In the afternoon trains left Taunton at 2.06, 2.17, 2.21, 2.23, two at 2.29, 2.35, 2.39, two at 2.48 and 2.59. Between Taunton and Norton Fitzwarren there is a relief as well as a mainline, but beyond all down trains have to use one track.

Some would have found a clear 'path' but those leaving less than six minutes after the previous one would of necessity be delayed by signals in the middle of the steep climb to Whiteball Tunnel, on the boundary of Somerset and Dorset.

The timetable gives each train a theoretically clear run. The trains come from places as far apart as London, Newcastle, Wolverhampton, Liverpool and Cardiff, and what happens at Bradford on Friday night may upset things at Taunton the following morning. Accurate timekeeping on a Saturday is impossible, and trains, as they do not always run in prescribed order, carry a number in front of the engine by which they can be identified.

Taunton station on Saturday was a schoolboy's dream. Every few minutes an express, though delayed on the outskirts of the town, raced through the station, and during the day most of the best engines of the Western Region passed through.

There were some pretty old-fashioned coaches too, in the kaleidoscope. Many other long-distance trains, each carrying 700 to 1,500 passengers, stopped and disgorged crowds for the Barnstaple and Ilfracombe and the Minehead branch trains.

Dialects of all parts of Britain intermingled on the platforms. Call the West Country sleepy? Not when 109 down long-distance trains passed through Taunton between midnight and 6.00pm.

The first time I spent a summer Saturday on Taunton station was in 1946. Though some trains were as crowded on Saturdays as during the grim war days, one could not help noticing how much happier people looked – especially the children, who had just broken up for their holidays.

The railway system is elastic but, even when all goods traffic is suspended, it is impossible to carry more than ten times the normal weekday passenger traffic without some inconvenience. But there were few complaints and much laughter could be heard on the platforms.

Some trains had empty seats, but others, particularly those from the North and Midlands, were definitely overcrowded. It is difficult for the railway authorities to estimate demand for each train, and while one express from Torquay to Wolverhampton was half empty. The next, only a little later, was overcrowded.

Though steam had ruled at Starcross along the Exe (the GWR ran a ferry service to Exmouth which used to carry the railway parcel traffic), this photograph shows an early Diesel-hauled Cornish Riviera Express, *while the tower of the atmospheric pumping station can be seen in the background near the signalbox. In that box, with no train on the board, it was eerie hearing the sound of a steam locomotive coming across the foggy water from the Southern's Exmouth branch.*

In the Torbay area, however, a new scheme is operating this summer. Passengers wishing to return to London on a Saturday have to be in possession of a ticket (issued free of charge) to board one of twelve trains. Though no specific seat is reserved, this arrangement ensures the balanced loading of each train.

Normally on a Saturday up to 10,000 passengers arrive in the Torbay area from London. A further 4,500 from the London Midland line, 5,500 from the Western line to Wolverhampton, 2,500 from the North, and 2,000 from South Wales go towards Torbay's grand total of about 30,000 – a figure excluding all joining west of Bristol.

A large number of people travelled overnight and arrived in Devon during the early hours of Saturday morning, By the evening there was a real crisis problem for those who had not booked accommodation, but eventually everyone seems to have found a bed.

It is impossible to form an accurate estimate, but probably 120,000 or more people moved into Devon and Cornwall on Saturday. During the next fortnight I hope to describe how some of them spend their holidays, and how satisfied they are with the amenities offered by the resorts.

A RAILWAY BYWAY

I also frequently contributed to the West Country's Sunday paper, The Independent. *This on the Callington branch was in September 1952.*

EVEN the enthusiastic motorist must admit that some of the grandest river and moorland scenery is best revealed to the traveller on railway branch lines.

Who can forget the journeys along the Fowey or the Camel estuaries, through the upper reaches of river valleys, or over the moor to Princetown? In many cases the train has almost become part of the countryside through which it passes.

One railway byway that has perhaps been unduly neglected is the Bere Alston to Callington line. There is something magic in the ascent from the picturesque Calstock viaduct up the ledge along the cliffside overlooking the romantic Tamar Valley – the squat little engine all the while shrieking its whistle to warn road users of its approach to the unprotected level crossings.

It was about ninety years ago, when there were many mines and quarries, that a scheme originated for a railway in the district. In 1869 the Callington & Calstock Railway Company was incorporated with a capital of £60,000 and empowered to build an 8-mile line of 3ft 6in gauge for mineral traffic.

From Calstock Quay, which was rebuilt and improved by the company, the line rose by an inclined plane to the marshalling yards some 300ft above. Worked by the system of counterbalancing, the weight of two full trucks drawing up three empty ones, the inclined plane was of single track with a passing loop in the middle. Beyond, the line proceeded to Gunnislake and Kelly Bray, the site of the present Callington station, 680ft above sea level. Numerous sidings connected with mineral workings.

During its first years the railway prospered, and Calstock became a thriving port dealing with quite large vessels. Half a dozen boats would sometimes be loading or unloading at the same time, and in those pre-viaduct days a regular service of passenger boats took people to market at Plymouth.

Throughout my long life I've travelled through Sonning Cutting on every conceivable kind of train, from GW steam ones, but also hauled by a variety of locomotives from other systems in the exchanges of the 1950s, including this experimental gas turbine No. 18000, shown here on a Cheltenham Spa train in July 1955.

Encouraged by their success the proprietors of the railway proposed to convert the line to standard gauge, and to build a branch to Morwellham Quay, outlet of the Tavistock Canal traffic, whence a tramway already led to the famous Devon Great Consols Mine. But mining became depressed, and nothing had been done about constructing the 8-mile extension when, in 1884, a Plymouth, Devonport & South Western Junction Railway (with powers to absorb the mineral line) came into being. This line – giving LSWR trains separate access to Plymouth (hitherto they had shared the GW line from Lydford) – was opened in 1890.

The Mineral Railway was officially absorbed in the following year, but only in 1908 was it rebuilt into a standard-gauge passenger line and extended across the twelve-arch 120ft high viaduct to Bere Alston.

The line was slow to yield returns, but by 1913 a half-yearly dividend of 3½ per cent was being paid, and 112,639 passengers were carried in a year. A scheme to link Callington with the North Cornwall line near Launceston raised high hopes but came to nothing.

The passenger train service has altered little in over forty years, there now being six up and seven down weekday trains plus a late evening special on Saturdays, and four trains in each direction on Sundays, with a few additional 'short' trains run between Bere

Alston and Gunnislake. On average, about 1,400 tickets are sold each month at Calstock and nearly 3,000 at Gunnislake. Above Gunnislake passenger traffic is light.

The mineral traffic for which the line was built is now small, the only mine in the district (at Luckett) providing the railway with little freight. Yet, for its length and considering it is only maintained as a Light Railway, the branch must surely be among the most remunerative in the West. In the season large quantities of fruit and flowers from the Tamar Valley are sent to London, Wales, the Midlands and Scotland. Last year, 404 vans and 50,000 packages of flowers, and 314 vans and 66,000 packages of fruit were dispatched from the district. Large bogie vehicles for express parcels trains work right through from Gunnislake to places like Cardiff, London and Newcastle. Much organisation has to be done behind the scenes before two tank engines noisily start to pull a string of vehicles laden with flowers or fruit up the gradients and round the curves from the viaduct to the mainline at Bere Alston.

A NIGHT ON THE GREAT WESTERN TPO

In December 1952, when mail was still exchanged at speed with lineside apparatus, I wrote about a trip on the Great Western westbound Travelling Post Office which then seemed as permanent an institution as Brunel's main line itself. I was then on the staff of the Western Morning News.

THE scene is Paddington on a cold December evening. Though a stream of long-distance expresses is arriving from the West and from Wales, there is comparatively little activity on the departure platforms. But at 8.45pm a tank locomotive pulls into platform 5, a train of eleven vehicles, which will carry mail touching the lives of several million people.

Barrow load after barrow load of mailbags is brought onto the platform, and at 9.00pm a staff of thirty-four leading postmen (more generally known as sorters) joins the train. Until 10.00pm large quantities of mail continue to arrive from places as far apart as Hull, Doncaster, Dover and Cambridge.

Even when the electric telegraph was used, trains on many lines were started on verbal command. When the signalman who crossed trains at the Menheniot passing loop said 'Right away, Dick,' the wrong engine driver (both were called Dick) started, resulting in a head-on crash, in which this South Devon Railway engine was destroyed and so never entered the GWR's stock. This photograph is a real period piece (note the universal headgear).

Some comes to the station by motor van, but most travels by the private narrow-gauge underground railway which links the main line termini and the large Mount Pleasant Post Office. Meanwhile the sorters have begun opening large numbers of mailbags and are organising things on board the Travelling Post Office.

By 10.00pm order is restored on the platform, and only a few late-arriving consignments remain to be stowed aboard. A commercial traveller posts a letter in the late box on the train itself. The letter, which should bear an extra halfpenny stamp, will be delivered at Penzance first post next morning.

At 10.09pm a letter is posted to a London address. The correspondent evidently knows something of Post Office working. If put in a London pillar box the letter would not be collected till the following morning; if posted on the train it is taken to Bristol, transferred to the up Travelling Post Office, and delivered in London by first post.

Punctually at 10.10pm, driver A.V. Coleman opens the regulator of *Ince Castle* and the train slides out of Brunel's great station, carrying its thousands of letters with good and bad news, parcels, cheques and bills, Christmas cards and court summonses. Throughout its journey the train is given top priority. If it is delayed a high proportion of people living in half of Wales and in five English counties will be affected.

Many times I have watched the smooth way in which the Great Western Travelling Post Office is loaded and dispatched. But on this particular night I was able to see for myself something of the working of the train and partake of the friendly atmosphere that exists on board. Great Britain has a network of forty-eight Travelling Post Offices, which cover 2,500,000 miles a year. About 7½ per cent of all letters are actually sorted on them, a large proportion of the ready-made-up bags of letters and parcels also being distributed.

The existence of the trains has enabled the Post Office to cope with the vastly increased mail of recent decades and yet still deliver in the far West by the morning's first post, letters collected in London or beyond at 6.00pm. The West has the distinction of being served by one of the two pairs of trains which are kept exclusively for postal purposes. The Paddington–Penzance and the Euston–Aberdeen trains – and their corresponding up numbers – are the backbone of the whole British mail service. Nearly all the night organisation of the Post Office is dependent on them.

The Paddington–Penzance train is an unusual one of three 60ft sorting coaches, three letter mail stowage coaches, and five vans for parcel mail. The parcel vans, which do not have corridor connection, contain bags of parcel mail already sorted for destination. The rest of the train is vestibuled with through side corridor connection. Into the three stowage coaches are placed bags of letters posted early enough in the day for them to be sorted prior to dispatch on the train. Some bags are distributed at each stopping place.

The three sorting coaches are arranged to give the maximum movement and comfort in the 8½ft by 60ft area. Fittings are padded to save sorters from possible knocks as the train sways at speed. On a normal run the sorters handle about 2,000 bags of mail and 90,000 separate items. When the train reaches Maidenhead the automatic exchange apparatus is brought into use. By the lineside there is a standard and a strong movable net, both of which are turned towards the track. Similar dispatching arms and receiving nets are opened on the side of the coach, and at high speed almost instantaneous exchange of mail takes place. The lineside and coach nets snatch the pouches hanging from the respective arms.

First stop is Reading, where mail from the southern route by Basingstoke and from the western line to the North is taken on. The train collects mail from places much farther away than the Great Western main line would normally serve for passenger purposes. The three sorting carriages are now the scene of greatest activity. Most of the thirty-four sorters are dealing with the 'immediate' mail (for destinations before and round Bristol) and the Welsh mail. It is an ordered activity. Each sorter has his particular job, the whole working together as a team. Some sorters place a letter a second into the pigeonholes on which have been chalked up West and Welsh place names. At this stage of the journey there is little conversation and an almost grim determination to complete the job.

At Swindon and again at Chippenham I watched Mr L.W. Gullis – known as the 'iron man' – work the exchange apparatus. Though it was snowing hard, he knew exactly when to pull the lever to open the dispatching arms and receiving net. These had been placed in position only a few moments before several pouches containing mailbags came hurtling in. Though the exchange apparatus remains the showpiece of the Travelling Post Office, it is not used so much as formerly. The London mail uses it only once more – at Liskeard.

Better road connecting services have enabled the dispatch from the train to be made in bulk at fewer places, and today towns like Dawlish and Teignmouth (which once had their own apparatus) are served through Newton Abbot. The day-time North mail between Bristol and Plymouth and Plymouth and Bristol does, however, still exchange at Totnes, Cullompton, Bridgwater and Highbridge.

At Bath the Wiltshire mail is put out, and by this time (12.12am) nearly all the Welsh and Somerset post is sorted. Mail for big towns in South Wales is put in bags ready for destination; letters for smaller places are packed in bulk and are re-sorted on the Welsh Travelling Post Office from Bristol. Between Bath and Bristol things were a little more leisurely, and the sorters found time for a cup of that rare beverage – TPO tea.

Attention was now given to some odd items – a registered letter packed in such poor wrapping that the pound notes were falling out, a package addressed to 'Newport' without stating the county of any one of the ten British towns by that name, and several letters addressed in such appalling writing that they were passed up and down the train before it was decided what should be done with them.

The sorters, whose ages range from twenty-one to sixty, are experienced men and know the exact whereabouts not only of each town and village, but also of many suburbs and scattered hamlets. By working as a team they pool their knowledge and the information they enter in their 'tip' book. On this train Mr R. Cox was the inspector. He made it his personal responsibility to see that not a moment was wasted, but he was full of praise for the team spirit in which the sorters work.

Bristol Temple Meads becomes extremely busy when the Travelling Post Office arrives at platform 6 at 12.38am. Already the corresponding up train has arrived and the Travelling Post Offices from and to Carmarthen and Derby are standing in the station.

Altogether eight trains are involved in an exchange of mail, the scope of which is only exceeded by Crewe. Twelve London sorters leave the down train and prepare to help on the up one. Sorters who have just arrived from South Wales take over the train going back to Carmarthen. Leaving Temple Meads at 12.55am the down train has a swift run to Taunton, where the rest of the Somerset mail is cleared. At Exeter goes the post for all North and East Devon, as well as for the immediate district.

From the Devon sorting coach are sent separate bags made up for every postal address in the county. To watch the sorters at work is in itself a valuable lesson in geography. At Newton Abbot is sent out the post for the Torbay and South Hams area. At Exeter three

A once-popular service that disappeared along with things such as slip coaches, Post Office trains exchanging mail with lineside apparatus at full speed, and water troughs in the days of Dieselisation and standardisation.

Penzance sorters join the train and the emphasis is now on the Cornish mail. Already the Penzance post is being sorted according to the rounds of individual postmen.

Beyond Newton Abbot I began to find the weariness of night travel creep on – but not so my guide, Chief Inspector Ben Hall, whose supply of information, mixed with good wit, never languished. Mr Hall proved no ordinary guide, and such was his keenness to make me learned in Travelling Post Office matters that at Bristol and other stops we ran round like schoolboys.

Mr Hall, who began life as a telegraph messenger boy, and is now in charge of a group of postal trains, is retiring next month. His comments on people who cannot address envelopes properly were so strong that I will never be caught *not* writing the name of the town in block letters. 'And to think we provide all this service for tuppence-ha'penny,' he said as I left him at Plymouth. 'And then people talk about restoring the penny post.'

When Plymouth is reached at 4.09am, fourteen more London sorters sign off and the post for Torpoint, Ivybridge and Launceston is put out. Two more Penzance men come aboard the train which now consists of seven coaches.

At Saltash letters for Calstock are dispatched, and at Liskeard the Looe post goes by the automatic exchange. A stop at Bodmin Road serves places such as Camelford, Lostwithiel, Newquay, Padstow and Wadebridge. The next stop is St Austell and then Truro, where the remaining Londoners leave. At Redruth goes the Helston and Camborne post, and at Hayle letters for St Ives. Penzance is reached at 6.45am, by which time the majority of the town's post is already sorted for delivery.

The up Travelling Post Office leaves Penzance at 6.40pm, Plymouth at 9.13pm and arrives at Paddington at 3.40am. Altogether 100 minutes are allowed for stops, and it is only through the excellent co-operation between railway and Post Office staff that station work can be accomplished according to schedule.

As the Travelling Post Offices run mostly by night, the public sees little of them. Even when ice brings road traffic to a standstill there are complaints if letters are delivered an

Two routes to Lydford, where unusually the signalbox had GWR and Southern lever frames back-to-back. The train is a Western Region one from Plymouth to Launceston, while the double track is that of the Southern's Exeter–Plymouth mainline around the north of Dartmoor.

hour late. It is taken for granted that a letter posted at Penzance in the evening will reach London for first delivery. It is, however, only through the high standard of service given by the postal and railway staff that our mail is delivered so efficiently.

It may not be everybody's idea of a pleasant life, travelling through each night, working against the clock sorting letters, but the men of the Travelling Post Office find their task anything but monotonous. They take pride in the tradition that every letter should be sorted in time for dispatch at the proper place.

RAILWAY STRIKE

This is the script of the first of my hundreds of broadcasts, many on railways. It went out live on the BBC's West Home Service on 6 June 1955 as the national railway strike began to bite.

I was driving along a North Devon lane running parallel with a now-rusty branch line, when a farm labourer stopped me to ask the time. The trains usually told him what o'clock it was, he explained. It was awkward without the trains. 'Of course,' he added, 'I never travel on 'em, but it's nice to know they are there.' The remark is typical. These days only a small proportion of West Country people actually travel by the trains, but everybody misses them when they stop running and when letters posted at Truro are not delivered at Exeter till three days later.

It was the silence and lack of activity which impressed me most in Devon and Cornwall. Not once did I hear an engine whistle or see a puff of smoke rising above some distant hill. There is only a little extra road traffic, and taken as a whole the West seems remarkably inactive. Judging by the number of people on the promenades at the resorts, it might be mid-winter. I thought a Post Office official hit the nail on the head. 'The strike has made London seem further away,' he said, 'and that has made the West even sleepier that usual.'

West Country people are not prone to strike. The fact is, however, the further West you go, the more complete is the stoppage. Some days only two trains have reached Plymouth, and on three quarters of the branch lines in Devon and Cornwall there have been none at all. Today, for the first time since last Tuesday, a passenger train left Penzance. Yesterday the only service on the Cornish mainline was in the opposite direction. All the way down, stations were completely deserted. And this is the beginning of the holiday season!

A fair number of goods trucks have been moved on the mainline, and so far everybody has been able to crowd onto the passenger trains which have run. A few more crews are working today, and there should be a better service in Cornwall tomorrow. But in the marshalling yards, where there are no engines for shunting, there are rows and rows of unsorted trucks.

Engine drivers on strike at Barnstaple have played cricket to pass away the time. It is the station staffs, who must each day report for duty but have very little to do, who find time heavy on their hands. Porters are reduced to reading the papers. Signalmen without signals to pull are cultivating their lineside gardens. And so the weary days drag on.

PARLIAMENT DEFIED

Parts of the introduction to A Regional History of the Railways of Great Britain: Volume 1 The West Country, *1960.*

ON 29 November 1952, inhabitants of Bridgwater's northern outskirts peered cautiously through their windows. Outside, two men ran to crouch in a doorway, automatically covering their heads as a whistle blew and explosions thudded. An accident at a local armaments factory was fresh in memory, and anyway the evening itself was eerie: after a wild, gusty day, snow was falling silently, stealthily subduing the suburb.

The noise was merely a few railwaymen's way of paying their last respects to the Bridgwater branch of the Somerset & Dorset Railway. Detonators had been placed every few yards along the track and the locomotive's whistle was tied down. Residents were taken unawares: for most of them the railway had virtually ceased to exist years ago, and nobody had troubled to spread the news that this would be the last train to set out across Horsey Level and Chilton Moor to Edington Junction.

The only passengers were a handful of railway enthusiasts and one or two reporters. At the Junction we waited for trains in either direction on the Somerset & Dorset's Highbridge line. One arrived empty; the other's sole fare was a red-faced Victorian-looking gentleman soundly asleep. The theoretic connections having been fulfilled, we recrossed the moor and at intermediate Cossington saw the guard extinguish the solitary lamp. The station was closed – in defiance of Parliament. The unrepealed Bridgwater Railway Act of 1882 states that at Cossington, 'The Company shall construct and for ever hereafter maintain . . . a fit and suitable stone or brick building with convenient approaches and proper goods sidings.'

As we alighted at Bridgwater North, quite deserted, snow dripping through the wooden roof, it was hard to believe that when this Act of 1882 was passed church bells rang out in wild rejoicing. Originally the town was served by the Bristol & Exeter Railway, a continuation of the Great Western, whose monopolistic service was not good enough for the merchants. They had made three unsuccessful applications to Parliament for powers for a rival route before the triumph of 1882. Friendships were made and broken according to whether families supported the ending or the continuance of the Bristol & Exeter's monopoly. Meetings and petitions were common; so were 'casuistry and cunning'.

The rest of the story is typical. The Bridgwater Railway brought little direct financial reward to its local proprietors but benefited the larger Somerset & Dorset and the still larger London & South Western a great deal. For example, they persuaded Bridgwater people to use the new line to join their route to London (*via* Templecombe) instead of going by the Great Western (with which the Bristol & Exeter had amalgamated). But this competition in itself made the Great Western belatedly improve its service, which eventually far exceeded anything possible by the indirect single-track Edington Junction route. In the automobile age even local patronage of this declined, and the one-time well-supported fourteen daily trains to and from Bridgwater North fell to four carrying a mere handful of passengers. So the Transport Commission decided to risk closure, despite Cossington's 'for ever hereafter' clause. No legal objections were raised.

Economically there was no justification for a second railway at Bridgwater – or there would not have been had the first one produced a good service. As, however, the Great Western would not do this until faced by a competitor, the town does owe the latter a debt. The improved service and reduced goods rates enabled expansion and consolidation at a crucial period.

It was after making that journey in 1952 and reflecting how much more auspiciously the era had began than it ended that the idea for this book and then for the series occurred – the idea of showing something of what railways have meant in social history, as well as telling the story of their development. The best way to do this is obviously to divide the regions into reasonably self-contained areas, not necessarily corresponding to those served by the individual railways.

Take a quick glance at the railway revolution in regional perspective. Consider what happened in a single generation, 1830 to 1860.

In 1830, though there were already a few isolated goods railways, particularly in Cornwall, virtually everyone and everything had to travel by sailing ship, on horseback or by horse-drawn vehicle. Several resorts had begun to grow, but for the most part only people compelled to travel did so. The vast majority of workers neither needed nor desired to go afield. The region had largely missed the industrial revolution, and – with one or two notable exceptions – sources of employment had changed little for many years. The owners of most of the small town mills of various kinds felt secure at the head of their tiny empires. Road towns such as Launceston were expanding steadily. Local and not Greenwich time was still used, while few national newspapers penetrated the far West. Though thanks to turnpikes and faster coach services they had improved greatly during the previous decade, postal arrangements remained crude.

Stage coaches did much to pave the way for the railways, but in the West they never carried heavy traffic, and limited seating meant that often passengers had to be refused. The point to be emphasised is that the coaches had an incredibly short heyday. In 1780 it still took nearly two days to travel from Plymouth to London; and some parts of the West, relying on the traditional packhorses, saw no wheeled vehicles. But by 1830 average speeds of 10mph were fairly common and in 1835 London to Devonport was regularly performed in 21¼ hours. The number as well as the speed of coaches increased – mainly after 1830 and thus within the generation whose beginning and ending we are comparing. Coaches were now timed in half-minutes. The opening of the London & Manchester Railway in 1830 put speed at a premium everywhere. As the railway network increased, the declining coaches made speedy connections with trains.

By 1860 the mainline railway system had been completed and its power demonstrated. The places it by-passed, such as Launceston, were already falling back, while a host of new resorts had been created and the holiday trade become firmly established in most of the region as a major source of livelihood (not in Cornwall, exceptional in this and some other respects). Everyone came directly or indirectly under railway influence and a surprisingly large section of the population actually used the trains, if only once a year and mainly for local journeys. Comings and goings between London and the West

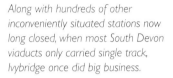

Along with hundreds of other inconveniently situated stations now long closed, when most South Devon viaducts only carried single track, Ivybridge once did big business.

were at least a dozen times more numerous than in 1830. The increased travelling, the universal adoption of Greenwich time, the rising popularity of national newspapers and the greater space given to national events by local newspapers which could now use the telegraph, a vital railway adjunct – all this had begun to blend the West into the rest of the country. The process of standardisation and centralisation had been set in motion, the closure of many of the small mills whose future had seemed so secure in 1830 being only one indication of the way things were moving. Indeed, most of the trends still in evidence today were firmly established a century ago.

NARROW GAUGE TO KILLYBEGS

This is my publisher's Postscript to The County Donegal Railways *by Edward M. Patterson, 1962, an early David & Charles title commissioned as a result of my visit.*

ONE of my most prized possessions is a ticket issued by the County Donegal Railways Joint Committee. It reads: 'PASS Mr and Mrs Thomas TO all stations FROM all stations AND BACK'. Alas, during a short tour of Ireland to study transport problems we had little time to take advantage of this magical document, and to my lasting regret I was unable to accept the offer of a footplate ride through the Barnesmore Gap.

We did, however, travel down the main line from Strabane to Killybegs and back, and it was during this journey that the idea of a book on the system was born. The railway immediately struck me, a dispassionate observer, as a remarkable enterprise. The first surprise, of course was that there should be a narrow-gauge railway at all in so thinly peopled an area as late as the mid-1950s. Merely to travel on the trains seemed to be stepping back in history. But any thoughts of it being a mere quaint anachronism were rapidly dispelled. Until the end, the railway played a vital part in the life of the community it served, and it was run with exemplary efficiency.

Above all, the system impressed me with its friendliness. Here were none of the formalities and none of the dignity which so often seem designed to reduce the stature of passengers on standard-gauge railways. The County Donegal Railways were simple, domesticated – no impersonal organisation sheltering behind a mystique. Relations between staff and passengers, and among the staff themselves, were eminently human. Another attractive feature was the railway's unselfconsciousness; being so far removed from big centres it was relatively little visited by enthusiasts. There was no temptation to become a show or museum piece: the local population always came first.

Although my visit was short, I came away with many memories to cherish. Some of these centre on the enthusiastic welcome given me at the Stranorlar headquarters, with its loco and carriage shops, its sweet-stall in the booking hall, its diminutive footbridge and its incongruous clock-tower above the gentlemen's lavatory. The coaches stabled in the bay platform pending the departure of the next steam-hauled excursion were unlocked for examination, and the railcars were run out from the maintenance shed especially for me to photograph them. On departure, I sat beside the driver for the journey on to Killybegs.

The grim grandeur of the Barnesmore Gap was impressive enough, but what most excited me was the last section, along the rough, tortuous and quite undeveloped Atlantic

Rural exotica. A Teign Valley train from Exeter to Heathfield climbs away from Ide in 1958. On summer Saturdays, a bus took passengers from Ide to Exeter to save branch-line trains using scarce capacity.

seaboard. The Diesel horn echoed: the crossing keepers opened the gates; mothers and children rushed to the doorways of the whitewashed crossing cottages; and labourers digging tiny patches of peaty soil at the cliff's edge set their watches as we rollicked by. The driver apologised for the rough riding: I should have come when the track was as good as anything I would have seen in England, he said. Talking about England, 'My daddy once went there. I've never been myself, of course.' And so into the dilapidated little port of Killybegs, where the most modern object was an oil tank wagon, a neat miniature of Esso's British wagons, standing in the sidings.

Here was a service worth recording.

Even since nationalisation, route 'rationalisation' has continued. Weymouth passengers for London now all go via Bournemouth, but in 1962 there were Paddington expresses such as this passing Bruton.

STRESS AND STORM

The Great Western's Launceston branch was often in the news. These two pieces, published in the Western Morning News *in December 1962, record my last actual journey and how the greatest twentieth-century blizzard in the West Country prevented me participating in the closure night funeral, when the last four trains didn't run or complete their journeys, but I kept in touch with stations by phone. Reprinted in* Double Headed: Two Generations of Railway Enthusiasm *(1963, 1981) written jointly with my father.*

I have just taken my final daylight journey on the branch between Plymouth, Tavistock and Launceston. The rich pattern of memories it evokes took me aback: memories of first boyhood sorties to Dartmoor; of attendances at village functions when I was junior reporter stationed at Plymouth; of journeys for the sake of journeying with mother, sister and fiancée; of adventures into industrial archaeology in Bickleigh Vale and Tavistock. The railway seems woven into the very fabric of my life; yet I have known it only during its decline – and but part of that. Its brighter days had already receded deep into history when I took a ticket from Plymouth to Yelverton in an auto-car or push-pull train powered by an 0-4-2 tank engine.

I cannot resist retelling the line's story. As early as 1845, the South Devon Railway (building the broad gauge line to Plymouth) had prudently proposed a Tavistock branch so as to avert possible narrow-gauge penetration to West Devon. This was only fifteen years after the opening of the Liverpool & Manchester Railway, stressing the speed of the Railway Revolution.

In 1848 the broad-gauge interests subscribed to a Plymouth Great Western Dock Company – the docks were built later – in retaliation to a London & South Western Railway narrow-gauge scheme linking a Plymouth branch *via* Okehampton and Tavistock with a Sutton Harbour development plan. But eventually the fight for Tavistock was between the South Devon and its former chairman, Thomas Gill. He had resigned after the rest of the board refused to sanction further trials of Brunel's unsuccessful atmospheric system, and now had narrow-gauge backing. Said the press:

'We trust that a timely coalition between the parties will take place so as to prevent a useless waste of money in the first instance, and the probable Parliamentary defeat of both in the next. The ambition of Mr Gill to regain a footing in the district may be laudable enough, but times, seasons, events and probabilities should be consulted quite as much as personal whims or lawyers' quarrels.'

Newspaper circulations soared as editors campaigned for the rival schemes: in 1852 whole pages (each with eight tightly packed columns) were frequently given to reports of meetings. Friendships were made and broken. Only solicitors thrived.

As foreseen, both schemes were defeated in Parliament in 1853. Gill collected help from far and wide for the next session's effort. His scheme was now magnificently entitled the Plymouth, Tavistock & Devon Central, and would have given Barnstaple and Bideford direct access to Plymouth. But the battle was won by the South Devon, with the timely help of Lord Morley, who struck a personal bargain to aid his own coffers. (The South Devon built the Lee Moor Tramway for him – but so poorly that it quickly had to be rebuilt.)

Construction of the single line from Tavistock Junction near Marsh Mills was slow and costly. Engineering works included Shaugh, Yelverton and Grenofen tunnels, and six large timber viaducts, that at Walkham being 376yds long and 132ft high. Hundreds of workers and horses were employed, but apart from press reports of the occasional brawl, we can only guess what the invasion of navvies meant to the villages and hamlets along the route. We do know, however, that progress was not rapid enough for the mining interests in Tavistock and the Tamar Valley, and that many people travelling from Tavistock to Exeter and beyond found it more convenient to catch a coach to Copplestone on the North Devon Railway than to Plymouth.

Opening day was 21 June 1859. The Royal Albert Bridge and the Cornwall Railway had been opened only the previous month, but that did not slacken the appetite for rejoicing. The local newspaper recorded:

Not a few of the inhabitants of the Plymouth end of the line were willing to make a
holiday, and, as the whole people of Tavistock seemed to participate in that feeling,
it appears to have been tactfully resolved that all who were on pleasure bent should
make that agreeable little town the scene of general festivity. And most assuredly
everything was done which could be done to give éclat to an event which will
evermore make the 21st of June one of the brightest red letter days in its annals.

Regular services started next day. At first the line was busier with minerals than with passengers. Adjoining the Tavistock station was the wealthy Wheal Crelake, whose ores were carried 'at especially favourable rates'. So unimportant was the local passenger traffic that intermediate stations were built only at Bickleigh and Horrabridge. Marsh Mills was added in 1861. Passenger business was, however, boosted by the extension to Launceston in 1865.

Launceston's fortunes had declined deplorably since, upon the opening of the Cornwall Railway, through traffic had deserted what is now the A30 road. The town worked frantically to be placed on the railway map. Again broad and narrow-gauge interests clashed. After many frustrations, the broad-gauge bill passed the Lords on 30 May 1862 'We well remember the trial of Queen Caroline . . . and the capture of Sebastopol, but on these occasions there was not the hundredth part felt by Launceston people as at present.'

Victory for the broad-gauge was brief. In 1876 the LSWR reached Lydford *via* Okehampton, and had obtained powers to lay a third rail, and run its trains over the broad-gauge from there through Tavistock to Plymouth and on to a handsome new terminus at Devonport.

Such had been the broad-gauge stranglehold on Plymouth, Stonehouse and Devonport that the inhabitants welcomed their second mainline service (albeit routed over the rival's branch) more enthusiastically than the first, though the mere site of an engine had then been a novelty to many. The three towns were *en fête*. All shops and offices closed '. . . apart from the GWR offices in Fore Street, which, resplendent in front with gilt letters on a black ground, tried to look as if nothing out of the common was going on'.

The track between Lydford and Marsh Mills was still single – as it remains – and station, siding and signalling were hopelessly inadequate. As both gauges' traffic grew, working the railway became ever more complex. For a short time a mineral branch ran from Shaugh Bridge to a quarry at the Dewerstone Rock; and on 11 August 1883 part of the route was further enlivened by the advent of the narrow-gauge Princetown Railway, whose trains at first ran through from the junction to Horrabridge. Throughout the 1880s, the LSWR was fretting for its own independent route to Plymouth. This was opened – *via* Bere Alston – in 1890.

Since then, the original branch between Tavistock and Launceston has had one of the poorest services of any West Country line. The occasional two-coach local puffing up the

Once it brought new life to the village of Moretonhampstead, but in the motor age it became an irrelevance. The station didn't change in the ninety-three years that people walked up and down the path, though the engine shed was closed, the locomotive arriving from Newton Abbot in early morning and returning to it after the last train. Yet the very last train, long after normal services had ceased, ran much faster than traffic on the parallel road.

single track was not infrequently overtaken by Southern's on their double mainline where the two railways run parallel for some miles.

But local passenger traffic continued to increase on the Plymouth–Tavistock section until well into the 1930s. When a platform at the junction between the Tavistock and Princetown lines was opened and called Yelverton in 1885, it gave the name to a village which rapidly became an important dormitory for Plymouth. Later halts were added at Plym Bridge, Shaugh Bridge, Clearbrook and Whitchurch: they would of course have been even more useful had they been built in the days of railway supremacy. Services were improved in the 1920s, especially in the early mornings for workers going to Plymouth and late in the evenings for those returning from meetings and theatres. An 11.10pm left Millbay for Tavistock each weekday, while for returning workers a semi-fast at 5.15pm was at one time followed by a stopping train all the way to Tavistock only ten minutes later. On Wednesdays and Saturdays, the regular service of about a train an hour in each direction was supplemented by special excursions. Some of these ran through from Plymouth to Princetown, but most terminated at Yelverton – occasionally hauled there by a '*Castle*'. On fine Bank Holidays and Sundays between the wars, 20,000 Plymouth people would go by train to destinations between Plym Bridge and Princetown – and three quarters of them to Bickleigh, Shaugh Bridge, Clearbrook and Yelverton.

The last day of normal steam to East Grinstead, with empty stock of the 18.07 Three Bridges–East Grinstead, 11 June 1965. One says normal but the conversion of a section of the route into the steam Bluebell Railway now has a long history of successes.

It is the collapse of this excursion traffic which has robbed the branch of any place in the Beeching era. Where 20,000 used to go by train, rarely do 200 muster now. This is not only because people own cars and train services have deteriorated: the public's taste in excursions has changed. Once all guide books to Plymouth waxed warm about Bickleigh Vale, but probably half of today's Plymothians have never been there.

The *pièce de résistance* of the journey has always been the climb through the vale to the Dartmoor foothills. What scenery the train commands as it climbs and winds through the rocks and woods, miles from a main road; and what a hunting-ground for the transport enthusiast, with the railway, a canal, the route of the pioneer Plymouth & Dartmoor Railway and its Cann Quarry branch, and of the Lee Moor Tramway, all running together.

For the last time I have followed the familiar curves of these abandoned transport routes playing hide-and-seek with one another. The round-faced guard (GWR branch line in every feature) issued tickets and grimaced at the babies in the perambulators parked down the gangway of the spacious auto-car, a veritable public hall on wheels – displaying the same GWR notice about passengers joining 'Rail-Motors' at stations having to obtain tickets from the booking office which I first read as a schoolboy. Nothing had changed.

The railway has remained a self-contained little world. It has had its own code of conduct, its own traditions. For many railwaymen (retired and still working) it represents a way of life. During its history of 120 years, including its conception and building, the lives of thousands have been intimately concerned with it, and altered by it. Ghosts will walk – or ride – when it closes on Saturday.

*   *   *

West Devon's worst blizzard of the century hit the Plymouth to Tavistock and Launceston branch railway on its closing night. This was not a typical railway 'funeral' but a grim and unsuccessful struggle to keep the wheels moving until the end. Over 100 people were stranded when the last trains ever to run on the line failed to reach their destinations.

There could scarcely be a more appropriate finish for the line which has stirred more controversy in its turbulent career of 120 years than any other in the West Country.

The final two scheduled trains did not run at all, and the two previous ones were abandoned – at Tavistock and Bickleigh – after railwaymen had vainly battled for many hours in appalling conditions to keep the tracks clear.

The 6.20pm from Plymouth to Launceston reached Tavistock at 12.25am yesterday (Sunday) morning, and remains there, the bedraggled 'funeral' wreath still hanging on the front of the locomotive which may complete the trip back to Plymouth today or tomorrow. The 7.10pm from Tavistock to Plymouth was frozen to the ground on Saturday night, but was rescued yesterday afternoon.

Staying in a Dartmoor village, I was cut off by the snow and among those unable to attend. But I followed the dying hours of the branch by telephone. From 8.00pm until 2.30am I was in constant touch with most of the stations, and gained a broader picture of the line's death throes than I could have done if stuck in one of the trains. As the blizzard howled outside, it was indeed a unique experience to talk to stationmasters long after they should have ceased duty and their stations closed for good.

Delays caused by frozen points and poor visibility first became serious about 5.00pm, but it was not until 8.00pm that the timetable began to disappear. Surprisingly, the first trouble spot was not on the moorland wilds, but at the junction with the mainline at Marsh Mills. The last goods train from Launceston to Plymouth stuck because of point trouble. The 5.40pm passenger train from Launceston was also delayed at Marsh Mills, while the following 7.10pm from Tavistock to Plymouth was kept back at Bickleigh, waiting there to 'cross' the 6.20pm from Plymouth to Launceston.

With sixty-seven passengers in its four coaches, hauled by 2-6-2 tank engine No. 5568, the 6.20pm had left Plymouth an hour late, spent an hour standing still a short distance out of the city, and was again seriously delayed outside Marsh Mills, which it did not reach until 10.35pm – 3 hours 10 minutes for 3 miles along the mainline, during which time only one train passed on the down road.

It took another hour to struggle up the Vale to Bickleigh and, as already said, reached Tavistock at 12.25am. One or two local people had stayed up to see the passing of the era, but the band engaged for the occasion had dispersed long ago.

A signalling failure between Tavistock and Lydford, coupled with the inability of the Lydford stationmaster to reach Tavistock to institute emergency block working (a cutting on the Southern line he was to have used was brimful of snow and remained blocked for several days), finally ended the chance of the train reaching Launceston. At about 2.00am the twenty passengers settled down in their compartments for the rest of the night; they were given breakfast by the WVS. Those bound for Launceston, including the engine crew, finished the journey in two taxis yesterday afternoon.

As soon as the 6.20pm from Plymouth to Launceston had passed Bickleigh, at about 11.30pm, the section was clear for the 7.00pm Tavistock to Plymouth train to continue its journey. But the points were frozen and had to be changed by hand. 'As fast as we dug out the snow, it filled in again,' said Bickleigh's stationmaster, Mr S. Taylor. 'The blizzard was so terrible that we almost collapsed for want of breath.' And when the points were eventually cleared, the engine was unable to move the coaches. Soon

after 2.00am, Mr Taylor telephoned to say that the train was to be abandoned. Steam was kept up as long as possible, but as water ran out the engine's fire had to be dropped. The three passengers – all fourteen-year-old boys – had breakfast in the signalbox. Yesterday afternoon, joined by six other young people who could scarcely believe their luck on seeing a train ready to leave Bickleigh for Plymouth, they were the very last passengers to use the branch. A relief engine and gang had fought their way out from Plymouth in the morning.

These are the bare facts. Behind them, of course, was human drama. People were stranded at all the chief stations – and incidentally sometimes answered the telephone while the staff were out contesting the elements. Passengers were full of praise for the staff; the staff were bitterly disappointed that on this final night, with buses and cars useless, they could not keep the railway going.

In a recent article, I said that ghosts would be abroad on closing night, and so it seemed. At Launceston people waited hours in the snow for the last trains which never came; they recalled that opening day was so wet that the term 'railway weather' is still in the local vocabulary. Up the line, the nocturnal activity reminded one of the 1880s, when the Lydford–Plymouth section was open round the clock to handle the Waterloo–Devonport traffic of the LSWR. Memories of the rivalry between Paddington and Waterloo were renewed in the small hours round signalbox and booking office fires. Ironically, the Western Region withdraws from Tavistock and Launceston only a day before the regional boundary adjustments. Today the two towns are exclusively in the Southern Region; tomorrow the Western takes control of the entire 'withered arm'.

When tracing the progress of the train up through Bickleigh Vale, I recalled the crowds who once went for picnics at fine weekends; at Yelverton the thousands of convicts who changed *en route* for 'Dartmoor'; at Horrabridge the unemployed miners who joined the trains in the 1880s and 1890s on their way to ply their craft in the New World. And when at length No. 5568 drew into Tavistock's ugly wooden station, I thought of the hopes and fears of Thomas Gill, of the train-loads of ore sent from Wheal Crelake, and of the special which brought 160 troops from Plymouth to quell a miners' rising in 1866.

OPPOSITE *Once the Isle of Wight was known for its network, with speedy steam trains. On 30 December 1966, the penultimate day of steam on the island, 02 Class 04-4-T No. 16 Ventnor, calls at Brading, which has already lost its junction station en route to Shanklin.*

LEFT *Little has changed since this 1969 photograph. Rannoch, only reached by a narrow, winding road terminating at the station, still hosts moments of activity between trainless hours. Unusually for single-track routes in the Highlands, it still carries freight as well as the Fort William coaches of the sleeper. Breakfast in the lounge car in high summer is unforgettable.*

CHAPTER 5
A DAY TO REMEMBER

IT WAS IN 1950 WHEN I WAS TWENTY-ONE and beginning to explore the West Country for material for articles I could write. Every detail shows how things have changed.

I set out on the 5.53am from Teignmouth with a workman's ticket costing 1s 5d, or about seven new pence. The ticket was mainly used by dockyard workers. It was issued to *bona fide* workmen and I was nervous lest I didn't qualify, though by the end of the day I was satisfied that I did. Such tickets were available on very early services all over the country, too early for office staff though, if hard up, they might save by arriving much earlier than necessary.

The steam train crawled up the stiff gradients west of Newton Abbot. There was a sleeping car next to my coach – four-berth compartments with no segregation of the sexes. Only a rug was provided.

At Plymouth I rebooked, not strictly allowed, but there were different ticket collectors for those leaving and entering the station, so nobody questioned me. My day return to Tavistock allowed travel out by one route and return by another. Both are now closed.

Horse-drawn trucks off the Lee Moor Tramway on their own right of way, heading for Sutton Harbour on their 4ft 6in 'Dartmoor' gauge.

What joy the ex-Great Western single-line offered. I'd studied the map, and in the narrow valley of Plymouth saw us running alongside the shallow, abandoned tub-boat canal to the former Cann Quarry and its tramway extension – and the horse-drawn Lee Moor Tramway which at one part crossed our track diagonally. China clay was still being taken down to Sutton Harbour, crossing the mainline by a level crossing boarded for the horses to walk on.

We accelerated up the hill and steamed into Bickleigh where most passengers, commandos, alighted. Their Devon base has been switched to Lympstone, where they now have their own station on the Exmouth branch.

Then through Yelverton, where I saw the Princetown branch climb by a steep curve, replacing the pre-railway age horse-drawn Plymouth & Dartmoor opened in 1823, of which the Yeo Mill Tramway was a branch and the only survivor of the unique 'Dartmoor gauge' of 4ft 6in. And so to Tavistock, with its station, roofed all-over with wood and an empty space between the platform tracks, a legacy of Brunel's broad gauge, for this was an early line – opened in 1859. The town's population had risen rapidly owing to the prosperity of local mines.

It was my first visit to Tavistock, but time was precious so I quickly found the Tavistock Canal with water from the Tavy, attractively flowing through the centre of the Abbey Bridge and West Bridge Gardens laid out in 1953. The swift flow of the water was to provide power for the pumping engines of several mines and make it easy for laden boats to float down. The towpath on which I was walking was for horses to pull boats back against the stream. They were loaded with coal, lime and general cargoes including the cider much

Plym Bridge Halt, just rebuilt (note the engineering train) and now served by a short stretch of voluntary railway.

loved by miners. The boats were the first metal ones to be built in Britain and were made by the Bedford Foundry, one of three then in Tavistock.

Soon the canal took its own winding course including an aqueduct over a river. There was a branch to Mill Hill quarry, which, because of water shortage, had been replaced by a tramway, long lifted. The slates from the quarry were popular for cisterns and chimney pieces.

Continuing along the canal, round a sharp bend, I could hear the passage of Southern trains entering or bursting out of a tunnel overhead. Then, as expected, the canal disappeared into a tunnel.

OPPOSITE *My train still standing in Tavistock South's dark station.*

ABOVE *The canal wharf at Tavistock.*

LEFT *The south portal of Tavistock Canal's tunnel. The wharf from where miners set off to work is just out of sight to the left.*

To reach a small landing stage by its mouth, I needed permission to cross a private garden. It was readily given; I was one of the first ever to request it. When industrial archaeology – a term then not invented – became popular, so many requested permission that it was usually refused. So I descended steeply to the small landing stage – or in canal parlance – wharf.

At about a mile and three quarters, it was by far the longest tunnel, and several railway historians made the mistake of calling a much later tunnel the country's longest. Cutting it was a Herculean task lasting thirteen years, constructed from both ends and joining perfectly in the middle. Poor air in the small bore prevented too many men working together,

especially in hot summers. The compensation we are told was that: 'Great discoveries have been made in the tunnel under Morwell Down which form part of this canal, rich veins of copper of amazing thickness begin to show themselves, and promise an abundant harvest of profit to the proprietors of this spirited undertaking.'

Standing at the entrance wharf, I saw 1808 displayed on this northern portal, the year the portal itself was started. I reflected on the miners who went to work by boat to spend their twelve-hour shifts at what was called Wheal Crebor. When other traffic had been lost after the railway at Tavistock was opened in 1859, the ore from this mine was the last to be carried down the canal.

I also thought about the gallant crowd taken through the tunnel on opening day. The *Plymouth and Devonport Telegraph* announced:

> On Tuesday last a most novel and pleasing ceremony took place in consequence of the completion of that arduous of laborious undertakings, the Tavistock Canal. It was begun in 1803, and has been continued with unremitting assiduity until the accomplishment of it, which has occupied a period of 14 years, during which the most incredible exertions have been made at the expense of nearly £70,000.
>
> The advantages derivable from this important undertaking are incalculable, and there is every reason to hope that not only Tavistock and this vicinity will be benefited, but that the port of Plymouth will also feel the good effects resulting from the increased inland navigation thus created.
>
> At eight o'clock some 400 gaily decorated persons of all ranks entered nine of the small iron boats. The whole party proceeded in their aquatic subterranean excursion with the greatest order and regularity, and prepared to take leave of daylight for about two hours.

OPPOSITE *One of the many pumping wheels at Devon Great Consols worked by the force of water flowing through the tunnel.*

LEFT *What I found at Morwellham Quay.*

Morwellham Quay in its heyday.

There were few whose fears induced them to quit the boats, and more than 300 entered the monument of industry and perseverance with rather awful and somewhat sublime sensations. The timidity of the ladies was, however, soon relieved by the reverberating sound of music from the band of local performers in the several boats, which contributed much to dispel the gloom and so lessed the apprehension at a depth of 450ft from the summit of the hill. The pleasurable sensations excited by the approach to daylight on again enjoying open sunshine were indescribable.

On emerging from the tunnel the grotesque appearance of the company, who had protected themselves against the occasional droppings of the roof, considerably amused the excited and shouting crowd of 5,000 spectators. When the boats moored a 21-gun salute was fired and the operation of the inclined plane demonstrated.

Refreshments, toasts and dancing followed, and the occasion will long be remembered not only for the important event which it intended to commemorate, but for the harmony and general satisfaction that prevailed. The polite attention of Mrs Gill [wife of the chairman of the South Devon Railway] to her friends merits their warmest acknowledgements.

Until the railway came to Tavistock in 1859, considerable traffic was carried. In 1820, 20,000 tons of goods were conveyed in the metal barges. The return loads had to be poled up through the tunnel against the flow.

Since I couldn't float through the tunnel, I had to climb over Morwell Down, to pick up the canal at its southern portal, where the flow of water was put to further use by powering the largest incline plane in Southern England, 720ft long with a maximum drop of 237ft, at a slope of 15 degrees.

Water from the canal drove this inclined plane with a huge water wheel. The metal boats were designed for tipping into the trucks of the incline, whose own trucks were higher at one end than the other to keep the load level. In fact the incline had two sets of tracks, one for the canal and the other for Devon Great Consols mine. Hansford Worth, a Plymouth consulting engineer describes how it worked.

MUCH HATED

It shows how unpopular the new railways were when, after the Duke of Bedford had purchased the canal after its abandonment, it was felt that its very existence would prevent the South Devon & Tavistock, opened in 1859, from charging higher rates.

A local spokesman said: 'It would have been quite in the interests of the railway had they purchased the land at a considerably higher price' to prevent possible competition.

In those days there were no standard rates, but fixed locally according to circumstances and were often unnecessarily high for heavy goods, even if at those rates the price of coal still fell by 50 per cent compared to pre-railway days.

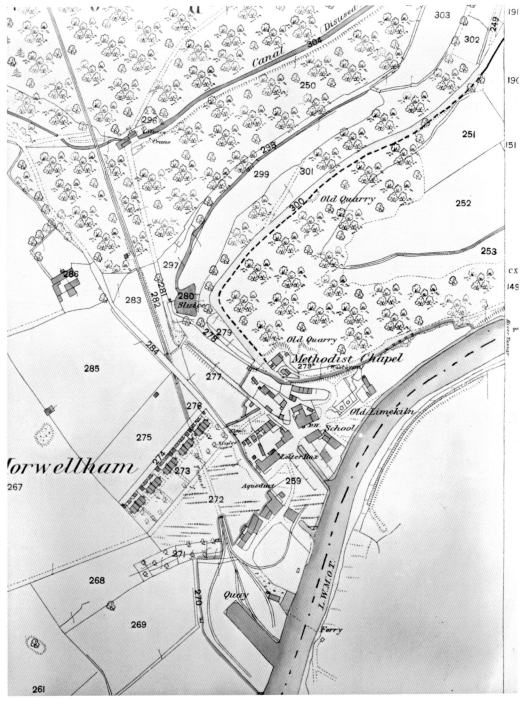

The wheel itself is about 3ft abreast and 25–30ft in diameter. On its side is fitted a somewhat ponderous bevelled cog wheel into which fitted gears of another smaller dimension. This is on a stout wooden axle which rises almost vertically and moves by the aid of another pair of bevelled wheels on a horizontal wooden axle . . . On this last is fitted a large drum on to which winds a chain of 4in link and ¾in iron which used to draw the ascending trucks . . . Another large drum with a wire rope on it is so connected with this last by a pair of ordinary toothed wheels after the descending train laden with copper ore was made to assist the water wheel in drawing up the ascending trucks.

Desertion followed the closure of the mines, the inclined plane being dismantled in 1888. Ships were built on both sides of the river.

The graceful Calstock viaduct being built (see also page 219).

We are told that at the foot, Morwellham Quay was once:

> A scene of busy industry, with its unloading of barges, and shouting sailors, and hammering workmen, and trains of wagons ascending and descending the inclined planes. A quantity of ore is here shipped off to distant smelting houses. It is curious to enter the well-swept yard, and observe the different wooden shafts down which distinct ores are poured. These ships in return bring coals, and limestone and many other commodities.

There was a limekiln at Morwellham. Boats of up to 300 tons had lined the quays at what was the Empire's largest inland port. In the evening there were drunken brawls. No policemen came near.

What I found was dereliction. Not a soul was to be seen. The water was choked with trees, but the quays themselves lined with bollards where ships had tied up were weedless, since one of the commodities mined had been arsenic. Many of the paving stones that once lined the whole area had been taken by locals. Arsenic was mainly sent to the cotton growing areas of the USA where it is still used on the crop to control fungus. Tracks would have lined the quays.

I shall never forget the scene, and am delighted to have been there. I particularly recall a drunken notice about to fall into the river: 'The proprietors of the Tamar Manure Navigation give notice that the Navigation is unfit for navigation'.

The Tamar Manure Navigation amounted only to a single but massive lock, 70ft long by 12ft wide with meticulously squared granite blocks, but enjoyed a long life enabling

boats to go up the river for a further 3 miles. Manure, building materials and lime were carried well into the twentieth century (7,740 tons in 1905), powered by teams of men pulling on ropes attached to the masts of their vessels. Gunnislake gas works, opened in 1872, was supplied by coal. Only after 1918 did the cost of dredging the basin and its approaches overtake the income.

Earlier there were great ambitions including a 30-mile canal to near the Tamar's source with a branch to Launceston. Turner's 'Crossing the Brook' (hanging in the Tate Gallery), probably of this location, suggests a tramway ran beside the Navigation. Eventually a standard-gauge tramway was built on the opposite bank, enabling ore from Devon Great Consols to reach Morwellham after the inclined plane closed.

'The mine of mines', Devon Great Consols, had 33 pumping wheels powered by water from the canal. A watercourse was skilfully contoured for miles from the canal's southern portal.

High up across the river the scene was accompanied by the occasional haunting whistle of a locomotive on the line crossing the viaduct at Calstock on its way to the then terminus at Callington as it approached open level crossings on what was a Light Railway, built to lower standards. Once this was only an isolated mineral line, the East Cornwall Mineral Railway. When the viaduct was built in 1907, there was a hoist down to the quay, for the river was the natural highway. Eventually long trains carrying strawberries crossed the viaduct on their way to Bere Alston and up country. For generations previously they had gone to Plymouth by boat. There were indeed rival market boats, overtaking each other and serving a series of quays now all abandoned.

But I discovered that the canal was still serving a purpose, for near the quay at Morwellham was a hydro-electric station powered by water descending through a 500ft stout pipe from a small reservoir above. It opened in 1933 after the West Devon Electric Power Company leased the canal for a nominal £1 a day. They had to recondition it and among other things dredge up coal that had been spilled from the boats. The Central Electricity Generating Board still repairs the tunnel. Apart from the glorious scenery, its the

Gunnislake station on its opening by the Plymouth, Devonport & South Western Junction Railway in 1908. Its busiest years were in the Second World War, when thousands of evacuees from Plymouth moved here, but commuters still start their journey from here for Plymouth since the railway is far more direct than the road.

only thing that remains the same today as it was fifty years ago on my day to remember and the plant remains the largest hydro-electric one in England.

After industrialisation and then suburbanisation swept across Britain, we now have the great leisure industry into which Morwellham Quay has been absorbed. Restored as a first-class visitor attraction, it includes a narrow-gauge train journey into an abandoned mine and restored ships and a nearby pub once used by miners and quarry workers.

Frank Booker, a friend, wrote a bestselling title on *The Industrial Archaeology of the Tamar Valley* and was instrumental in bringing the transition about, giving it has to be said new confidence to places such as Calstock on the opposite side. The regatta was brought back to life, and I organised two boats to come up the river on the rising tide carrying hundreds of people to view the remains and go further to the entrance to the Tamar Manure Navigation.

Within a few weeks I was on the early workman's train again, this time to cross the viaduct to Calstock, where I found magic of another kind. The narrow streets under the shadow of the viaduct were full of interest, and I recalled how a burst of enterprise including brickmaking, shipbuilding and the making of long, strong ropes helped reduce the hardship following the abandonment of mining. Fruit growing on a hillside free of north winds was still booming, and at the station I heard how many thousands of packages had been despatched last season. Staff remembered the days when the lift from viaduct to quayside was still in regular use, and I traced the earlier inclined plane that had carried the East Cornwall Mineral Railway down from the high ground to shipside.

But on my day to remember, back in Tavistock, without notice I called at the Bedford Estate office, was given an enthusiastic welcome and allowed to examine their records, something which, with so many enquiring writers, would not happen today. Among other things, I found the quote about the opening day party going through the tunnel. I used it in an article for *The Western Morning News* that helped me get a job and start on a career in journalism and broadcasting. The quote and other material was also used by the Charles of David & Charles, my publishing company, in his book on *The Canals of Southern England*.

Outside, I asked the way to the Southern station. 'You mean the new station?' It had only been opened in 1890. And at the station I was in luck, seeing and indeed travelling behind my last-ever sighting of a GWR *Dukedog*. It was a pilot engine added to the front of a stopping train to Plymouth Friary. Though the Western and Southern region ran a daily

route-familiarisation trip over each others' lines so that the crews could drive trains in emergency diversions, I've no idea how the *Dukedog* came to be in Tavistock as a Light Engine, and in those days was too shy to ask.

Introduced as recently as 1936 for light passenger duties, especially over the Cambrian lines where weight restrictions were severe, they were made of the chassis and boilers of different earlier classes. Originally they were named Earls, but those dignitaries objected to such ancient machines bearing their names, and were given Castle class engines instead.

It was then home by another train for Dockyard workers, basically a parcels service with a couple of carriages which stopped at Cornwood's little-served station only minutes after the 5.40 advertised departure, just too early for them and me.

Every detail of that day is etched on my memory.

CHAPTER 6
24 HOURS OF MEMORY

At most times of day or night I can summon up memories of what happened at that moment in some point of railway history. This 24 hours of memory is, as far as I am aware, the first time such a thing has been attempted. The selection is necessarily personal, including many of my own memories as well as historic ones across the country. Enjoy the spirit and think of your own memories. Even when the timetables of the GWR and the Western Region's early days seemed ordained by God, times may vary by a minute or so.

12.00am (midnight), New Year's Day, 1948. With engine whistles sounding everywhere (those at Newton Abbot clearly heard in Teignmouth), the moment that Britain's railways were nationalised. It is now hard to recall the enthusiasm for bringing 'the means of production and distribution' into public control.

But already there were warning signs. Not merely would the GWR, LMS, LNER and SR lose their identity, but they would be swallowed into a heavy bureaucracy.

Said the *Manchester Guardian*: 'If the dual loyalty in the regions should lead to confusion in control, the results may affect the public service. It is not pleasant to greet the announcement of the nationalised transport system with such diffidence. We hope to be proved wrong. But this country can afford no more mistakes in its essential activities. The nation wanted to own its own transport system. It did not want bureaucracy to take charge.'

Such fears proved all too real. Decades of ceaseless reorganisation bled confidence. Morale dropped, and the railways lost much freight traffic that could easily have been retained. Most efforts of modernisation were ill thought out and resulted in huge waste.

In later days the Teign Valley branch's single auto-car carried few passengers, but in the days before much motor competition even inconveniently situated stations such as Chudleigh needed real trains.

Thus a thousand steam locomotives were built before the rush to Dieselisation; thousands of loose-coupled goods wagons were built along with fancy new marshalling yards . . . all rapidly to be discarded.

On that New Year's Day, my boyhood special sorrow was for the passing of the GWR – God's Wonderful Railway. Because it had been the best, lower standards hit its staff hardest. There was even talk of a strike when it seemed likely that its automatic train control, uniquely pioneered and used over much of the system, would be abandoned. The mood of frustration was indicated by the non-political West Country Writers' Association passing and publicising a resolution: 'Bring back Great Western Railway'.

12.27am On a clear, moonlit night, the 6.25pm up Postal Express from Glasgow to Euston runs into the back of a stationary 5.40pm Glasgow to Euston passenger express in mid-section between Winsford Junction and Winsford station on double-track mainline. A soldier, lambasted in the press as the cause of the accident, has pulled a communication cord in his compartment to get home on leave sooner. The date: 17 April 1948.

Though the soldier may have been selfish, stopping a train in mid section should not in itself have caused danger, and the signalman who had given out-of-section bell code and accepted a following train before the first had passed was primarily blamed. Doing so involved no equipment failure, but his belief that he must have seen the passenger train pass complete with tail lamp. It was not the only accident caused by a signalman on night duty gambling that he must have seen a train pass without actually having done so, but it was the most notorious. Sixteen passengers at the rear of the passenger train were killed outright and a further eight died of injuries in hospital.

As always seems to happen with accidents, there were a number or irregularities, starting with the fact that unusually, the Postal Express was late (it should have overtaken the express 64 miles earlier at Lancaster), but mainly involving conflicting evidence between signalmen, and especially a delay in safeguarding the stationary express by placing detonators on the track while the man responsible for doing so wasted valuable moments trying to find out why and where his train had stopped.

It had been stationary for 17 minutes when the accident happened. Just two detonators were laid, both heard by the driver of the Postal, who rammed on the brakes but whose speed was still around 45mph at the moment of impact. Mercifully, the down Postal was stopped just before being allowed into the section. With wreckage strewn across both tracks, it was a night of major disruption, but normal working was restored far sooner than would be possible today when the police cordon off a 'crime scene'.

5.53am With a workman's return from Teignmouth to Plymouth for 1s 5d in old money (less than 7½p), an early start is cheap and gives ample time to explore most places in Cornwall on a day trip (see Chapter 5: 'A Day to Remember'). The train left Paddington at 11.50 last night and has sleeping cars to Plymouth. *The Owl* as the train is nicknamed, has a leisurely lay-over in Plymouth allowing time to purchase a day return ticket onward. It has come *via* Bristol the first direct train from Paddington to Exeter not being until the *Torbay Express* at noon. The *Cornish Riviera Express* (see 10.30am) calls only to pick up passengers.

Once *The Owl* got going again at Plymouth North Road, it only missed a couple of suburban halts all the way to Penzance which it didn't reach until 11.00, having taken only 50 minutes less than 24 hours.

ABOVE *Before the age of the tokenless block, along with many other minor stations, Forsinard on the Far North Line was fully signalled. Once, two trains were snowed up here for several days, their crews paid continuous overtime.*

OPPOSITE *Many stations attracted as many people to witness their last steam train as for their final demise. On 21 September 1961 this was the scene at High Barnet.*

6.39am The first up train to leave Teignmouth on weekdays. Poorly heated and the lights fading at every station stop since the dynamo isn't yet fully charged (the train originated a few minutes ago at Newton Abbot), the journey in winter begins uncomfortably and at all times seems interminably long to Bristol, the twenty-sixth stop not being reached until 10.08. It connects with the 10.15 LMS train waiting in Brunel's original terminal part of Temple Meads station, which the following 'express' to Cardiff (allowed fifteen minutes at Exeter St David's, seven at Taunton and four at Weston-super-Mare) doesn't.

I used the 6.39 for many purposes: working at Taunton or Bridgwater, or changing at Exeter St David's for the Exe Valley, Barnstaple, and (until the Western ran an earlier train to Paddington) even to walk from St David's to Central for a Southern train giving an earlier London arrival.

The 6.39 wasn't particularly friendly and wasn't missed when services improved. Moreover, having stopped so frequently, using the loop line platforms at many stations, even in those days it was apt to be held up outside Bristol.

An interesting point is that we were due in Taunton simultaneously with a train from Minehead and five minutes after one from Barnstaple. In common with those living near other junctions where branch line trains strengthened the service for the last few miles into a major town, workers were spoilt for choice. For westbound passengers, there were connections to all three routes.

This is almost exactly the scene I remember when I first became familiar with Newton Abbot. But between 1926 and the 1950s, a wartime bomb destroyed the railway cottages to the right and flattened the ground which became the site for the headquarters of David & Charles publishers. On my landing there is a photograph of children playing while watching the train and I often wonder what happened to them.

7.40am As the carriage and wagon depot hooter reverberates down the estuary, the 7.40 departs Newton Abbot. It frequently serves my newspaper and broadcasting duties and is at a more civilised hour than *The Owl*. No workmen's tickets are issued, but there's ample time to rebook in Plymouth. In fact I sometimes travel by auto-car with my girlfriend (who joins at Cornwood and works at St Budeaux) and I rejoin the 7.40 at Saltash.

The 7.40 was a Newton Abbot train hauled by a Newton Abbot engine, *Chepstow Castle*. Passing it at the buffer stop at Penzance one day made me decide to buy the nameplate if it were ever available. It is now the most expensive thing in our home.

Sitting in the front compartment and sticking my head out of the window, I got to know many stationmasters and learnt tit-bits of information traded down the line. Once we were delayed on the Royal Albert Bridge at Saltash by a swan on the track who wouldn't move until a shunter arrived with a pole. Phoning the BBC (reverse charge) an item for the West Country evening news earned a welcome half guinea.

8.15am The time selected by a Southern advertising campaign to emphasise the frequency of morning rush-hour services to London. 'Every one of the forty stations marked here has an "Eight-fifteen to Town" on weekday mornings,' it explains.

8.18am To be precise: 8.18½ on 8 October 1952, a late-running Perth–Euston overnight express with sleeping cars runs at speed into the rear of a commuter train at Harrow & Wealdstone. A minute later, a double-headed down express crashes into the wreckage. England's worst and Britain's second worst accident, it claims 122 lives, shocks post-war public opinion and paves the way for the universal introduction of an automatic warning system.

Possibly going on mainline duty, a railwayman at Thorpeness Halt on the Saxmundham–Aldeburgh branch in 1947.

Most lives were lost on the crowded commuter train which had crossed to slow from mainline, for its now non-stop journey into London, and whose guard (a key witness at the enquiry) was just about to step on board having given the right-away signal. Precautionary fog signalling had only just been abandoned and there was much discussion as to whether the driver of the Perth train failed to respond to a signal because of a returning fog pocket or low early-morning light.

8.23am After breakfast, in the 1950s I am either on the platform to see off this departure from Glasgow Central to Gourock or, if running a bit late, in my room on the top floor of the Central Hotel which, though cheaper, I choose mainly to enjoy the station announcements. What lovely place names the 8.23 invoke: Gourock with steamer connections to Dunoon, Innellan, Rothesay, Tighnabruaich and, by other steamers, Largs, Lochranza, Campbeltown and Ardrishaig.

The Gourock route brought the last regular steam locomotives to use Glasgow Central. Occasionally I travelled on the 8.23 which had a spirited run along the then quadruple track to Paisley Gilmour Street and was in Gourock (26½ miles) at 9.23. A wonderful choice of ferry and cruise routes was on offer, all at inclusive rates.

Five columns of the timetable were devoted to the 8.23 and its steamer connections, while the branch from Paisley to Wemyss Bay offered further routes and, both from Paisley Gilmour Street and Canal, there were extensions south. Occasionally I used the sleeper that picked up passengers at Gilmour Street. One evening the train was hit by boulders being thrown in the Gorbals, which broke windows in the cabins on either side of mine. I was told not to worry but go to sleep: pretty impossible with the noise of the rest of the glass being

knocked out by talkative staff at Paisley and temporary repairs effected and more permanent ones made in Carlisle.

Former LMS and LNER services had not yet been integrated, and further steamers left from Greenock and Craigendoran. Once a day you could do a round trip, out by sea and back by the *Lady of the Lake* on Loch Lomond returning *via* Balloch Pier. And naturally you could go through the Kyles of Bute having been joined by more passengers at Rothesay, where you listened to station-like announcements for the position or 'station' along the pier of your steamer.

Before the 1923 Grouping, three companies ran rival steamers for commuters to some destinations, many passengers showing great loyalty to their chosen line.

The Glasgow & South Western had been a serious rival to the Caledonian, swept into the same ownership in 1923 but not really integrated until well after nationalisation. Both the Caledonian and the North British had massive hotels at their principal stations. The G & SWR's St Enoch station was a major affair whose operations I greatly enjoyed studying. However, possibly nothing could beat the marvellous teak departure display at Central, men physically inserting trains' individual boards at the appropriate time (it was replaced not so long ago) for Britain's busiest station in terms of train numbers. Many platforms were – and are – routinely used by pairs of trains.

The point work at the extended station throat out over the Clyde was something else, once freely viewed from the platform ends. Now you need special permission to reach there, and Glasgow Central's signalbox has been replaced by panels that also control Queen Street on the arch-rival's route. St Enoch is now a shopping centre, and the two remaining hotels have had very different post-privatisation lives. Central, which once had three restaurants and where the LMS band was in residence in winter (in summer it moved to Gleneagles), has lost its glamour while the Caledonian has gone up market but lacks any railway 'feel'.

I'm not sure if I naturally ended with more authors in Glasgow than in Greater London or if I found them as the result of enjoying the marvels of the city, its stations and steamer connections. Especially in summer, it was a truly wonderful playground.

ABOVE LEFT *Station architecture Kelvedon & Tollesbury Light Railway style: Feering Halt.*

A Midland 4-4-0 Compound heads along splendid quadruple track near Duffield.

8.46am On a crisp Friday morning, 28 February 1975, a slightly late-running train bursts out of the tunnel leading into Moorgate Tube station and positively accelerates going over a crossover into platform 9. The signalman is alarmed, and another railwayman on the platform sees the driver, motorman Leslie Newsome, sitting bolt upright with his cap on and his hands on the controls. At 30mph the train bursts through the hydraulic buffers and crashes into the tunnel's end wall. It is still 8.46.

It is undoubtedly the accident I would like least to have been involved in. Just thinking about it induces insomnia.

The signalman alerted HQ, though he still had no idea just how serious things were.

It also took a moment for the first police motorcyclist to take it in, but soon a fleet of ambulances and fire engines were on their way, nurses and doctors rushed to the scene, and emergency arrangements made at St Bartholomew's Hospital.

The train's first three coaches were telescoped into each other and horrendously compacted, having been bounced back somewhat from the effect of the impact. Alive and dead people sitting upright were trapped. Heat rose.

The harrowing details were broadcast every few hours. It took 13 hours to bring out the last of the seventy-four injured passengers, and four days to clear the forty-three dead, the last being that of motorman Newsome.

A week passed before the wreckage was finally cleared. Not merely was the heat indescribable, but with the presence of rats there was a real danger of plague, and at the end the firemen were allowed into the tunnel only for a third of their hour shift, for which they had to wear protective clothing and be disinfected after. Drawn from virtually every London brigade, 1,324 firemen were involved, horrible memories still vividly lingering with many.

Nothing was found wrong with the equipment, and one can only guess at whether motorman Newsome was in a trance or dead at the controls. Approach control now means that power is cut off until a train has reduced speed to the level the new buffer could cope with, 12.5mph. Was it an accident waiting to happen? Maybe, but things had been the same for seventy-four years.

9.26am The departure time from Newton Abbot of traditionally the day's first express, the 8.30 from Plymouth, after it has been strengthened by a section from the Torbay line. The elaborate shunting operation is performed many times daily, full use made of the scissors crossovers on the outer faces of Newton Abbot's two island platforms in the station's 1929 rebuild.

First to arrive, and often spending fifteen minutes at the Paddington end of the platform, were the Torbay coaches, whose engine cut off and disappeared into the locomotive depot. The engine of the Plymouth train stopped before the cross-over and used it to run round the Torbay coaches. One of the pair of Newton Abbot shunters meanwhile attached itself to the rear of the Plymouth train (the last coach traditionally a slip-coach for Reading) and then propelling it onto the Torbay coaches. A wheel tapper meanwhile was busily at work, while a catering attendant sold beverages through open windows. On a cold morning when the train was late, a customer complaining that his tea was cold was told: 'Can't be. It was boiling hot when I made it.'

In the same way that full-length (fifty-four trucks) goods trains were shortened at nearby Hackney marshalling yard for the climb over Dartmoor's foothills, it made sense for passenger trains to be lightened by the removal of their Paignton or Kingswear sections. And though every day the *Cornish Riviera*, as many summer Saturday trains, was technically a 'runner' through Newton Abbot, when the load was increased in busy times, it frequently stopped for the addition of a pilot locomotive.

The shunting procedure varied. For example, the second train to arrive might overtake the first by using the scissors crossover. Trains were being joined or divided much of the day, a practice that was only abandoned in the 1960s.

10.00am Attended by LNER officers and watched by boys of all ages, Britain's most famous train leaves platform 9 at King's Cross with slightly later departures alongside it. The gleaming green Pacific at the head of a long line of bow-ended teak carriages displaying destination boards makes a sight that later generations will sorely miss.

However, the 'Top Link' driver sometimes struggled up the steep gradient into the tunnel, which the locomotive could enter at 10mph though its driving wheels were whizzing round at 40mph. The crowd waited till the tail lamp has disappeared into the dark, steam-filled hole before slowly dispersing.

The LNER was by far the poorest of the Big Four of the Grouping era, its shares almost worthless (a fraction of the GWR's) and at the final meeting of the Board in 1948, the directors faced the ignominy of the proposal for compensation for their loss of office being voted down. The North East saw an especial decline of traditional industry, and make-do-and-mend 'Razor Gangs' sought to cut head counts. Slow and dirty local trains were the order of the day.

Yet the LNER was a well-run railway, with good track and far better management than that of the larger LMS and, though the best known, the *Flying Scotsman*

The Somerset & Dorset gradients were steep, but were two locomotives (Ivatt 2-6-2T 41307 and Standard 2-6-4T 80138) really needed to haul this three-coach local train heading toward Bath on the Somerset & Dorset near Shepton Mallet on 5 March 1966?

(which once carried a stenographer and hairdresser), was by no means the only quality express. Others included the *Scarborough Flier*, *West Riding Limited*, Pullman *Queen of Scots* and the *Jubilee* followed by the *Coronation* with an innovative beaver tail and lounge.

Incidentally following the end of the 'railway races' between the East and West Coast routes to Aberdeen, the agreement not to reach Edinburgh in less than 8¼ hours only ceased (under the pressure of GWR publicity for its speedier trains) in 1932. After which things steadily speeded up, the LNER being the natural holder of steam speed records.

10.17am The moment I fall irretrievably in love with the country railway as the day's first train from Taunton to Barnstaple pulls into South Molton station, which is to become my hobby and support system during two difficult years evacuated from Teignmouth (for its size England's worst-bombed town).

There is always an element of the irrational about falling in love with anyone or anything. I was desperately lonely, and needing companionship was undoubtedly a factor. Another was the railway itself, the station layout, signals and signalbox. On this occasion I was a mere bystander. On my third visit I was invited into the signalbox where I was to spend many happy times, pulling levers, working the single-line tokens and putting them into their holders, discovering the facts of life over the omnibus telephone circuit serving every station on the branch, cuddling Blackie the mongrel who I'd take for walks between trains and – especially by lamp light after dark – reading the rule book and other documents.

I enjoyed the banter between train crew and station staff, three of each, of course loved the softly gurgling 2-6-0 Mogul still in GWR green, as the coaches were in chocolate and cream (though wartime all-over brown steadily took over).

Above all I studied the handful of people including soldiers on leave alighting from the outside world and the single woman joining it, and the cascade of rabbit empties and parcels disgorged from the guard's van (after the train had chugged up the hill and the signals replaced to danger) collected by barrow for the parcels office where there was hardly a spare inch of space.

From one of those broad-sheet timetables that used to grace station boards, I noticed that the day's first up train must have crossed the down one at East Anstey, two stations and a halt up the line, while as soon as the one I had watched set off reached the next station, Filleigh, the South Molton signalman gave permission for another up train, which turned out to be a pick-up goods shunted for a full two hours at South Molton after its engine had run round it.

10.30am The legendary departure time of the *Cornish Riviera Express* or one-time *Limited*, with compulsory seat reservations. Although the working timetable did not exort staff to ensure punctuality as was the case of the 10.10pm Great Western Travelling Post Office (see page 51), everyone treated it with special respect. Once it carried two slip portions, but in my day the first place to be served was Exeter in winter and Plymouth in summer. For many years it was Britain's, and once the world's, longest non-stop run.

Enthusiasts felt the tingle factor as they checked its punctuality with their watches; some staff stood to attention as it ran through intermediate stations.

The restaurant car running through to Penzance, naturally held a special status in Cornwall. It was a prestige holiday train, west of Plymouth serving only Par (for

At low tide on a cold morning, a Southern locomotive leaves a long steam trail beside the River Taw near Barnstaple.

Newquay), Truro (for Falmouth), Gwinear Road (for Helston) and St Erth (for St Ives), and missing the populous industrial centres of St Austell, Redruth and Camborne. On summer Saturdays the main train was diverted down the winding cliff-top branch to St Ives. With special stock, it was one of the few Great Western trains with a uniform roofline.

Once when the up train was delayed by a signal error early on its journey, I heard the signalman ask the driver if he'd be on time by Plymouth and when assured he would be, so no enquiry would be instituted, organised false entries in the train register 'because the Company set such store by this train'. Well after nationalisation, it was still 'the Company'.

10.30am On Whit Monday 1951, a locomotive already in its mid-eighties starts the first public service on the Talyllyn Railway in North Wales under voluntary control. The toy-like 0-4-0T *Dolgoch* is followed by a crude vehicle of the same vintage looking like a horse-drawn thing on rails, and a miscellany of other carriages ending with a guard's van with benches around its sides offering overflow seating and a window through which tickets can be sold at intermediate stations. *Dolgoch* still has its original boiler which started work before Stirling's first 8ft single-driver had left the drawing board and the GWR was still partly broad-gauge. The departure not only marks the eighty-fifth birthday of the individualistic 2ft 3in gauge line up to an old slate mine but the beginning of a new era in railway history: the restoration railways for pleasure as part of the tourist industry.

The date is July 1939 but it could equally as well been post-war. Dundee Castle heads a Wolverhampton train too long to be totally under the ugly wooden roof (which still survives) at Penzance.

As L.T.C. Rolt vividly tells in *Railway Adventure*, the first season on the Talyllyn was distinctly hairy, with frequent derailments and breakdowns. It also took time for the generous efforts of the volunteers to be bedded down. But the Talyllyn steadily became a reliable, charming and especially friendly railway, still among the best. It was one of several lines built for slate traffic and the only one never to close, the volunteers appearing just in time.

Along with steam centres and museums, there are now dozens of operating railways in the leisure industry carrying well over a million passengers a year. Two 15in gauge lines, the Romney, Hythe & Dymchurch and the Ravenglass & Eskdale were really already part of the leisure industry as was the Snowdon Mountain Railway, though run as commercial affairs. Voluntary enthusiasm has been the driving force for the rest, which include numerous parts of the closed national rail system reopened if only on a seasonal basis, as well as other narrow-gauge lines such as the also slate-orientated Ffestiniog and the rebuilt Welsh Highland to which it is now connected. That excludes pier and cliff railways, some with a long history, and short pleasure lines in parks and at the seaside.

Altogether it is a vast movement, many lines now supplementing volunteers with a core of paid staff. Occasionally it is felt that some lines are now almost too business-like, while the Talyllyn and the South Devon (of which I am Patron) are among those retaining a friendly, informal attitude. The same applies to many mainline steam specials, together with the pair of British *Orient Express* trains now also an important part of the leisure industry.

10.43am It happened on an Irish line which closed when I was four, and is unknown by many of today's enthusiasts but, often over mid-morning tea, I recall it as the most significant accident in the history of railways in the British Isles: the Runaway Train or Armagh disaster.

On 12 June 1889, two more people, mainly children, were killed than lost their lives in the Tay Bridge disaster (see 7.16pm). It was by no means the worst accident in railway history, but it exerted more influence than any other – an accident that need not have happened but was waiting to do so.

A Methodist Sunday School excursion from Armagh to Warrenpoint on what had been an impoverished independent line but, taken over by the Great North of Ireland (I), was carrying 941 people in its heavy load of fifteen coaches. The single engine stalled on a long 1:75 incline out of Armagh.

It was decided to split the train but, with inadequate precautions and general confusion between staff, the ten rear coaches slipped back and ran into the following regular train. The inquest and public inquiry revealed the usual miscellany of irregularities which make fascinating study, but three things stood out: the lack of *continuous* automatic brake; reliance on the time-interval system, a second train being permitted to follow before there was any proof that the first had cleared; and the lack of a telegraph which accompanied the opening of most trunk lines.

The public and Parliament were so moved that by 30 August of the same year the Regulation of Railways Act was in force, allowing the Board of Trade to compel railways to introduce *continuous* brakes on all vehicles of trains carrying passengers, install the block system which meant that signalboxes could communicate with each other, and have safety locking between points and signals. With continuous brake, any carriage is at a standstill until a locomotive creates a vacuum. One consequence was that boilers generally became larger.

Thus the Runaway Train was instrumental in making our railways much safer, and marked the end of *laissez-faire*. Most companies were quickly compelled to make improvements. Only excepted were a few remote rural lines with scant traffic.

The GN(I) wasn't among those complaining of the costs involved, and went on to be a highly efficient railway whose lovely 4-4-0 blue express engines and imaginative timetables many still remember.

11.52am Having enjoyed a compartment to myself, an airman joins me at Chiseldon just as I'm starting my railway sandwiches. I'm on the 10.10 from Cheltenham Lansdown (the London Midland Region station) to Southampton Terminus, though I'll be getting off at Andover Town. Since as I've just counted there are only eight people on the three-coach train, and the airman is the only one getting on at Chiseldon, I wonder why he picks my compartment; but he's a jovial fellow and, as so often happens, while trying to seek isolation, I enjoy a talkative companion. It is mid-June 1958.

When staying in Cheltenham, sometimes I stood on the road bridge watching this train cross the complicated junction between London Midland and the Western tracks. The double track of the Midland from Birmingham and Western from Malvern Road serving the North Warwick line and also the terminus of St James, has as a wartime improvement been quadrupled on to Gloucester. The train from Lansdown diverges left off this to the double-track line through Cheltenham's fourth station, remote Leckhampton.

SUMMER SATURDAY KESWICK

Memories of an afternoon and evening spent on Keswick station in the early 1950s emphasise how utterly different our railways have become.

With the first generation of green-painted Diesel cars reviving passenger traffic, nobody would have thought about possible closure. There were signalboxes at either end of the station, signal arms dropping for a succession of Diesel and steam-hauled trains, the latter including the *Lakes Express* (which was strengthened here on its up journey on summer Saturdays, and an evening through train from Manchester whose front two vehicles were trucks for cattle for Cockermouth). That meant Cockermouth signalbox forwarding them to what was grandly called Cockermouth Junction, where a separate signalbox controlled access to the yard.

Everywhere along the branch one could see how economies could be made but were resisted. When an intermediate station was closed to passengers, its signalbox was retained and trains had to slow for manual token exchange, breaking up what was anyway only a short section.

At Andoversford the train I was travelling on then left that double track to Kingham to join the single-track picturesque and often isolated former South West & Midland Junction Railway, once made famously busy by its manager, Sam Fay, who went on to do greater things.

Though it passed by the GWR's Swindon Works and threw off a branch from its own Swindon Town to the GW's Swindon Junction, many people felt that in the 1923 Grouping it would have fared better under LMS or Southern control, possibly jointly like the Somerset & Dorset. The GWR lost no time in Great Westernising it, but showed little enterprise of the kind it did for the Welsh lines it also absorbed. With so few passengers, how long could this fascinating cross-country byway last?

The answer came almost immediately, for from the last day of that same June the Western, especially seriously in the red, withdrew three of the four main trains. The one-a-day, serving places such as South Cerney, where I used to stay with Charles Hadfield in the early days of David & Charles, seldom carried more than a few enthusiasts wishing to ink in the route on their map, but regulations stipulated that at least one daily service had to be provided until authority was given for closure – a prolonged but often futile process.

There were a few more trains – empty ones to give driver training on the new Diesel multiple units coming from Swindon. If only they had come earlier, as so many of us had urged, there would have been far less waste. For steam mileage was costly, and the almost random cuts made that 30 June across the Western destroyed useful traffic which in many cases could have been developed with simplified track and the faster, cleaner and far cheaper units.

12.00pm On 13 June 1842, Queen Victoria takes her first train journey, from Slough to Paddington, the first of many Royal associations for the Great Western. Daniel Gooch, the mechanical engineer, drives his broad-gauge Firefly class locomotive *Phlegethon*, and supremo Isambard Kingdom Brunel is in attendance.

The Queen was said to be enchanted, sharing the cost of the building of special carriages from her private purse. Yet she was never really comfortable with railway travel, and imperiously laid down expensive and time-consuming rules: top speed 40mph, 30mph at night, meal breaks stationary. She opposed electric lights in her saloon, though liked the electric bell to summon her attendants.

A light engine always ran ahead, no trains passed in the opposite direction, and so on. She was scared by accident reports, and horrified when the driver of her train on a Scottish journey had his head sliced by a bridge. Without looking ahead, he had climbed onto the tender to repair the emergency brake. Queen Victoria sent a bouquet to the funeral and paid for a handsome headstone.

Soon Royal waiting rooms were prepared at the stations closest to her palaces, including Windsor and Ballater for Balmoral. Her annual train to Ballater involved monumental detail and much disturbance to ordinary travel. The only Sunday trains on the Deeside branch were specials carrying Government dispatches during the Queen's visit.

Eventually Queen Victoria was the first monarch whose body was carried from Paddington to Windsor by a special funeral train.

OPPOSITE *Only slightly spoilt by the fact that BR were yet again changing livery, in 1967 the up express ran through the Lune Gorge before its scenic value enjoyed by discerning passengers was spoilt by the building of the M6.*

12.15pm On a Sunday lunchtime toward the end of the 1960s, I am half asleep at the front of a train from Derby to Birmingham when the brakes come sharply on, and looking out of the window I see the station nameplate Sutton Coldfield. Unconsciously I become alert with dread.

It took only a few seconds to realise my anxiety was because the accident to a Sunday train (diverted as obviously mine had been) came to grief at exactly this spot. Details of the 23 January 1955 crash that killed seventeen and resulted in forty others going to hospital had obviously been etched into my memory.

The station was closed and its signalbox switched out, for normally no trains ran this way on Sundays. Why the driver entered the sharp left hand curve at 55–60mph instead of the maximum of 30mph we will never know.

With commendable speed, various actions were taken to halt a Bristol–York express about to reach the station where the partially destroyed train and platform awning blocked both tracks. These incidentally were the days when many carriages even on steel frames were wooden-built. With modern integral steel coaches, many fewer would now be killed or injured.

12.23pm The 12.10 GNER electric 225 express to Leeds crashes at 115mph half a mile south of Hatfield. Soon after, near Princetown on Dartmoor, I'm contacted by the BBC on my mobile, told the bare facts of the accident and asked to return to our hotel to report live on radio by telephone. The surmise that it had to be track fault is correct.

Involving no other train, or a signalling or driving mistake, and killing just four passengers, the uncomplicated accident nonetheless had profound consequences. Making hefty profits as a private company, knowing about track wearing out on curves (or gauge corner cracking), but to swell profits Railtrack had postponed remedial work including that on the very section involved. Its chairman was further vilified by talking about the heavy wear caused by freight trains, of which hardly any use this section.

Such was the magnitude of risk that later the same day, the speed of all trains was reduced by a third everywhere that track was to be renewed, and a 20mph limit imposed where there were signs of fragments of rails broken off, mainly on curves. Trains ran late throughout Britain, and the Highland sleeper was temporarily withdrawn since the delays meant the journey length became impractical. Railtrack itself fell (causing its shareholders hefty loss), replaced by State-owned Network Rail.

1.06pm A double-headed through train from Newcastle with a section from Darlington (joined up at Penrith) arrives at Keswick on summer Sundays with the only catering vehicle ever to travel west of Penrith from which it runs non-stop. The number of passengers varies according to the weather, but is often considerable.

I made a point of seeing its arrival while conducting the Lake District Enquiry based at Keswick. Later, when on holiday at the Keswick Hotel, it arrived before our Sunday lunch but could still be seen and heard shunting when we retired to our room afterwards. It took two hours to turn and tend the locomotives and place them in position having moved the train from the single down platform to one of the up ones.

Especially at summer weekends, Keswick was a busy station. The Saturday *Lakes Express* from Workington, for example, was doubled in length and given a second locomotive.

Historic oddity. Designed by Francis Trevithick, son of Richard, who was the first to build a full-size locomotive, this single-driver (wheels 6ft 3in diameter) of 1845 happened to be the first engine built at Crewe.

1.39pm A tank engine and single coach, with only a fat schoolboy and a guard on board, comes squeakily round the sharp curve of the Hemel Hempstead branch, the single-line token being given up, onto the Midland's down mainline before immediately crossing to the up main for the last mile into Harpenden station. A favourite train-spotting point during the brief period we live in Harpenden in 1938–9 is nicknamed The Hole, at track level where queues of coal trains under permissive working wait for their turn to head toward London.

Since there were only two daily trains on the Hemel Hempstead (three on Saturdays including the one mentioned), Harpenden Junction signalbox's main function was to allow stopping services from the north to switch to the relief line. Down ones had to cross the up main and, better seen from the high bridge over the tracks, once that had happened I waited to see how quickly an express would follow. The tall semaphore signals were stylish – and so were the frequent feather-weight expresses all with restaurant car.

If a train reached much more than half the length of a major GWR express, the Midland put on an extra locomotive. In 1923, when the Midland dominated the new LMS, it is said that some North Western men at Euston cried when it was insisted that a second engine was needed for their heavier trains when one had been sufficient.

The Hemel Hempstead branch was one of those minor lines planned with unjustified optimism. There had originally been a triangular junction, the abandoned cuttings to the north showing that access from there had a gentler curve than the one then still in use. With these deep cuttings and a high embankment over a bridge (still intact when I last used the road), it was an expensive line to build. And though it was called the Hemel Hempstead branch, trains terminated and started at Heath Park Halt, three quarters of a mile beyond Hemel Hempstead.

Summer Saturday lunchtimes were especially busy on the mainline. I never did understand why I once saw an immaculate GWR train head toward London. A mystery I still occasionally try to solve.

2.03pm Shortly after my office reopened after lunch in the late 1960s and early 1970s, three trains from or to Leeds pass outside simultaneously. The first down one departs Newton Abbot at 2.01. The second, which has been catching it up nearly all the way, is *The Cornishman*, which if things are bang on time (as they usually are) passes the up *Cornishman*, so the three trains are side by side.

The Cornishman was among trains being given names when the still fiercely independent Western Region gained authority to re-introduce chocolate-and-cream livery for its named services.

Some years earlier I used to use the Torbay portion of the up *Cornishman*. At Churston, after a down train had been crossed, it waited while the Brixham auto-car engine shunted a fish van onto the back. The train took over an hour to get from Kingswear to Newton Abbot where, during the stop-over there was time to get out and see both up and down *Cornish Rivieras* pass through non-stop. What silly yet haunting memories enthusiasts retain.

The Torbay section of the up *Cornishman* joined the main train at Exeter, the general manager once causing delay by insisting that a rogue non chocolate-and-cream coach be placed at the very front to give the rest of the train a continuous traditional appearance.

3.11pm The boat train from Folkestone carrying Charles Dickens on 9 June 1865 derails on a girder bridge across the River Beult near Staplehurst for the simple reason that two rails are missing.

In those days the cross-channel ferries to Folkestone were dependent on the tide and ran at differing times. The foreman laying new track had not expected it so soon, his lookout man was not stationed far enough back, and detonators that should have been placed on the track were not: the usual chapter of mishappenings.

Most of the carriages fell alongside the cracked girders into the river – there was no protective balustrade – and ten people were killed and forty injured. Dickens was in the front first-class coach with his companions Ellen Ternan and her mother, and his first thought was to help them out of the suspended vehicle.

Famously, he then crawled back in to rescue the last part of the manuscript of one of his best novels, *Our Mutual Friend*, at the end of which he writes of the 'terribly destructive accident'. 'When I had done what I could to help others, I climbed back into my carriage, nearly turned over a viaduct – to extricate the couple [two of his characters, Mr and Mrs Lammle, at breakfast]. They were much soiled, but otherwise unhurt.'

Already upsettingly separated from his wife and suffering from overwork, he was returning from a trip to recuperate. His nerves never fully recovered from the accident and he died five years later to the day. Meanwhile he tired himself out with public readings and being jittery of train travel necessary to reach them. He wrote little beside the unfinished *Edwin Drood* and a ghost story, *The Signalman*, drawing gloomily on his experience.

3.27pm In 1956, the day's first (but also last) train arrives at Hawes on the eastern fringes of the Lake District. There is quite a gathering on the platform, railway enthusiasts travelling or coming to see this oddity of a single daily train on the truncated Northallerton branch from Garsdale on the Settle & Carlisle. Parcels traffic on the daily service is brisk. At least Hawes is still connected to the national system. The train was a through one from the once-important junction of Hellifield, with southerly connections, as had the return service. It was retained when other trains to Hawes were chopped because, as a through service, it had been relatively well used. The delay in closing Hawes possibly gave the impetus to replace a section of track with a vehicle placed on it and open a heritage centre so that people remember its railway. Today some drive to Garsdale to catch trains on the revitalised Settle & Carlisle.

There was a curious history of the east end of the minor cross-country route to Northallerton. British Rail ran a freight service which often carried military vehicles. After that had ceased, volunteers reopened part of it, but that scheme went into liquidation, though the new organisation now running trains for pleasure dreams of providing a Diesel commuter service into Northallerton.

3.50pm In the days when stations and towns are truly competitive, Teignmouth welcomes one of two daily trains not to call at Dawlish. Ironically the other twelve hours earlier, sometimes exactly so to the minute, picking up early birds for Devonport Dockyard.

The 3.50pm was the forerunner of *The Cornishman*, unnamed and coming from Wolverhampton, Birmingham Snow Hill and the North Warwick line *via* Stratford-upon-Avon, which in the post-war years carried about the same number of summer Saturday trains for the West Country as the Midland down the Lickey Bank. Until later times, there were only two daily services to and from the West and Birmingham.

Busy opening-day traffic on the narrow-gauge Leek & Manifold Valley Light Railway, but it was not to prove typical. Despite the fact that narrow-gauge trains conveyed standard-gauge trucks and sidings were also built to standard gauge, the railway was a wildcat scheme that never could be profitable. Yet its folklore remains well known among today's enthusiasts.

I recall a woman passenger asking Teignmouth's booking clerk the times of trains to Birmingham. 'Do you want the Bradford or the Hampton?' had her somewhat puzzled. The Bradford would have been *The Devonian*, so named pre-war.

Passengers from the West to the North still went *via* the Severn Tunnel and Shrewsbury, though in preference to spending nearly two hours stationary in Crewe on a through coach, I used to take the day's first train to London and *The Mid-Day Scot* from Euston, an exhilarating train I greatly enjoyed in steam days.

4.05pm The electric train on the circuit from Newcastle to the coast and back takes me to Whitley Bay ('Newcastle-on-Sea') where large crowds are bathing, making sand castles and eating ice creams. I continue on at 5.10 on the sole evening train running back to Newcastle *via* the docks. They are fascinating but already well past their heyday, and this little-used loop off the circuit (as the little-used North Wylam loop off the line to Hexham) won't last much longer. The litter of abandoned lines in the North East, the cradle of railways, is steadily increasing.

In 1959 there was basically a 20-minute interval service on the 20-mile circuit, an isolated piece of non-standard electrification which BR later abandoned, using Diesel cars instead. Now, however, it is part of the Metro, much admired by other cities, re-electrified with an excellent service attracting increasing usage.

5.40pm The commonest time for stopping trains on main and branch lines to set out from large towns taking workers home but also, in 1962, when I first travel by it, the starting time of the main part of the *Royal Highlander* from Inverness to Euston. With seating, sleeping and restaurant car, it isn't exactly quick.

At Aviemore, coaches and a first-class sleeping car that had left Inverness at 4.20pm were picked up. I still know people who used to join it at Nairn. Perth wasn't reached until 9.30pm, Crewe at 4.37am and Euston at 8.25am.

Between the departure of the two sections from Inverness, there was a 5.00pm all-stations to Aviemore *via* Carrbridge and a 5.30pm to Aberdeen. The latter was one of the then four new Diesel-car expresses with miniature buffet between Inverness and Aberdeen stopping only at Nairn, Forres, Keith Junction and Huntly. At 5.53pm it was followed by a slower steam-hauled train to Aberdeen *via* the Coast route between Elgin and Keith. Only a few years earlier there had been only one daily through train. Times were changing, but the great economy drive with its many closures lay in the future.

Though it still feels a long journey, especially over the high passes in winter darkness, today's *Royal Highlander* leaves Inverness at 8.46pm and arrives in Euston at 7.47am. The train now has sections from Fort William, Inverness and Aberdeen, combined in Edinburgh Waverley, where united it becomes the country's longest passenger train, reverses, and runs non-stop through Haymarket for a second time, now under electric power and heading for the West Coast mainline.

Today the longest journey is from Fort William, the train losing time having to wend its way through the northern suburbs of Glasgow to reverse in Edinburgh and return west. In 1962, when the railways followed traditional allegiances, the separate Fort William train made the quicker journey, terminating at King's Cross, as did the nightly *Aberdonian*.

What memories they all evoke: different ex-LMS and LNER stock and smells, the potties next to the berths in which passengers were implored to place no solid matter, and some stewards who might have climbed out of Dickens.

Trains called at Truthall Platform on the Helston branch in daylight only. Platforms had a booking office, if only open part time, while in GWR speak 'halts' were unstaffed.

6.55pm Possibly the most embarrassing time of my life: a train crowded with a new wave of evacuees following the start of V2 rocket attacks on London in early September 1944, comes to a prolonged halt at South Molton.

The signalman was 'having a quick one' at the nearby Tinto, and I was proudly in charge of the signalbox with Mum paying a rare visit to the station. Possibly feeling under pressure, I became confused where the evening trains in each direction were, and incorrectly arranged for them to cross at South Molton.

The down train with the evacuees entered the section as the signalman arrived; there was nothing unusual in that. 'Why haven't you asked for it to go forward?' he asked. On hearing what had happened, he tried calling the box at Filleigh, the next station in the other direction. There was no reply, but it seemed ages before we heard that it was entering the section.

My signalman friend explained the position to the guard, who said that his passengers, squashed closely together, would welcome a break. They didn't need another invitation to pour out onto the platform. Many had never seen a cow or rabbit before, and were enchanted in the evening sunshine of double summer time.

'You've made them very happy,' was the comment of guard and signalman, echoed by Mum's 'They've had the time of their life.' But to this day I still feel guilty about my only serious misjudgement in amateur signalling days.

7.10pm A train arrives in Broadstone from Southampton. Before it has left, a second (due one minute later) also arrives from Southampton. This seeming intensity of service is due to Dorset's odd railway geography. Though leaving Southampton within a few minutes of each other and having taken the same route for the first 13 miles, when they arrive virtually simultaneously they are travelling in opposite directions.

East of Broadstone they were on the original mainline to Weymouth, nicknamed Castleman's Corkscrew for having been built cheaply by its founder. Curves were sharp and gradients steep. Bournemouth was Britain's last major resort to develop, and at first was served by branch lines from either end. After they were joined up, that became the mainline, and the Corkscrew declined into almost branch line status, though in the 1950s two summer Saturday Weymouth expresses still used it. That involved a steep descent down from Broadstone to Holton Heath on the Weymouth line.

Though there were long gaps between trains (barely sixty passenger trains on summer Mondays to Fridays, but many more on Saturdays) I found Broadstone's four-platform crossroad station fascinating. The pair of platforms to the east were the most used, carrying trains from Brockenhurst, where the new mainline through Bournemouth left the Corkscrew on the branch from Salisbury, which joined the Corkscrew at West Moors, and trains from the Somerset & Dorset going on to Bournemouth, mainly to Bournemouth West but a few to Bournemouth Central.

The day's first train, too early for the most ardent enthusiast, was the third-class-only passenger, mail and newspaper 4.39am from Salisbury to Weymouth. That used the much quieter western side of the station, and emphasised the huge assortment of routes taken by Broadstone trains. They included the summer Saturday Waterloo–Weymouth, other trains from Salisbury to Weymouth, but (back to the eastern platforms) also a summer Saturday Bournemouth to Cardiff followed by a New Milton to Swansea *via* Salisbury, and everything down the Somerset & Dorset. On summer Saturdays, that included trains from many northern and Midland starting points supplementing the daily *Pines Express* which didn't always stop at Broadstone, meaning that local passengers had to join at Poole.

To complicate the history, it should be mentioned that originally the Somerset & Dorset linked up with the Corkscrew at Wimborne, once described as 'the most important railway centre in Dorset . . . the key to the metropolitan connections of the county'. Wimborne's importance declined sharply when Broadstone became a crossroads. All the secondary and cross-country routes that made Broadstone so fascinating have alas long been abandoned. But I continue to recall those happy hours on the station, and especially the thrill of hearing the exhaust of a Merchant Navy coming up the steep slope and cut across the layout to continue on the Corkscrew with returning holidaymakers from Weymouth and Swanage.

7.16pm The probable moment that a northbound train on Bouch's original Tay Bridge plunges into the water, killing all seventy-five passengers and crew in the only major railway accident from which no survivors emerge. It is on 18 December 1879, the year after the bridge had been triumphantly opened and Sir Thomas Bouch had been knighted.

Bouch was disgraced by what emerged about shoddy design and workmanship. Though the storm on that Sunday night was possibly the fiercest ever, the bridge was supposed to withstand such pressures. Its failure at least ensured that subsequent viaducts were better constructed – the Forth Bridge perhaps unnecessarily over-engineered, more so than the ultimate replacement Tay Bridge. The accident was one of few to enter folklore, obliterating the memory of earlier but less spectacular bridge disasters.

Had not Queen Victoria, ever nervous of rail journeys, crossed by it? The Tay Bridge disaster still ranks alongside the sinking of the *Titanic* in many people's minds. Because of wind funnelling up the Tay estuary, the ferry journey was often rough and immediately on its opening many workers in particular had crowded into trains just for the trip across the bridge.

It is not surprising that, especially on dark stormy nights, today's passengers think of the stumps of the piers of the old bridge retained to give extra protection to the exactly

parallel new structure seven and a half years later and a permanent monument to the fallen. Unsentimentally the North British Railway fished the 4-4-0 tank engine No. 138 out of the water and reconditioned it to run for another forty years, but Bouch died within months of the disaster and the enquiry that humiliated him. The very engineering journal that had lauded his bridge gave him a bitter obituary.

8.08pm On 24 November 2008, we arrive back at Inverness on the noon *Highland Chieftain* High Speed Train from King's Cross. We joined it at Edinburgh watching ingredients for dinner being loaded into the restaurant car. The meal, as a few days earlier had been the breakfast, is of the highest order in a relaxing environment helped by familiar friendly crew, who had a short layover between down and up trains at Newcastle. The only thing that is different is that the price has risen since National Express have taken over the East Coast franchise from GNER.

Though there were rumours of money troubles as the recession deepened, little did we realise it would be our last East Coast restaurant car meal, and probably one of the very last ever to be served north of Edinburgh. A few days later most restaurant cars out of King's Cross were abandoned . . . and then National Express lost the franchise: see 11.59pm.

When I moved to Scotland just over twenty years ago, there were two day trains and two night ones from Inverness to London, one of each routed *via* Birmingham. Now the single day and night trains both go direct. Such is the length of their journeys that one of them is in transit continuously night and day apart from the HST's arrival at 8.08pm until the down sleeper leaves half an hour later.

9.50pm Starting time for a short-lived Manchester London Road to Plymouth sleeper, a single car attached to the long-established train which runs as other north-west to south-west services *via* Hereford and the Severn Tunnel.

I used to host dinners of North Country authors at the grand Midland Hotel, the last to use page boys in Britain, before taking a taxi to Piccadilly station, and would arrive only a few minutes late for work at Newton Abbot. For a time the train began with electric power (Crewe–Manchester being the first stage of the West Coast electrification) switched to steam to Bristol and then be Diesel hauled.

Later I had to wait at Crewe to join the Edinburgh–Plymouth sleeper, which I usually crossed on the bridge near my office, as I did when walking from home to be at there for a sharp 8.30 start.

10.03pm Having left Paddington at 7.31am, the time Daniel Gooch, locomotive engineer to the Great Western, returns after driving himself to Exeter and back on the day the Bristol & Exeter opens to Devon's capital city, 1 May 1844.

'It was a very hard day's work for me as apart from driving the engine a distance of 387 miles, I had to be out early in the morning to see that all was right for our trip, and while at Exeter was busy with matters connected with the opening, so my only chance for sitting down was for an hour while we were at dinner. Next day my back ached so I could hardly walk. Mr Brunel wrote me a very handsome letter thanking me for what I had done.'

Genius though he was, Brunel was no locomotive engineer, and he and Gooch, who lived much longer and eventually built engines that would be adapted for standard gauge, in skill and temperament, happily balanced each other.

Ivo Peters, whom I knew as a friend when he lived at No. 1, The Royal Crescent, Bath, and who epitomises the Somerset & Dorset, catches a Southern Pacific drifting down to Milford with the 9.05 Bristol to Bournemouth in July 1953.

In 1844 a sharp look out had to be kept for trains in front, but excluding stopping time, the return trip was accomplished at an average of 44.5mph. May Day 1844 became known as 'Gooch's Good Day'.

11.17pm Just up the road at Gidea Park station from where I had earlier lived as a boy, a delayed Liverpool Street–Peterborough express crashes into the rear of a Southend-on-Sea train which it should have preceded, killing seven and injuring forty-five. The date is 2 January 1947 at the start of LNER's somewhat down-at-heel last year and a terrible one for Britain as a whole.

There were multiple failures behind the accident, but most blame went to the Peterborough train's driver for going too fast in the fog. What is interesting to note here is that six years later (see 8.18am) when Britain was still climbing out of its post-war blues it took another more serious fog-caused accident to bring about the widespread introduction of automatic train control or warning system.

11.30pm The one-time almost nightly seasonal car-carrying sleeper leaves Stirling for Newton Abbot complete with restaurant car serving late dinner before departure, all-night drinks and snacks, and several sittings of breakfast before arrival at 9.35am. It has replaced an earlier Edinburgh to Newton Abbot, and is convenient for much of northern Scotland. Most of the passengers are holidaymakers, both Scottish and West Country, but is also useful for business, visiting authors and booksellers.

In the reverse direction, some passengers detraining at Stirling drove to Perth to join another Motorail to Inverness to avoid the then awful A9. Later the Newton Abbot train was switched to daylight with a picnic box rather than restaurant car but a first-class compartment for each car's passengers. I was on the final run south with the train at maximum capacity. It was withdrawn earlier than it might have been because of the simplification of Newton Abbot's layout. Once a dozen car-carrying routes served Newton Abbot, including one to Dover. Cars were loaded and unloaded by busy porters at the old Moretonhampstead platform 9.

As roads improved, the demand naturally reduced but, until killed by privatisation because it awkwardly straddled franchises, Edinburgh–Plymouth sleepers carried a few cars to Bristol.

11.59pm The moment that the operation of the East Coast mainline is brought back under State control to give a time of stability after standards have dropped dramatically after a short period in the hands of National Express. The latter had taken over from the highly popular GNER, renowned for quality on-board service both at seat and in the restaurant car, and for a keen management anxious to restore normal running after any disruptive incident.

Both lost the franchise as a result of money shortage in their holding companies, the GNER suffering a drop in traffic growth after the Hatfield accident (see 12.23pm) and National Express in the recession at the start of the twenty-first century. Two failures in a row has resulted in discussion about the whole franchise system on our privatised railways, and especially the risks run and doubtful public service rendered by accepting the highest tenders to reduce the nation's taxes.

CHAPTER 7
PICTURES FOR PLEASURE

OVER THE YEARS I'VE BUILT UP A FORMIDABLE GALLERY of railway art. Inevitably the collection is personal, but I hope readers will enjoy the pictures and their stories – and that a museum or perhaps steam railway might have sufficient hanging space to keep the collection intact when the time comes to part with it. While the rest, mainly in the hall, stairs and landing, are treated as a whole, what is in the study is naturally the most personally nostalgic.

On the way to school I loved peeping at railway pictures in a couple of other people's porches, but my own first has pride of place over the mantelpiece: GWR *King Henry V* No. 6018 battling through a storm along the Sea Wall near Dawlish (below).

It is easy to dismiss it as a touch romantic or even unrealistic, but the sea did actually break over trains and one can imagine the fireman on a down train sheltering with the driver on the right hand side, where (unlike on other railways) the controls were. It was on the recommendation of a director of my publishing house David & Charles, who had seen it displayed at the Barbican Gallery in Plymouth, that I popped down to purchase it – almost as soon as it had been painted in 1974. That was following storm damage that washed away part of the down platform at Dawlish.

The price was a modest £120. Don was then unknown, but his fame spread rapidly, and in less than a year the gallery offered to buy it back for £1,200. Later Don Breckons cost much more.

My study commands a view of the Moray Firth and occasionally, when a north-easterly gale blows, I compare the waves outside with those in the picture. The walk along the Sea Wall has always been a favourite, though it ends on the Teignmouth side of Parson's Tunnel, the last of the five from Dawlish going through the sandstone cliffs. Realistic though the painting is, nobody could actually have seen a train at a rough high tide from that perspective. But it was around this point that once I had a Great Western porridge changed after a splash of sea water had come through the not-quite-closed restaurant car window, and that on an up train.

I love the power and movement of the picture, though for me the scene is so familiar that perhaps I do not spend as long looking at it as I do some of Don's later work, capturing those magic branch line moments where there is a real story to tell. Yet if I could only retain one Don Breckon, it would have to be this.

Though the subject is still the Sea Wall, this 'art' is of a quite different kind: the four-colour letterpress blocks for the jacket of the fourth and subsequent David & Charles editions of my most deeply researched railway title, *The West Country*, Vol. 1 of *A Regional History of the Railways of Great Britain*, together with a reproduction of the jacket (right). In six hard-back and three paperback editions, this key volume of the only series ever to tell the story of all railways in a region against the economic and social background sold over 40,000 copies.

All the type of the front and back of the jacket is here, but the main attraction is naturally the contemporary 'painting' of a 1852 landslip near Parson's Tunnel, showing passengers clambering over the fallen rocks between the broad-gauge trains halted on either side of a gap in the track. The saddle tank locos were going to back their carriages to Dawlish and Teignmouth respectively. Health and Safety was not a phrase known to Brunel. In the early 1960s this set of blocks cost £120, making colour prohibitively expensive for anything but the jacket. Digital colour is cheap and encourages much greater use in today's books, but I don't know of a printer who can now use four-colour blocks, so our illustration is reproduced from the printed jacket.

Next comes a large 1924 framed map of the Great Western Railway. Mainly taken from timetables, hundreds if not thousands of these maps must still survive, though few will be decently framed and none looked at more frequently or in greater detail than this one facing my desk and reminding me of my successful journalistic, broadcasting and publishing careers, as well as that of author. They were all initially greatly helped by my love and knowledge of God's Wonderful Railway.

Over the years I have become familiar with many of the details that elude brief study: the parallel lines running up the Welsh valleys, the score of Company Docks, including Brentford, Newquay and Aberdovery, the tracks owned to Clapham Junction, running

A Regional History of the Railways of Great Britain

Volume 1 THE WEST COUNTRY
David St John Thomas

Volume 2 SOUTHERN ENGLAND
H. P. White

Volume 3 GREATER LONDON
H. P. White

Volume 4 THE NORTH EAST
K. Hoole

Volume 5 THE EASTERN COUNTIES
D. I. Gordon

Volume 6 SCOTLAND
The Lowlands and the Borders
John Thomas

Volume 7 THE WEST MIDLANDS
Rex Christiansen

Volume 8 SOUTH AND WEST YORKSHIRE
David Joy

Volume 9 THE EAST MIDLANDS
Robin Leleux

Volume 10 THE NORTH WEST
G. O. Holt

Volume 11 NORTH AND MID WALES
Peter E. Baughan

Volume 12 SOUTH WALES
D. S. M. Barrie

Volume 13 THAMES AND SEVERN
Rex Christiansen

Volume 14 THE LAKE COUNTIES
David Joy

In preparation
Volume 15 THE NORTH OF SCOTLAND
David Turnock

ISBN 0-946537-17-8

9 780946 537174

Vol 1
The West
Country

A Regional History of the Railways
of Great Britain
Volume 1 THE WEST
COUNTRY

DAVID ST JOHN THOMAS

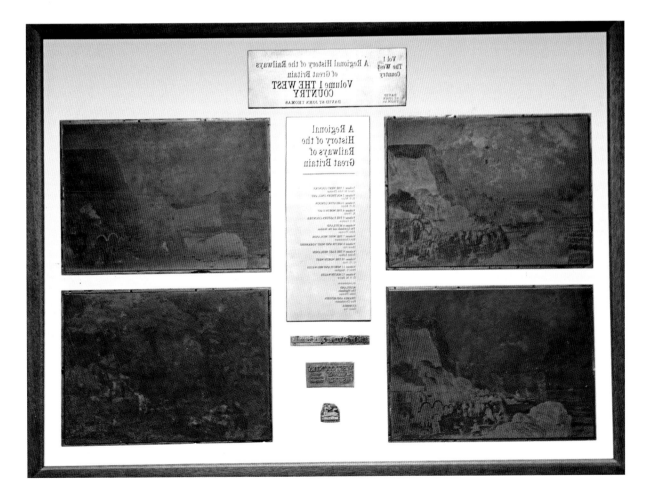

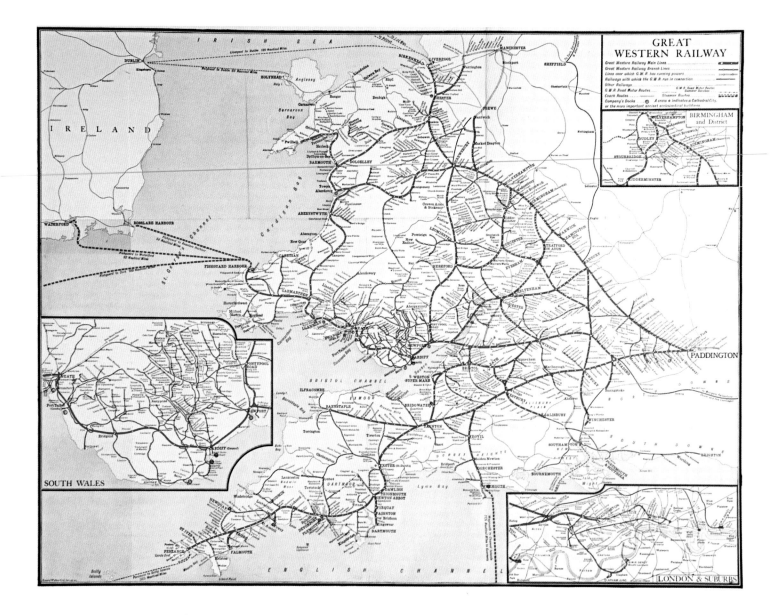

powers to Aldgate, Victoria and by two routes to Manchester, depots at Poplar and Victoria & Albert Dock, and the 'G.W.R. Road Motor Services', some of them seasonal, and the company's shipping routes to Ireland and the Channel Islands.

The map is post the 1923 Grouping and includes those of the absorbed companies, mainly in Wales, but before the opening of the Southern's North Devon & Cornwall Junction Light Railway from Torrington to Hallwill in 1926. Though all passenger lines adjoining and penetrating GWR territory are shown, including the Weston, Clevedon & Portishead and the Welsh Highland, the GW's cartographers were skilled at making *their* route look the obvious choice. Thus the undulating, curvy branch from Taunton to Barnstaple looks superior even to the GW's own mainline to Exeter and in a totally different league from the Southern's route to North Devon. It is also made to look more obvious to travel by coach to Lynton from Minehead or Dulverton than by the Lynton & Barnstaple line, then still open.

I could (indeed do) look at this map for hours, noting the lines I have travelled on and those that closed before I could find time and money to visit them. The one thing missing are the GWR hotels; they and air services were added later, by which time, however, the

'Road Motors' had been taken over by the separate bus companies in which the railways could have shareholdings but not control. Since the 1930 Road Traffic Act, train–bus connections have never been as good as they were in the 1920s.

A King bursts out of Box Tunnel, from a painting by George Heiron. Though the original hangs on the landing, this tea towel version (right) is on the inside of my study door and was itself a good seller, stocked in many shops. It is from the jacket of *The Great Western Railway: 150 Glorious Years*, the only title that earned (very modest) tea towel rights. The official souvenir of the Western Region, with an introduction by Bill (now Lord) Bradshaw, in retail terms the public spent a million pounds on the book.

Finally, in my study, a small black-and-white photograph underneath one end of the mantelpiece brings back many memories. John Arlott of cricket commentary fame (but also a good author), myself the David, and Charles Hadfield the Charles of David & Charles are caught holding on to each other on a miniature train set up in the garden of Forde House, Newton Abbot, for our twenty-first garden party in 1981.

Moving to the general gallery, we start with several works by Don Breckon, all except the last being commissioned for the over-large format books we published of his work. Most tell a story. In the painting above, we are on the former Cambrian Railways, absorbed into the GWR in 1923. As on other absorbed lines, better locomotives were soon provided. However, the weight restriction on the Cambrian meant that the new power took the form of the 3200 (later 9000) class Dukedogs. Introduced in 1936, incredibly they were basically an amalgam of the boilers of a Duke on the chassis of a Bulldog – the latter having been introduced way back in 1898. When you think of the changes in the competition from motor transport that had taken place in that generation-plus, it really is mind boggling – though of cherished memory for older enthusiasts who enjoyed travelling by and photographing the Dukedogs on their early post-war Welsh holidays. Not pleased were the Earls after whom some of the Dukedogs were first named. When protesting that they didn't appreciate their names on such ancient machines, they were quickly given Castle Class locos named after them instead.

Here we see a couple of Dukedogs, Nos 3210 and 3208, when nearly 'new', crossing Barmouth Bridge with the LNWR Royal train, on the Coronation tour of the realm by the newly crowned King George VI and Queen Elizabeth. Note the royal headcode, the little boy on the beach waving his Union Jack and the two fishermen standing to attention with their feet in the water . . . just enough to show it is a special occasion in this very familiar situation without detracting from the sheer grandeur of the scenery. I always felt that especially on Great Western lines in Central and North Wales, the railway frequently enhanced the natural landscape.

When I look at the picture, which I do daily going up and down the stairs, many memories are brought to life . . . of walking over the viaduct as well as taking all manner of

trains. One recollection is of when I was describing the scene for a broadcast and a gaggle of schoolgirls on their way to Barmouth collapsed in laughter thinking I was talking to myself. They hadn't spotted the lapel microphone.

Like a great piece of music, a good picture unlocks a host of memories . . . which in this case include those fine LNWR clerestory coaches which even on ordinary trains gave a luxurious ride. It was often said LNWR stock on GW metals was the best of all. Then there is the pleasure in knowing that despite those marine insects which were gnawing away at the wooden piles, which for years threatened the coast line's very existence, we can still travel by train to reach the Talyllyn and Ffestiniog and Welsh Highland Railway. This picture was commissioned to give us sufficient Welsh element in *Don Breckon's Great Western Railway*.

Also commissioned for that book, *Dulverton* (above), painted in 1986, twenty years after its closure, captures the atmosphere of what was simultaneously a much under-used station yet still the most important trading establishment of any kind for miles around. It also delightfully shows things not going quite right, for the Barnstaple-bound passenger headed by a 2-6-0 Mogul is delayed for the arrival of an up goods sauntering into the platform. We can perhaps gauge the length of the delay by the position of passengers who have alighted. Anyone changing onto the Exe Valley auto-car train has already boarded it.

Looking at this picture recalls the purring, wheezing noise of the Moguls when idling. They may not have been the most glamorous of engines, but they spent long careers struggling up inclines and were prevented from catching up time by being limited to 60mph going downhill on the Barnstaple branch. They were fitted with token catchers which the fireman extended from his cabside for automatic exchange on non-stopping goods trains (usually made up of twenty-eight wagons including brake van) and on summer Saturday expresses to and from Ilfracombe.

The picture emphasises that freight was still more profitable than passengers. Only on summer Saturdays, and for special events such as Bampton's 1974 horse fair, were passenger trains longer than the standard three coaches, usually only one with corridor and lavatory composite. Nearly always 1400 class 0-4-2 tanks propelled two auto-cars to Exeter, usually with few passengers from Dulverton but more at the southern end.

Back From Town (below) was the name Don Breckon chose for what is perhaps my most-loved portrayal of the country railway. I can do no better than quote what he wrote in *The Railway Paintings of Don Breckon*:

> Over a cup of coffee David St John Thomas talked about his concept of the typical country branch-line station scene. The engine shunting a wagon from the train, the people taking the footpath home, the station forecourt with the hotel taxi etc. David's interest was mainly with the people and the activity surrounding the station; the landscape and the locomotive were of interest to me.
>
> After a few rough sketches I reached the compromise of running the footpath parallel with the railway – the people and the engine shunting could than have a prominent position in the painting. The station forecourt would have to be pushed back but its size would mean that the area would still convey the activity there.
>
> I began work on a larger rough sketch of the layout for David to see. Dividing the picture into three, vertically and horizontally, gave me a good proportion division for the main shapes and focal points. I took a viewpoint to one side of the foot path on a rising slope with a tree to the right casting a shadow across the foreground 'linking' right to left. By running the footpath into a dip in the ground the main figures did not obscure the station area and the fencing post could be lowered so as not to get too involved with the wheels of the engine.
>
> I was rather bothered about the shunting of the cattle truck because, despite the shunter with the pole, it did seem as though part of the train had broken away accidentally.

David was happy with the rough layout and came up with a further suggestion about the shunting – a bracket signal with siding arm. As he tells in his *Country Railway*, David enjoyed pulling such a signal as a boy at South Molton when a truck of cattle was detached from the evening passenger train. Here it is lowered to show that the engine was not off down the mainline.

Now it was time to pick up a 30 × 20in canvas and get to work on the painting. As it progressed, however, there was still some research work to do. The station building was based on Avonwick, the goods shed at Fairford and the engine on five or six good photos of a 45XX 2-6-2T. I looked through old family photographs for details of old ladies' hats and coats of the late 1940s and a photograph of an old Dennis taken at Crich Tramway Museum was just right for my village transport.

One of the good things about painting in oils is the chance to make alterations as the work progresses. The old lady, like the boy, was looking at the engine until I reckon that she's too tired after a day's shopping to be looking around her. Then the small pond beside the footpath 'grew' into a stream so that I could insert the little plank bridge and add interest to the flow of the footpath.

When the painting was finished I looked back at the early sketches and felt it had worked out reasonably well. I'm still not sure about that shunting though!

There was always something special about the junction between two branch lines. *Rush Hour at Heathfield* (below) shows that, unlike Dulverton, the multi-track curved divergence is almost as eye catching as the trains. During much of its history, Heathfield only saw three passenger trains together once daily . . . but look at the huge infrastructure needed for this mid-morning performance. It is perhaps not surprising that the layout was one of Devon's first to be totally track circuited, so that the signalman could see exactly where everything was. By the way, back in the 1930s, in summer the Moretonhampstead train we see disappearing into the background ran non-stop from Torquay to Bovey Tracey. It must have kept the signalman on his toes.

In fairness, the track circuiting and overall infrastructure (bar the platforms) were more justified by freight. In the 1950s, for example, though only one daily freight ran from

Newton Abbot to Moretonhampstead, there were two on the Teign Valley: one carrying heavy mineral traffic from Christow, and an express freight to and from Exeter run for crew-training purposes for, if the Sea Wall at Dawlish was closed, many trains were diverted by the Teign Valley and Heathfield, which had a wider loading gauge than the Southern's double-track mainline from Exeter *via* Okehampton to Plymouth. I have never seen a photograph of Heathfield with diverted trains though I did see one of the up *Cornish Riviera* with its tail set back through hand-locked points in the refuge siding at Christow.

Heathfield itself provided considerable lignite or white coal, pipes and earthenware from the pottery served by the siding in the left foreground and, such was the shunting activity that, if the express freight from Exeter was not punctual, the signalman insisted it be held at Trusham for up to two hours.

Like so many country stations, Heathfield died a lingering death. First to go were the Teign Valley passenger trains from 9 June 1958, followed by Teign Valley freight tracks in Autumn 1960. Moretonhampstead passenger trains ceased on 2 March 1959, freight continuing to Bovey Tracey till 1970.

Heathfield then had new freight to a banana ripening store given wasteful and quite unnecessarily full signalling in 1970. The banana plant had a short life and the last freight was oil to Heathfield and clay from Teigngrace by which time the signalbox ceased to function and the last passenger excursion carried the 'one engine in steam' wooden token.

Another reminder of how radically things have changed is provided by the photograph of the daily shunt in progress at Penryn on the Falmouth branch (below). There are almost thirty trucks in the yard or across the trailing diamond crossing, with more on the main train in the platform.

The daily shunt at a small market town might last anything up to a couple of hours, and usually included sorting trucks left by other goods trains or leaving them ready to be collected by a later one. Shunts had to be fitted in carefully between passenger trains and often (as obviously here) involved a midday lull in passenger activities.

The next group is of Newton Abbot and nearby. Over the years, thousands of photographs have been taken from the bridge carrying the Torquay road over the railway. Half a century separates this pair. The first (above) shows the old and to say the least inconvenient station, with its series of wooden sheds further to the east at the twentieth century's beginning. Note the short trains and the children on the path alongside Railway Cottages which, after suffering a direct hit in the 1940s, in the 1960s became the site of David & Charles's offices. The small Brunel building beyond remained intact and was incorporated by us along with the Carriage & Wagon building and repair depot shorn of its tall chimneys which had been needed when internal power was provided by an old locomotive boiler.

The 1953 photograph showing the new (1929) station (right), depicts a later age but still one very different from ours: semaphores, telegraph posts and wires, steam, smoke and general gloom aided by the cooling tower of the coal-fired electricity works and emphasised by a vapour trail. Soot was occasionally as thick in the air as in a London smog.

The signal gantry at the end of the down platform was replaced by a larger one including Aller Junction distant arms. When made redundant by multiple aspect signalling controlled from Exeter, I purchased it. Early on a Sunday morning it was put on a low-loader and we toured the town causing surprise especially to those who had only just woken and wondered if they were still the worse for the local scrumpy (rough cider).

In its new position (where it still stands) the gantry was warmly welcomed by the townspeople as a memorial to the railways' past contribution to local life. Motorists hooted and waved at it; until it became an accepted part of the landscape, the police said it caused a string of minor bumps.

The last-ever 'crossing' in the loop at Christow on the Teign Valley branch sees trains replace auto-cars and produces this romantic scene (above). Reporting the branch's closure for radio, I was also unofficial signalman. Watched by the stationmaster, is Bob Wyse, who was later to become my much-loved gardener, leaves his locomotive to grab the bag of the water tower – and, not unusually, Ivo Peters, of Somerset & Dorset photo fame, has abandoned his distinctive car with the door open in a rush to take a photograph, though I am not sure if it was this one or not. The date is 7 June 1958, and in a few hours the final train, Newton Abbot to Exeter *via* Christow, will carry greater crowds. Though much inconvenience was caused by the closure and replacement bus services were a joke, no savings were made on track maintenance between Heathfield and Christow, retained for a daily goods. (See also picture on page 20.)

Many of the best pictures in the gallery relate to the seaside railway. Chapter 10 of this book shows that it has always been of special interest.

What especially captures my eyes in both of these original pictures are the beach huts where many passengers will spend much of their holiday. This one is titled *Arrival at St Ives on a Hot Summer's Day in the Early 1950s*, and it is by A.L. Hammonds. It was included in *To the Seaside*, which we published in association with the Guild of Railway Artists.

The book has a splendid mix of paintings and drawings from all over coastal Britain and I'd love to have been able to purchase several more of them, but this was the opening one and very special. The collection was exhibited in a Torquay gallery and, seeing the full painting for the first time while going through the display on West Country television, I actually said on air that I was going to buy it.

With a summer Saturday *Cornish Riviera Express* diverted along the cliffs to St Ives, it shows a lot of rolling stock in a confined layout. Once the train had stopped, a locomotive, out of sight in the engine shed on the far right, will go forward and reverse onto it to take it (carrying a few passengers) to Penzance ready for its normal route next day.

Then released, the Prairie tank will follow Light soon after. Then the engine at the front of the train in the short loop (which hurriedly cleared the way for the *Cornish Riviera*) will take its three carriages into the platform and run round for a normal run to the branch's junction at St Erth. Through services to branch line terminals were expensive to operate including many interesting manoeuvres but it was still profitable.

Like all good pictures, it gives you plenty to look at – was PLA (passenger luggage in advance) carried in those box wagons? – as well as splendidly capturing the atmosphere of what the stationmaster of St Ives once described as 'Great Western on Sea'. Typically the 'layout' is now a single line ending at a buffer stop well back, most of the station being converted into a car park, though in summer trains bring a record number of passengers from the new park-and-ride halt at Lelant.

The other picture (below), by Alan Fernley, who did splendidly evocative work, shows the South Eastern Railway's Ramsgate Harbour, an operator's nightmare, a terminus with

IM TAKING AN
EARLY HOLIDAY COS
i KNOW SUMMER
COMES SOONEST IN THE SOUTH
SOUTHERN RAILWAY

short platforms that couldn't ever be lengthened because of the tight site.

It must have been fascinating to watch the movements . . . which I frequently imagine when studying the painting. Amazingly, it wasn't until 1926 that traffic used the short but vital new link to the through Town Station, and Harbour was closed. Electrification came much later. Now there is scant holiday traffic but heavy commuter business at Ramsgate.

This poster was published in the early days of the Southern Railway, soon after Grouping (right). It shows an early season *Atlantic Coast Express*, the loco at the platform's end under the old manual signalbox, shortly before departure to the west. A young lad carrying a small case is telling the engine driver: 'I'm taking an early holiday cos I know summer comes soonest in the South.'

In a very different era to today's, the Southern's first supremo Sir Herbert Walker, and his new publicity assistant J.B. Elliot, who later himself became the Southern's last general manager, personally selected the young lad on the Saturday morning and supervised the taking of the photograph on which the painting is based.

Fast forward to my seventy-fifth birthday at Buckfastleigh on the South Devon Railway, when I hired a special with Devonshire cream tea for friends and a few fare-paying passengers.

Among the latter was an elderly gentleman who approached me on a rain-sodden platform where I'd just welcomed guests and said he was the young lad in the poster. From the very same case, he removed a copy of it which he had autographed as a present. Marvellous.

Next to it is another picture of the *Atlantic Coast Express* waiting departure (right), a true Southern Railway scene just before nationalisation. The old signalbox has gone and electric light signalling taken over, while the new Merchant Navy Class 21C9 *Shaw Savill Line* heads a longer train whose front two coaches are beyond the platform.

A 'portmanteau' express, apart from the Ilfracombe section, most of it was a series of single composite carriages for different destinations, though on summer Saturdays complete trains, some with restaurant cars, worked through to some of the Atlantic resorts.

First stop will be Salisbury, for a locomotive change. Excellent though it was, the Southern never had water troughs. Though with Diesels, longer non-stop journeys are technically possible, there are now none even from Waterloo to Salisbury.

Once it got control of the Southern lines in the West, the Western Region made sure the route was reduced to second-class status, sections of what had been singled have now been redoubled at great cost. Yet after the introduction of Diesels on the Western, I recall reporting how a steam-hauled *Atlantic Coast Express* made it faster on the once-excellent route to Exeter than the *Cornish Riviera Express.*

The Forth Bridge crossing a wide expanse of tidal water is a pen-and-ink sketch by Arthur Spence and reminds one how unnecessarily over-engineered it was . . . in reaction to the earlier collapse of the Tay Bridge with a train whose every passenger uniquely in Britain was killed. The picture is not a favourite yet a gallery in Scotland would be incomplete without one of the most famous of bridges.

Though we have finished with the maritime theme, the next picture makes me feel positively wet. Commissioned for the jacket of *LMS 150*, it shows the *Royal Scot* from Euston to Glasgow overtaking an electric local to Watford, while the Stanier 4-6-2 *Princess Elizabeth* is picking up water from Bushey troughs. From the perspective, we're in for a right soaking.

Here, a delightful period piece: Alan R. Guston's 'Going Home', children in buoyant mood, presumably transferring from train to the Bedford bus almost in the same livery. It was bought from an exhibition of paintings by members of the Guild of Railway Artists in Warwick after I had given a short talk to them.

A work for which the artist was paid a phenomenal sum and made a huge impact, over 21,000 people paying to view it in seven weeks: *Paddington Station*, by W.P. Frith, RA (bottom).

His fee was £4,500 plus a further £750 for waiving his right to send it for exhibition at the Royal Academy. It was commissioned by a Haymarket picture dealer, L.V. Flatlow,

who no doubt did well by exhibiting it at his own gallery. Subsequently it was exhibited at various prestigious locations. The original measured an incredible 8ft 5in by 3ft 10in. My reduced copy is still 3ft 8in by 1ft 8in, and was bought by my wife in Hay-on-Wye as a birthday present.

It too has an interesting story. The gallery's sale note on the back (and taking it off the wall to read it was a major engineering job), says:

'Brilliant open letter Proof Engraving The Railway Station by Francis Hale after W.P. Frith in carved original gold frame. The property of Major killed in the war in France 1914 Braithwaite.'

The curved roofs of Brunel's train sheds and the transept were first seen by more people from the picture than actually used the station. The crowd is certainly exaggerated, not to mention all the things going on such as an arrest taking place, but there was naturally huge excitement when travelling in the early days – and it is well known that the telegraph which accompanied the railway had earlier been used to arrest a murderer on his arrival having hoped he'd made his escape from justice.

By contrast, the broad-gauge locomotive was a mere detail to the artist, and one wonders whether luggage was really piled on the roof and whether it would clear tunnels.

There's a great contrast between this and the painting of Bath Green Park with a Somerset & Dorset train (left), presumably bound for Bournemouth, at the platform mainly used by Midland trains from Bristol. Except on summer Saturdays, the station died during long intervals between trains, and on Sundays was undoubtedly more peaceful than most churches: something I recall when my parents walked out of a service they didn't like at a nearby church and asked us to sit quietly in the lifeless station.

This is another picture I commissioned from George Heiron, presumably for a jacket, though it didn't seem to be used and I cannot recall the circumstances. The site is now occupied by Sainsburys' who have retained the frontage of fond memories.

Below, we have glamour of an altogether more modest nature. GWR push-pull auto-cars, with their 0-4-2 tanks became popular on many branch lines, economical by saving the need to run round at reversal points and serving many new halts, often closer to the needs of passengers than fully fledged stations built when the railway had a monopoly and sites were selected more for the companies' convenience than those of customers. This evocation in a sketch by Don Breckon is accompanied by a copy of an actual notice displayed in all auto-cars.

The GWR expected passengers to be familiar with its terminology, halts were unstaffed while platforms had staff at least part of the time. At the first station the train stopped after a halt the stationmaster was on the platform to sell tickets and fetching them and any change needed from the booking office. On market days at another station along the line, such as those from Yeo Mill Halt going to South Molton, might cause considerable delay in this case at Bishop's Nympton & Molland.

The photograph of Inverness goods station (below), date uncertain, emphasises how much freight came up the Highland's mainline, with freight trains also to and from Aberdeen, Elgin, Kyle of Lochalsh and Wick and Thurso.

Almost all the rolling stock of the Manifold Valley Light Railway (between Hulme, Waterhouses on the North Staffordshire and Leek) is on this train (bottom). The narrow-gauge line ran a spartan service of mixed trains including a vehicle accommodating a standard-gauge milk churn. I seldom pass the picture, on our half-landing, without recalling that the engine driver and his fireman, his son, didn't speak to each other for years on end.

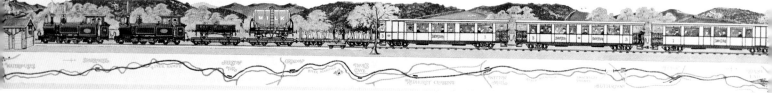

Two of the three pictures from overseas have a distinct cold feeling. I've always loved the period-piece train ferry pouring smoke into the frozen atmosphere (left). I've never known the date or exact whereabouts except that it is on one of America's Great Lakes. Note the well-wrapped passengers venturing outside.

The other (below) is of a steam snowplough shooting snow and steam as it battles through a deep drift on the Yukon & White Pass Railroad in Canada. The first time I visited Skagway by cruise ship the railway and its vast depot in the town in the American 'pan-handle' were closed. The second time, not only was it restored, but trains were backed into sidings alongside various ships to make an easy transfer for passengers who had paid their fares on board.

Rotary Snowplow on White Pass

Members of the boards of companies in the David & Charles Group are on Newton Abbot up platform, and staff on the down one and beside the company's train beyond. One of its vehicles we had bought was lost by British Rail which said they were not responsible since insurance against loss hadn't been paid. Through our network of enthusiasts, we traced it to a York marshalling yard, where the yardmaster said he had appropriated it as a mess van and there'd be a strike if it were taken away from his staff. We gave him a month to make other arrangements. Destination boards stated David & Charles and Readers Union. BR then said we were not allowed to advertise, but accepted the argument that destination boards merely said where they were going.

Everyone asked what the train 'was for'. Nobody could accept that it was just a talking point, yet even coach drivers slowed to point it out. All publicity is good.

Here we are looking up the Tamar to Calstock with its viaduct on what is now the Plymouth–Gunnislake branch but was once the Bere Alston–Callington line. Beyond Calstock, it replaced the East Cornwall Mineral Railway, which ran down an incline to the quay. When the viaduct opened, there was a hoist to lower trucks to the quay. To the left can just be seen the abandoned Morwellham Quay (see Chapter 5).

Now a few personal mementos, starting with the locomotive nameplate, the most expensive thing in the house but not easily stealable since it needed scaffolding and four men to fix it high up on the landing wall. The Great Western notice, from South Molton signalbox, guards my wine cellar and, on the garage roof weathervane, a reduced template image of a broad-gauge locomotive, half the size of that which stood over Newton Abbot locomotive works. The full original is in the town's railway collection. BR made a hefty charge for me to borrow it, but later someone then must have kept it since it was never returned to its original position.

The Whistle sign in our drive has had some odd effects. A lorry driver telephoned to say he'd found a house called Whistle but couldn't find ours, while several local people have said they never realised a railway had once run down the drive.

When I first displayed these fire buckets when my office was in Newton Abbot's railway station, I found an elderly official slumped under them saying: 'So it's come to this. We can't even have our own GWR fire buckets.' When I told him I had bought them from the relic shop then on Euston station, he was angry saying I should have known better.

The 'Engines must not pass this board' sign was once prominent on the front page of the *Sunday Times* Business section with my photograph accompanying an interview, later used in *Small Businesses: How they Survive and Succeed* by Philip Clarke. Of the seventeen firms profiled, David & Charles was one of only two survivors until, in 2011, its third owners after me killed the brand by renaming it the utterly unmemorable F & W International Media Services Ltd.

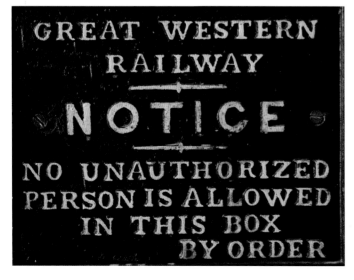

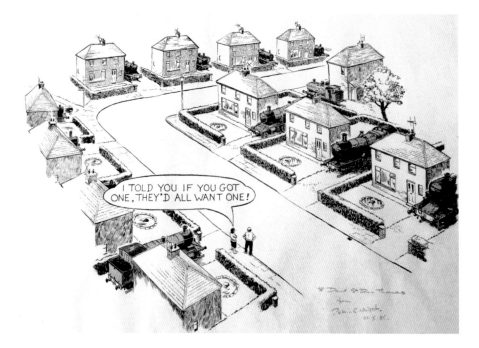

"I TOLD YOU IF YOU GOT ONE, THEY'D ALL WANT ONE!"

"BEG PARDON DRIVER, BUT THERE'S AN AXLE-BOX OVERHEATING UNDER MY COMPARTMENT."

Then a series of fun pictures (left). The first is a preliminary attempt at a jacket by Dennis Malet for my bestselling *The Country Railway*. It seemed just too light-hearted for what readers saw as a serious if nostalgic book. It has given me much enjoyment over the years.

The cartoons are other take-offs of railway enthusiasts. Both appeared in the original *The Country Railway* but were eliminated from the 2011 reprint by my present publisher.

Finally (below) the only photograph ever taken of my wife and me when we were boy and girlfriend in the 1950s but then didn't see each other for 45 years. Both of us had carefully kept a copy all that time.

The tickets are of a 5½d fare from Dawlish Warren to Dawlish. It started at 1½d when we first walked from Dawlish to Dawlish Warren for fresh air and hot-buttered toast but, as morale sank after nationalisation, soon the porter couldn't be bothered to cross the line to the booking office to fetch the tickets and we had to travel free. 'The Company' always earned more respect than its nationalised successor, not a political but a practical observation.

The photograph was taken on a summer Saturday at Spray Point, the small parcel of land that juts out from the Sea Wall. A schoolboy enthusiast was taking photographs of trains but said he could spare just one shot of us, film then being expensive. The building behind was once a café but, without running water, it didn't survive in the age of health and safety.

CHAPTER 8
RAILS, RAILS

THOUGH MANY CLOSURES HAD ALREADY HAPPENED, everyone knows that the national rail system was heavily pruned by the Beeching cuts. What is much less appreciated is how dependent we once were on rails in industry, farming – everywhere heavy weights had to be moved. The proportionate closures are probably greater of non-BR lines than of them.

Abandoned tracks soon deteriorate, especially at accommodation crossings. When there were plans to re-open most of the Ashburton branch, I was televised on the first plate-layers' motorised truck to use the rusting rails. Apart from an occasional missing or broken fish plate, all was well until we reached a level crossing where gravel had filled in the space needed by our wheels. 'Everybody off' as we had to manhandle the truck over the crossing.

Once there were rails everywhere: along docksides, deep up onto Dartmoor, and at innumerable works and quarries. As a boy, I was fascinated by the layout on either side and across a road at a quarry a few miles north of South Molton. Such curves and points, with a sturdy little steam engine pushing and pulling trucks busy all the working day. Much more interesting than girls.

A few miles away, just east of South Molton, the GWR's Barnstaple branch was fed traffic by a line from the north. Its opening and closing dates are obscure, such lines opportunistically coming and going as traffic warranted. They were remembered for a time but never formally recorded.

Many branch lines didn't neatly stop at station buffers, but had goods or mineral extensions and/or were fed by narrow-gauge lines whose gauges and characteristics varied and were much studied by enthusiasts. A few narrow-gauge ones, especially in North Wales, have been restored as major tourist attractions, but many more disappeared into history, though most narrow-gauge (and therefore sexier) ones are well described, their layouts and signalling systems recorded for posterity.

I especially recall the magic of the steeply graded, rope-worked extensions beyond Blaenau Ffestiniog, first seen well before the Ffestiniog Railway to Blaenau was restored. There were many rails, often at different levels, serving the North Wales slate quarries. Most locomotives spent much of their careers at one level.

The extensions to coal mines beyond the passenger terminal and loco depots of the branches of the South Wales valleys were also fascinating. A colourful though harsh way of life was lost with the sudden decline of the coal industry. How unreal it now feels that once lines such as the Barry Railway prospered carrying coal to the docks for export.

Today we import nearly all our coal. That has created new traffic such as from the former ore terminal at Hunterston on the Firth of Clyde filling to capacity both the former Glasgow & South Western route (now alas partly singled), and the Settle & Carlisle, which BR once fought hard to close.

Bickleigh Vale on the Great Western's Plymouth–Tavistock–Launceston line. Taken by Roger Sellick, a school friend, in 1957. He died shortly afterwards being the first friend I was to lose, but has left a great photographic legacy.

I've many memories of South Wales coal lines. It was fun overtaking coal trains and their empties on quadrupled track and learning about local conditions from miners packed into non-corridor stock always willing to talk to that rarity: an Englishman actually interested in their mining. Including reading and music, their own interests were sophisticatedly varied and civilised.

Much later, when the manager of Welsh railways asked what I'd be most interested in doing on a day out, I said travelling by coal trains. Fascinating it was, though the hours rapidly slipped by as we were looped to give priority to passenger services usually earning much less revenue. As so many traffics, they have disappeared and, by many, lamented as much as the demise of the *Brighton Belle*.

Railways were once everywhere. Though there were no passenger trains or a proper goods system, even Shetland and the Orkneys had sufficient quarry and other lines to warrant books being written about them.

On the mainland, northern Northumbria had so many minor (mainly colliery lines) that an Oakwood Press book about them runs to several volumes. Many lines taking coal to ports were shortlived, rising and falling with the local industry.

Steel and other works had their own internal railway systems, often with their own locomotives. Some were extensive where, as on the national system, successive generations of men were engine drivers.

A handful of industrial lines carried passengers. At its peak the system serving the three separate parts of Devonport Dockyard (originally broad gauge) had 20 miles of busy track

Yesterday's railway. I can veritably hear this steam train battling the ascent on the Settle & Carlisle near Blea Moor in 1967. Photo by John Goss.

and at one time or another seventy locomotives. It was renowned for its passenger trains with six different classes from workmen to admiral.

Where there were docks, there were railways, some with extensive systems needing their own signalling, such as the PLA (Port of London Authority) with its complicated network. Since port traffic has been concentrated into a handful of container ports, many abandoned ones have been fossilised. Pieces of track (including one of Brunel's broad gauge at Plymouth's Sutton Harbour) also survive as the result of improvement schemes. The rails that are still used along quaysides are mainly very broad ones for the movement of cranes.

It is perhaps not realised how short a journey many goods made. To cite a few Devon examples, Teignmouth Quay, once with its own signalbox, exported ball clay from Teigngrace, near Newton Abbot, and imported coal for that town's nearby rail-connected gas works. Coal trains from Kingswear went no further than the 8 miles to the gas works between Paignton and Torquay, which had their own signalbox, open to break the section on peak summer Saturdays.

Fremington, for many years Devon's busiest port, imported most of North Devon's coal including locomotive coal for Barnstaple only 2¾ miles away where all of the region's engines were stabled, and exported clay that hadn't come much further. Coal for Plymouth's main power station included some making an even shorter train journey.

Each traffic had its peculiarities. At Teignmouth, for example, a road vehicle nicknamed The Elephant pushed trucks around the quays. And once, such was the occupancy of the single line between Paignton and Kingswear, that a down passenger might cross an up coal and a passenger train at Churston where, incidentally, a school was built so that pupils could travel by train from three directions.

Wherever Britons worked overseas they would find railways. All six whaling stations on South Georgia had their lines for moving coal and whaling products. An abandoned 0-4-0 steam engine still lies rusting on a beach.

In Britain in the post-war years, the decline in BR's goods business was slowed by trains steadily taking over more from coastal shipping. It was a trend that worried many people at the time since, with predatory pricing, it was easier for BR to steal traffic from shipping than to slow the decline of general goods. Then suddenly the usage of coal dropped in the commercial as well as household worlds. Remains of the coal concentration schemes of the 1970s have joined the industry's rich archaeology.

There were so many rail-served industrial sites that inevitably many were forgotten, only to be rediscovered and recorded more recently. Thus in a recent issue of the newsletter of Plymouth Rail Circle (to which I have belonged for sixty years) we read about the MOD's Holming Beam Target Tramway at Merrivale Range, the Hillhay incline and the Caffa Mill tramway at Fowey, and the 18in gauge line at Kelly Iron Mine at Lustleigh.

In the first edition of my *West Country* in the Regional Railway History series, flatteringly referred to locally as 'The Bible', there was brief mention of the 2ft line linking Penlee Quarry (see box, above right), with loading ships, described as the most westerly

> ### PENLEE QUARRY
>
> Active only when a ship was loading at the harbour, the 2ft Penlee Quarry line at Newlyn had up to ten trains each carrying 40 tons hourly. Every few minutes a full train was 'crossed' by an empty one on the loop midway down the mainline, and the rattle of the rake of trucks being pulled or propelled by the small Diesels over the worn rails and points scarcely ever died away. The Diesels took over from steam locomotives in 1940. The ¾-mile line was replaced by a conveyor belt in July 1972.

Half tramway, half railway: what Wantage provided to link itself to the mainline 2½ miles away, which Brunel built as straight as an arrow bypassing many small places. Opened in 1875, passenger trains ceased in 1925.

Though most passengers kept checking, reading the destination board as well as the departure sign on the platform, asking the guard and other passengers (and then maybe getting confirmation from the driver) that this was the right train, many still somehow got on the wrong one. And in the days of much longer non-stop runs, scarcer return services, and before most private homes were on the telephone, this resulted in a lengthy disappearance off the face of the earth. But they were also the days before motorway pile-ups, abductions and most violent crime, so there was more puzzlement than anxiety. The attitude was rather that nobody could tell what would happen to you if you caught a train.

Great Days of Express Trains, 1990

line, but later editions added 'even further west' the Parknoweth tramway ran 2¼ miles linking mines. Many other industrial sites were steadily added, and many more again are now known by enthusiasts.

However, the much-reduced china clay network was always well known, and its changing workings (including through Cornwall's longest tunnel, between Par and Fowey) well documented. I've been through the tunnel both by train and then for a broadcast by lorry. BR sold the land to the clay company as part of an agreement to protect long-distance traffic to the Potteries.

It comes as a surprise to many to learn that Europe's largest system of industrial railways serves the peat bogs of the Irish Midlands. Up to 5 million tons of peat are carried annually, the system and its traffic being far greater than that of the Irish national system. Once one line even had a passenger service. It had to be abandoned since all capacity was needed for peat trains to West Offaly power station.

At busy times this power station (one of three) is served by rakes of sixteen wagons sixteen hours daily. Trains usually work in pairs, as they do to two briquette factories. Apart from the main system, there are several smaller ones in other areas. Altogether it is big business involving many miles of rails, some of which are laid temporarily alongside the peat beds being worked on, and moved back with the workings.

Diesels have long been used but Bord Na Mona's three steam engines are held by the Irish Steam Preservation Society at Stradbally, County Laois. There's an excellent website with a gazetteer of the railways of Bord Na Mona (the Irish Peat Commission).

Better known is perhaps the fact that railways served the battlefields of the First World War. Even today, at the York end of the line serving Harrogate, what was double track has been single since that of one line was sent to France and never replaced. The whole of the Bideford, Westward Ho! & Appledore Railway went that way in March 1917 after temporary track was laid across Bideford Bridge to allow the locomotives to reach the LSWR. Some British locomotives had a rusty end on the battlefields after being commandeered for the war effort.

Notably in the American Civil War, railways played an important part in warfare. In Britain they were vital, memorably in the dispersal of soldiers rescued from Dunkirk, though the popular recollection is perhaps still of overcrowded trains especially at night. We also remember the familiar news bulletins about the British bombing German marshalling yards.

Nor should one forget the potato railways of the Fens, which, like those serving overseas sugar fields, were part permanent and part movable. In recent years thousands of British enthusiasts have visited Cuba to relive steam serving agriculture, the engines burning the very cargo they carry. I recall being enthralled by the layouts, and their connections to each other, of the lines of the northern Queensland sugar fields running alongside the mainline north to Cairns.

Once there were aerial ropeways feeding railways. An example was stone from a quarry carried in successions of dangling buckets to Christow on the Teign Valley branch.

Where the traffic still exists, today it is more likely to be carried by unromantic road, conveyor belt or pipeline rather than by rail or aerial ropeway.

It could be added that rails were also found in many indoor locations. Narrow-gauge lines, on which heavy items were pushed, ran around factories, including around locomotive works. Underground, many mines had extensive systems, later succeeded by conveyor belts.

Some larger shops had their equivalent of aerial ropeways, money and change being catapulted around. As a boy I was disappointed if Mum gave the exact sum and we didn't need to wait for a return 'train' to be catapulted back with the change.

There were also indoor equivalents of pipelines. Some newspapers had an internal pipe system in which copy was catapulted around. Occasionally a container not given a sharp enough start might get stuck in the pipe, once necessitating staying in the office to rewrite the last story of the night to be sent to the compositors.

But back to real railways, many of us find magic in that pair of parallel rails with their gentle curves and gradients. And as time has gone on, we still enjoy following the course of abandoned routes, many with well-preserved embankments and cuttings and – in gentler country – the tell-tale linear woodland since, as explained in the chapter on natural history in my book *Railway Season*, railways open and closed are where woodland most advances in our overcrowded island.

Typical of thousands across the country, this narrow-gauge quarry line once served the Devon County Council's Wilminstone Quarry near Tavistock. Road transport took over in 1952, and the quarry is now a small industrial site. The picture was taken the year before the rails were lifted by Mr Starr of Camels Head, Plymouth, and has been digitally improved by Bernard Mills, to whom my thanks are due. Note the incline and the Plymouth & South Western Railway Viaduct, long closed but still standing.

PHOTOGRAPHY BY H.C. CASSERLEY

Here is a selection of photographs by H.C. Casserley, kindly sent by his son Richard. Richard has memories of his father visiting exotic railways in Britain and Ireland, involving much travelling. At first, the photographs were mainly of locomotives, usually in sheds, but more interesting scenes in stations or en route came later, and these are now most useful, often being the sole indication of what a particular rural railway was like. Since the ownership of cameras did not become common until later, his father probably recorded more railways than anyone else. By the time railway photography became more popular, many lines (including most narrow-gauge ones) had closed.

On this page, a double-decker train on the Dublin & Blessington and the Glyn Valley Tramway.

Towyn Wharf on the Talyllyn Railway in 1932, years before it was closed under private enterprise leave alone its long period in private preservation, 19 August 1933 the 11.15 Robertsbridge to Tenterden leaving Rolvenden, Atlantic at Machrihanish with the 2.15 to Campbeltown on 2 August 1930, and the Campbeltown end of the line.

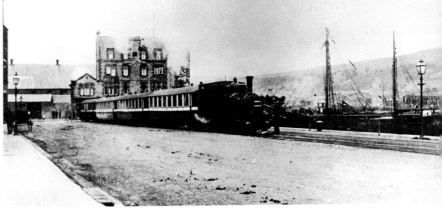

CHAPTER 9
65 YEARS OF RAILWAY WRITING
(2: 1963–84)

IF YOU GET ON IT WON'T BE EMPTY

One of many reports in The Western Morning News
on branch line closures, this one Helston in 1963.

FIREWORKS, fog signals, Diesel horns, bugles, top hats. 'Auld Lang Syne', wreaths, sandwich-board men proclaiming 'The end is at hand', cameras and tape recorders, and a lurid representation of 'Dr Beeching's axe' – these all contributed to Saturday's ticker-tape funeral of the Helston branch line.

Railway enthusiasts acclaimed it the 'best burial' to date. 'And it's just as well to be in practice with all the other threatened closures,' added one of them.

The enthusiasts had travelled from far and wide to see that the last trains were accorded full honours. A group of Plymouth Railway Circle members returned by road, reaching the city at 1.00am yesterday.

A young Birmingham enthusiast and his wife travelled down specially by sleeping car on Friday night and returned by sleeper on Saturday night. Others came from Bristol, Derby, Wolverhampton and Manchester.

Dereliction with memories. This was once platform 9, reached from outside Newton Abbot station and serving the Moretonhampstead line. From the main station one watched perhaps a couple of dozen passengers assemble for the last train up the branch – the warehouses were semi-derelict even then. Later, this was the platform where cars were driven by BR staff into motorway vans while passengers joined the carriages at the main station.

In common with many of the other 'mourners' I arrived in time to get a last daylight trip over the branch, which commands fine views of the tightly packed broccoli fields as it winds across the plateau land.

Cameras clicked and a generally festive air prevailed when the 4.11pm from Helston 'crossed' the 4.10pm from Gwinear Road at Nancegollan. This was the last time that two passenger trains were to use the branch line together. Then I saw the *Cornish Riviera Express* – drab in the standard maroon livery – make its last call at Gwinear Road. Only two passengers transferred to the Helston branch, although another ten alighted and left the station. From today the *Cornish Riviera* stops at Redruth instead.

The funeral proper began as crowds assembled for the departure of the 8.45pm from Helston. Money was piled high in the booking office as people bought tickets as souvenirs as well as for the final trip to Gwinear Road and back.

Hats were raised as 'the funeral' procession formally moved down the platform. The fully dressed mourners were former boys of Helston Grammar School who once used the train daily. 'We represent all stations on the branch and thought it a fitting farewell,' they said, proffering the wreath for inspection: 'In loving memory of the Helston–Gwinear Road express.'

All doors of the six-coach train were closed, the signal turned to green, and, amid the explosion of fireworks and fog signals, the 8.45pm started on its noisy way.

'It makes you very sad,' said Mrs Angove, whose father was employed on building the line before its opening in 1877. Her travelling companion was one of the youngest mourners, Christopher Oliver, aged seven, making his first as well as last trip.

While waiting for mainline connections at Gwinear Road most of the 300 passengers sang 'Auld Lang Syne' on the platform. Four people transferred from the 2.30pm from Paddington – three genuine travellers who would have had the branch train to themselves had it not been closure night, and Mr J.C.W. Jones, Clerk of Crowan Parish Council, who jokingly displayed a large 'For Sale' notice.

It was 'Auld Lang Syne' at all stations and halts on the way back to Helston – and violent whistles from the guard who disliked the passengers leaving their compartment.

'I'll be glad when tonight is over,' said the guard. He himself will remain one of the evening's memories. No inspector or even stationmaster remaining on duty, he bore the full brunt of the enthusiasts' criticism of a 'typical British Railways muddle'.

Normally the last train spent the night at Helston, but the enthusiasts thought that after the closure it would work back to Gwinear Road, and they asked permission to travel by it – as they had done in similar cases at other branch line funerals. Plymouth head office, however, was adamant that the train would not return.

In fact it did return. But passengers were prevented from using it. 'It's advertised as an empty train and if you get on it won't be empty,' said the guard.

After one final burst of song at Helston, Diesel No. D6312 – displaying a wreath – duly set off into the lights and went home.

But that was not quite the end. The privately run refreshment room had been granted an extension licence to commemorate its closure. Tongues continued to wag furiously about British Railways and Dr Beeching.

And outside in the station yard, buses and cars were entangled in one mighty traffic jam. It was here, of course, that the first railway sponsored bus service began in 1903 – an innovation which had been the railway's own undoing.

Today more people probably fly from London to Glasgow than take the train, but for most of railway history the train was the way to go. The Royal Scot, seen here leaving Lancaster, was the most popular train, though the Mid-Day Scot, which carried through carriages from Plymouth, was my favourite, though I usually ignored these and went via London, only necessitating leaving Newton Abbot about 45 minutes earlier. Travel by such trains, with long high-speed non-stop runs, buffet car and full meal services, offered real excitement.

RURAL TRANSPORT

Two extracts from The Rural Transport Problem, *1963.*

UNNECESSARY INCONVENIENCE

THIS book is written with considerable feeling. In the course of my research not only have I continuously met people whose enjoyment of life has been sapped by inadequate transport, but time and again it has seemed that much of the inconvenience to the rural population (and also much of the damage to the rural economy) is unnecessary.

The average standard of transport management in the countryside is, with outstanding exceptions, disconcertingly low. In many cases a more useful service could be provided at far less cost. Too frequently buses and trains are run with scant reference to the demand. Narrowly missed connections are perpetuated in the timetables year after year, sometimes decade after decade. The railways in particular are often guilty of useless expenditure; fully staffed signalboxes survive long after the removal of any possible justification for them.

Inevitably a study of the rural transport problem leads first to criticism of the operators, who could have done so much more to help themselves and the public. Sometimes indeed these men seem almost to enjoy the martyrdom of watching losses mount to the point where closure is inescapable. But examination of the difficulties in their wider context brings sympathy for railway and bus officials on the job and the realisation that the policy-makers are largely to blame.

The chief trouble has perhaps been the lack of foresight on the part of transport – especially railway – management. It was not realised in time that the railways could not pay their way and continue to provide extensive social service. If the Transport Commission had presented the Government with a forceful, clear-cut alternative between policies, probably some decision would have been reached early enough to prevent much of the damage. On the other hand, the Government need not have evaded taking the initiative in giving the industry the lead it so obviously needed.

Throughout the 1950s, arguments continued inside and outside the industry as to whether the railways should be regarded as a public utility or whether they should be run on strictly business lines disregarding the interests of minorities. Although it became increasingly clear toward the end of the decade that basically the Government insisted that the system should pay its way, loopholes remained, the question of the retention of social services was shunned even in the 1960 White Paper, and many railwaymen felt that 'justice' for British Railways still lay round the corner.

The result was a prolonged and extremely unhappy compromise. Although many services had been closed by the time British Railways entered a new era under the management of Dr Richard Beeching in 1962, thousands of miles of uneconomic routes were retained – including some branch lines which British Railways wished to close but could not because they were unable to meet the condition then in force that adequate bus alternatives had to be provided. Yet because so many routes had no assured future – closure was always potentially imminent – improvements and even short-term working economies were shelved. In addition, capital was not available for schemes on many lines more likely to have a future. With few exceptions, it was impossible for railwaymen at district headquarters to obtain sanction to spend even small sums of capital on schemes which would have yielded valuable annual savings. Some lines which could have been brought near to paying their way ten years ago had thus become hopelessly uneconomic by 1962.

CONISTON

CONISTON in the Lake District lost its passenger trains in October 1958. The story of events leading up to the closure, and of the aftermath, is one of the most complicated and controversial yet encountered in the study of rural transport.

The Coniston branch, 9¾ miles long, left the Coastal or Furness line at Foxfield, was single track, included heavy gradients, and commanded some fine Lakeland scenery. It carried fair local traffic all the year round, and summer passengers included long-distance travellers on their way to or from a Lake District holiday and numerous day trippers. It had eight daily trains, plus an additional service between Foxfield and Broughton, the most important intermediate station. In summer the regular services were supplemented by twice-weekly excursions from Blackpool and Morecambe.

The local authorities, the Friends of the Lake District, and the general public, including a number of well-known people, produced evidence which persuaded many members of the North Western Transport Users' Consultative Committee that this was a case where the withdrawal of trains might cause widespread inconvenience.

The majority of the independent members asked that British Railways should continue the service. But the votes of British Railways' own representatives gave a majority in favour of endorsing the closure proposal. It was, however, agreed that trains should continue until a satisfactory bus alternative had been provided. The complication here was that the Lancashire County Council was seeking an order prohibiting vehicles of more than fifty hundredweight laden weight from using the parallel road.

The Central Consultative Committee supported the recommendation that the line should be closed, but asked the North Western Committee to withdraw the condition about the bus service. At the same time the Central Committee gave a broad general hint to guide the North Western Committee: consequential expenditure by local authorities and other organisations should not be offset against the savings claimed by the Transport Committee. The saving to the railway was sufficient to justify a decision to recommend withdrawal of the service.

The North Western Committee did not accept the first directive, and reaffirmed their recommendation that trains should be withdrawn only when a suitable bus service was introduced. Further deadlock was avoided by British Railways agreeing to pay Ribble Motor Services to run the bus service, which was allowed to use the road upon certain

Throughout the Grouping period of 1923–45, the LNER was the poorest and usually the dirtiest of the Big Four. A train as heavy as this would almost invariably have been better powered on the other three, yet it has to be admitted the LNER showed dogged determination and enterprise in attracting custom in its poorer part of Britain – and with its economy seeking 'razor gangs' cut out much unnecessary expenditure.

conditions laid down by the Traffic Commissioners. Briefly, the restriction sought by the County Council on large vehicles was approved, but an exception was made for stage-service buses provided a number of passing places were built.

Ribble already operated their Ambleside–Coniston and Ulverston–Coniston routes at a loss, and felt disinclined to start another obviously uneconomic venture. They introduced the new service purely as agent for the railways, who paid about £5,000 a year – receiving back only about £2,000 in fares.

The number of bus journeys provided was little more than half the number of trains. In winter the service dropped to four daily trips each way, with an additional trip – paid for by the Lancashire County Council – for school children during term time. During the Lake District Transport Enquiry, it was found that only a small proportion of former train travellers were using the bus. Three classes of people were dependent on it:

1. Long-distance passengers without access to a car, who could not afford a taxi and had luggage too heavy to carry from the bus to the railway station at Ulverston. Some of these people said they would prefer to travel by Ulverston if the bus called at the railway station there, or by Windermere if there were a through Coniston–Windermere bus.

2. Workers, shoppers and others travelling from places formerly served by the branch line to places on the main Coastal line. For those bound for places north of Foxfield, the alternative bus services from Coniston were no use, and though Barrow could be reached *via* Ulverston, this was indirect. When the railway was working twelve Coniston people used to travel daily to Barrow; in 1961 only three. Several of the others were interviewed and complained that the journey by bus was too long and expensive to make it worth earning the higher wages obtainable in Barrow.

3. Residents along the bus route going to another place on the same route. These purely local passengers, not changing into trains at Foxfield, accounted for over half the traffic.

All three classes of passengers complained bitterly about the fares. The return from Coniston to Foxfield was 3s 1d for about 20 miles, compared with only 2s 3d from Coniston to Ambleside. To go to Barrow *via* Ulverston was cheaper than to use the more direct Foxfield route. There were no through road-rail bus fares.

The bus was paid for by one organisation and run by another. Local people alleged that because of the ease of passing the buck it was impossible to come to grips with either. They believed that British Railways were satisfied to see the traffic decline as this might hasten the day when the subsidy could be withdrawn. Certainly not even transport officials expected the arrangements to last indefinitely: Ribble Motors stated that they would not run the bus without a subsidy.

Not only was the bus lamentably failing to pay its way, but the inquiry team were left with the impression that a subsidy of £3,000 could be used more fruitfully elsewhere. Yet even here the money could have been better spent. Quite apart from *advertised* mis-connections, lost connections were frequent. The timetable failed to allow for the almost standard late running of some trains on the Furness route. And although the service was subsidised by British Railways, it was not mentioned in the railway timetable, so few visitors knew of it.

It might be argued that a transport operator who withdraws or intends to withdraw a service should allow a reasonable time for the public to adjust to the changed conditions. The bus was presumably intended as this stopgap. But in practice everyone who could make alternative arrangements did so, leaving the bus with mere oddments of traffic.

Two years since our main investigations the position remains substantially the same, although British Railways cannot be expected to continue the subsidy much longer.

It would be possible to reduce the service substantially and still cater for the essential local requirements on a minimum basis, while routing one daily Coniston–Ulverston bus each way *via* Ulverston station would greatly ease the problem of long-distance connections. But no matter how many cuts are made on the Foxfield service, it is highly unlikely to pay its costs, and although the Ulverston station diversion might be in the long-term interests of public transport as a whole, it would probably involve Ribble in a loss. Though much waste might have been avoided, we are still left with the question: who pays?

The Coniston–Foxfield service received national notoriety in January 1962 when in bad weather a school bus left the road and turned on its side in a field. Three children were seriously and four slightly injured. At the request of the parents and of Lancashire County Council, for a time the school bus was diverted by a much longer route (admitted to be no less dangerous) and the question of stopping the subsided service was also raised. No permanent changes have been effected, but the accident stressed the need for further improvements to the Class III road between Foxfield and Torver.

Passing places had to be built before the bus service could begin, and by 1961 the County Council had spent £13,000 on improving the route, while it was stated that eventually £40,000 would be required 'to put the road into something like a reasonable and safe condition'. The work already done has been at the expense of other schemes previously regarded as more urgent, and a County Council spokesman added: 'It would, we feel, be true to say that expenditure of the order of £40,000 would never have been contemplated on this road had not the rail service been withdrawn, although some minor improvements would have been made.'

The closure of the railway has necessitated heavy road expenditure, the basic bus service between Coniston and Foxfield loses £3,000 each year, and the inquiry into the school bus accident elicited the information that it was costing between £800 to £1,000 more a year to send children to school by road than by train. The Post Office and many businesses in Coniston have been put to extra expense, as have numerous individuals. The cessation of the trains has seriously lessened Coniston's tourist trade.

The closure of the railway has resulted in greater total expenditure and loss than its retention need have incurred, given a Diesel unit and simplified staff and signalling arrangements. The annual loss on the passenger side could have been reduced to £5,000 a year while goods traffic continued. The Lake District Transport Enquiry could not, however, recommend reopening. Most of the regular daily passenger traffic was lost for good. Reopening would inevitably have had to be experimental, making local people reluctant again to become dependent on the service. Indeed, once the decision to withdraw passenger trains had been taken, complete closure would have been wiser – although, while the line was still used for goods, it was churlish to refuse to run the occasional special excursion to Coniston.

Retaining the branch for goods alone proved extravagant. The engineering department claimed that cessation of passenger services allowed relatively little saving in track maintenance. In fact shortly after passenger trains were withdrawn part of the track was relaid. Compared with the standards of several other regions, notably the Eastern, the upkeep of the Coniston branch was needlessly elaborate and costly for three light goods trains a week. Staff costs alone amounted to almost twice the annual revenue.

Even that is not quite the end of the story. To handle traffic formerly dealt with at Broughton, British Railways have established a small goods depot at Foxfield, until then solely a passenger station. Although the capital cost of this work has not been stated, it must have been considerable. And it is now planned to close small goods stations everywhere, concentrating traffic at a few large centres.

An everyday scene on the Isle of Man Railway, when the system was at its greatest and people used trains such as this three-coach one for routine journeys. No hint of preservation here, though wouldn't we love to be on board? Fast speeds on the 3ft-gauge always characterised the island system, run very much as a mainland railway with substantial station facilities and a great signalbox, the heart of the system at Douglas.

BORDER COUNTIES

Written for Double Headed: Two Generations of Railway Enthusiasm, *with my father, Gilbert, 1963. Visiting mid-Northumberland in the summer of 1959 for research into the rural transport problem, I was brought into close contact with the Border Counties line, from Hexham to Riccarton Junction. This cross-country byway endeared itself to nearly a century of train lovers, and though I came too late to see it working I found its influence still heavy in the air.*

IT began as a local concern – great was the aplomb with which the first sod was cut at Tyne Green, Hexham, in 1855 – but was completed by the North British Railway as a wedge deep into North Eastern territory. Its construction, especially the last section across the almost uninhabited fells to Riccarton Junction, 800ft above sea level and 2 miles from a road, was a battle with geography. This part was opened in 1862 simultaneously with the completion of the Waverley route to Scotland. Eventually the North British obtained running powers into Newcastle, and at one time through trains ran from there to Edinburgh *via* Riccarton and Peebles. But most passengers were on purely local journeys and, even before the First World War, the traffic was so thin that several stations became unstaffed halts. The standard service was three trains each way daily, all calling at almost every station – excluding Thorneyburn, for many years a timetable oddity with a single service each way on Tuesdays only. In 41 miles there was only one station where two passenger trains could cross – Reedsmouth, junction for the Wansbeck Valley line to Morpeth.

Reedsmouth station is just within the parish of Birtley, where I worked for a fortnight, and was the first point I visited upon arrival in the district. Driving through the village, I regretted having missed seeing the passenger trains. The Morpeth branch was closed to passengers in 1952, and the Border Counties in 1956. The only trains still running were three goods weekly from Morpeth to Bellingham, reversing at Reedsmouth. The short section between Reedsmouth and Bellingham was thus the sole part of the Border Counties open for any purpose.

I intended to enquire on what days and at what times the goods trains ran, but was pleasantly forestalled. The gate being open, I had driven onto the triangular platform between the two branches, and was trying to evoke the scene at 7.45 on mornings years ago when three trains would stand at the station together. While I was still in the car a whistle sounded from the Bellingham direction. But more, before its echo had died away down the valley, another whistle shrilled, this time from the Morpeth line.

Ghosts of the North British arose during the next few minutes. An inspection train with a handful of officials enjoying a country jaunt pulled in from Bellingham; the thrice-weekly goods came round the curve on the Morpeth line. In addition to the usual single-line crossing manoeuvres, both trains had to be reversed. Signal wires squeaked, point rods grunted; steadily the rust of two days was worn off the tracks of the layout – which would have pleased even the most ambitious North British director. The vast capital tied up in the station, and its imposing signalbox with three tiers of windows, was making one more attempt to seem justified before the inevitable final withdrawal of railways from this outpost of civilisation. To see tracks and points and signals used is satisfying, albeit the movements are not profitable and could be performed in half the time with simpler equipment.

This was the only time I saw the goods; but though virtually trainless, the Border Counties line was still to an extraordinary extent the kingpin of local life. People dated events from its closure, and pointed out how much more cheaply it could have been run and what hardship the absence of trains had brought to families without cars. Hardship was especially acute at Redesmouth itself, a railway settlement, most of the houses still owned by British Railways, and well off a bus route. The retired enginemen who had spent their working lives taking others around on their lawful occasions now found themselves unable to reach Bellingham without a long walk or cycle ride or the expense of a taxi. Not only the railway but the community which had grown up round it was in ruins.

I also heard, of course, about the old days, when the railway was respected and big men skilfully coaxed large-wheeled engines up steep gradients, and cleared majestic

Inverness locomotive roundhouse. Everyone noticed how morale sank when the Highland Railway became part of the LMS. Locomotives which had once shone were left dirty.

snowdrifts. I assimilated so much history and legend that eventually each mile of the route assumed individuality; I learnt just who had used every station and why, and what were the idiosyncrasies of the gangers on the bleakest moorland beats and the postmistresses who held court in offices on station platforms; and wherever I went in the valley of the North Tyne there was the railway intruding itself in the best of the scenery. The grandeur of the engineering works was still apparent – how content the builders must have been with the grace of some of their curves on the bank of the boulder-strewn river! – although decay was far advanced and seemed to set the tone for the whole of the parched, inactive countryside that summer of summers.

The only other non-passenger train I saw was on my way home at Kielder Forest – just Kielder until 1948 when the 'Forest' was added to publicise the massive forestry project which was transforming the scene for miles around. This was the demolition train, removing the track which, several years earlier, the Northumberland County Development Plan had asserted would become increasingly busy transporting timber. The plan even discussed whether the single track would be adequate. Meanwhile, instead of three daily trains to the Waverley line at Riccarton Junction, the foresters and their families now had only two buses twice a week. Subsidised by British Railways, these ran to Steele Road, one of the most isolated stations in Britain, but the nearest with road access. A plea to change the destination to Newcastleton, a small market town which could have been reached by an easier road in an additional three minutes at most, was rejected with that perversity so often found in rural transport arrangements. Also, the morning bus was advertised to reach Steele Road a few minutes after the departure of the only train for hours to Carlisle market, although in practice by fast driving a connection was achieved.

Shortly after I had written this piece, my eye fell on an advertisement for an excursion via *Morpeth to Bellingham to celebrate Bellingham's September Fair. So I again found myself at Reedsmouth, on a Diesel train that reversed there. In view of my comments on how isolated the community had become, it was sad that residents including former railwaymen were not allowed to join at Reedsmouth.*

A DAY WITH CÓRAS IOMPAIR ÉIREANN

This was published in the Railway World Annual, *1964. On the occasion described, I saw Irish railways as passenger traffic began its dramatic increase but would have been amazed by the many improvements and re-openings that have followed, especially the much greater enlargement of Dublin's Heuston and the first piece of Irish quadrupling, a section of the mainline out of it with dedicated tracks for suburban trains, and the re-opening of Limerick to Galway as part of that planned of the Limerick–Sligo corridor.*

IRISH railways are very Irish, a greater contrast from British Rail than are the railways of most of the rest of the English-speaking world. That is the feeling I always return with after renewing an emotional acquaintance with Córas Iompair Éireann (CIE).

Not long ago, I had to pay an unexpected short visit for evening events in Dublin on Sunday and Cork on Monday. Having Monday morning and afternoon free, I decided to take the train to Waterford *via* Kilkenny (a route new to me) and then (since there is no afternoon train from Waterford to Limerick Junction) to go by hire car. BEA duly confirmed that Avis had a car available and that I could drop it off at Cork airport on my way home on Tuesday.

So at 7.00am on Monday morning I left one of Dublin's northern suburbs soon to be served by the electrified railway. I had to go by taxi since there is no convenient link to Heuston station, an imposing stone block of a building inconveniently far from the centre. Once it looked as though Heuston would be closed and trains from the south be rerouted *via* the outskirts to Connolly. Instead Heuston has gained two platforms, making five. The new ones, two sides of an island, have been fitted into the middle of the station where carriage sidings once stood. They make the station far more flexible, and prevent the delays that occurred over many years to up trains; extra services or late running often resulted in trains being halted at every appropriate signal many miles back out into the country.

Traditionally, rather less than a score of daily trains have arrived at Heuston, which has no suburban traffic, but they have always tended to be bunched, with periods of hectic activity after long lulls. This is still partially true, though among the twenty-one winter Tuesday–Saturday arrivals (two extras on Mondays) there is now a more evenly spaced service from Cork.

This was my first visit to Heuston since the new platforms had been opened and I was pleased to see that they had been given the chequered black-and-white tile treatment that is a feature of all major CIE stations. It was also the first time I had seen BR Mark 2 air-conditioned stock in CIE's black-and-tan livery bringing greater luxury though, of course, not making use of the wider loading gauge. A ten-coach set formed the 7.30 departure for Cork, the day's first train out of Heuston.

My 7.40 to Waterford, six coaches including the heating van, left from one of the new platforms with around a hundred passengers but minus the advertised buffet car; a story all too familiar in Britain – the steward had not turned up. Twenty minutes on our way we passed the day's first up train, one of the Monday-only extras, from Waterford.

Heuston used largely to be involved in handling Irish people going to Britain and overseas visitors bound for southern Ireland *via* Dun Laoghaire, transferring from the ship into a special train run around Dublin to Heuston. The train no longer runs, having been withdrawn as part of the electrification work and anyway traffic has declined: fewer visitors come to Ireland and, more of those who do, fly or bring their cars. Today, therefore, Heuston is more concerned with taking the Irish about their own business, and weekend traffic in particular has boomed. Fourteen trains now depart on Sundays in place of the single one of the immediate post-war era. And Friday evening and Monday morning traffic is also very heavy.

At our first stop, Droichead Nua, we were joined by a handful of passengers, but about seventy were on the up platform as an extremely full 5.00 from Cork arrived. At Kildare we stopped beside the next up service, a Mondays-only train from Galway.

And so on to track new to me, the single line of the Waterford branch, crossing another packed up train at Carlow, with a sniff of the bacon and eggs being served in the day's only full restaurant car on the route. At Kilkenny, following rationalisation of routes to Waterford, you reverse; one of the much-publicised Dublin–Waterford liner trains was in the freight yard.

As in most of inland Ireland, the scenery was pleasant, undulating without being dramatic, few signs of habitation away from the occasional village, but the inevitable ruin to remind of troubled days. The speed of CIE trains between stations on single lines is surprisingly high, but approaches to stations are always taken cautiously.

At Waterford, the Limerick line and then the rusting track of the long-closed Mallow route joined us as we slowly approached the station, already busy with people waiting for

the return 10.55 to Dublin. After a short look round, I crossed the river and began enquiring as to which garage had the Avis agency. None was the answer! BEA had boobed. Worse than that, no other car hire firm had a vehicle free, and a travel agent said there were no buses or planes. I could hitch, or wait for the 20.35 which would get me to Cork at 00.30 next morning (too late, of course, for my appointment) or, had I thought about it earlier, I could return by the 10.55. But now it was 10.50 and I'd never walk back in time. A request to be driven was at first refused but then accepted. Running through red lights, we just made it, in time indeed to buy a ticket.

At first I bemoaned the fact that I had only bought a Dublin–Waterford single at £12.50; a day return would have cost the same. But though I had to change at Droichead Nua, the very first station out of Dublin, and go roughly three times the mileage of the direct route, I was charged by the latter, £10. Yes, I went a lot of miles for £10!

The train was very full, the five-across seating in the open stock being put to good use. No catering service was even supposed to be provided, and by now feeling extremely hungry I dashed down the hill to buy biscuits while the locomotive was running round the train at the Kilkenny reversal. And so back to the mainline at Kildare. We were late and I thought we might delay the seasonal Mondays, Fridays and Saturdays 10.30 from Dublin to Tralee, first stop Rathluirc (between Limerick Junction and Mallow); but it passed us at speed near the Curragh racecourse.

At Droichead Nua, over the bridge to join the 12.55 from Dublin to Cork. 'I remember you,' said an employee. 'You used to be booking clerk here years ago.' I told him it was my first time ever at Droichead Nua. 'What a coincidence,' he said. 'You are just as tall as the man I remember.' It recalled the time when, sitting beside the driver of a County Donegal Railways train, I admitted that indeed I came from England. 'That is a great coincidence; my daddy was once there.'

It was now that the real Irishness of the traffic could be studied. Though no train had called since that on which I had travelled to Waterford, numerous passengers arrived and discussed their travel plans with the patient booking clerk. Pricing is even more complex than on BR, with concessions according to how many mainline rail journeys you make annually and the size of your family, as well as which trains you travel by and when you return.

'But supposing one of them should feel homesick, can they come back earlier?' Priests and nuns seemed the best informed on what the deal was. The employee who thought I was a former colleague confirmed that occasional freight (containers only) was still handled at the station – and shepherded us all (about forty, including five who had changed from the Waterford train) to the very rear of the platform. 'Even if you're going Super Standard class, they won't let you straight into it, and the restaurant that comes next will be locked.'

Of course I made straight for the restaurant car, with happy memories of CIE catering on former occasions. Meat dishes cost up to nearly £10, but egg, bacon and sausage automatically accompanied by a stock of brown and white bread, pats of butter, jam and tea or coffee, was a reasonable £4.45. No table setting, each person given his own tray. Business was brisk. But then again, the train was full.

At Kildare, which we should have run through non-stop, we crossed first to the up track and then into the up platform loop, crowded with passengers. There beside us on the down mainline was the 12.15 to Tralee, which nearly an hour before, we had passed at speed only a mile or so away.

Rathluirc, Mallow and Cork passengers – the last should have changed at Mallow – were transferring to us, though even if we regained our own lost time, they would still arrive an hour late.

'People are standing,' came the report from the stream of customers for lunch and for drinks at the bar. So, the £10 Waterford–Cork fare seeming a real bargain, I decided to splurge on a £5 supplement to get into Super Standard class, still labelled first-class, though first-class as such has long been abolished in Ireland. Most trains have only Standard class accommodation, but prestige expresses have a single Super Standard class coach, just like a BR open first, at the end furthest from Dublin, next to the restaurant car. You can indeed be served food and drink at your own seat, and as an afterthought I had dessert there.

Though the train as a whole was crowded, there were only a dozen of us in this little club. Predictably, several were priests, always among the keenest supporters of first class in the old days, and overseas visitors, notably Californian university students. Distinctly not the talkative cross-section of ordinary Irish people I had travelled with to and from Waterford.

A few years earlier I went down the mainline to Cork on the locomotive, single-manned by the father of sixteen children. I remember well, since his repeatedly telling me how poor he was, and how rich I must be, was mistaken by me as a hint he should be tipped. When I proffered a note at the end of the journey he made a pretty speech: 'I've no doubt I need it, and I've no doubt you can afford it – or more. But you've helped me bring the train into Cork on time as a good colleague and colleagues don't tip each other.'

Though much continuously welded rail has been put in, but I thought the general standard of maintenance had deteriorated, resulting in slower overall speeds. Most trains now make more stops, but this has encouraged traffic at the ten intermediate stations now open. Indeed, throughout Ireland, it is unusual for a train to stop without substantial business being transacted.

On my locomotive trip the busiest intermediate stop was of course Limerick Junction, where nearly 100 passengers alighted. Most of them were going to be delayed, the branch line for Limerick having left five minutes before so as to be able to maintain a connection from Limerick into the up afternoon mail. Mainline trains no longer have to back into Limerick Junction, an interesting, uniquely Irish place. I recall L.T.C. Rolt's colourful

For many decades crew familiarisation in case of emergency, the GWR ran a daily service around Dartmoor on the Southern and a Bulleid West Country Class Pacific ran via Newton Abbot. The latter is caught leaving Dawlish on an up train in the 1950s.

description of it with two steam locomotives facing each other only a few yards apart at the only time in the whole week that there was activity in a wartime Ireland starved of coal.

At Rathluirc, over thirty passengers alighted, and at Mallow more than I could sensibly count. Those for Killarney and Tralee were told to remain on the same platform and catch the next train; the 10.55 from Dublin was obviously behind us, well over an hour late, but was to precede the 15.40 Cork–Tralee, which arrived at the next platform during our stay. Further delays must have occurred as the two trains running block to block down the branch had to cross the evening Tralee–Cork train.

I had now spent nine hours on CIE, most of them on the mainline, and had not seen a single freight train on the move. But between Mallow and Cork we passed a container and a tanker train, and as I left Cork station and walked across the road bridge immediately in front of the tunnel-mouth, a second train of tankers came around the goods loop, its locomotive roaring as speed was gathered for the steep climb up through the tunnel. No station could be harder for mainline trains to start from than Cork, but I never tire of the station itself with its spacious concourse complete with steam locomotive on display and the suburban platforms for the Cobh line.

It was an enforced day on CIE, but one I shall always remember.

DEMISE OF THE MILK TRAIN

This appeared in Country Life, *31 March 1983. Today, railways in Britain
rarely carry milk, yet there was a time when nearly a half of the milk produced on
our dairy farms was carried by trains collecting it from the local station.*

THROUGHOUT the country the routine was the same. A shattering row broke the peace
at wayside stations as empty milk churns were disgorged from a down train of the morning.
Soon they were collected by the farmers' horse-drawn vehicles, to be brought back, loaded,
during the afternoon. Placed on trolleys at the platform edge, they were ready for the guard's
van or special milk-churn van of a late afternoon or evening up train, and the revenue they
provided often exceeded the fares of passengers.

Railwaymen of all ages performed the daily ritual with the precision that so important
a traffic demanded. Much attention to detail was necessary, such as checking the labelling
and ensuring that full churns were not left too long in the sun. The routine at many thousands of farms was regulated by the railway timetable, which changed little from year to
year – in many cases from decade to decade.

Dairy farmers were among the main rural beneficiaries from the coming of railways.
In many valleys the value of milk increased by 50–80 per cent when the railway arrived. In
the 1880s, for instance, milk that could be sent fresh to the cities was usually worth at least
a shilling a gallon, compared with a maximum of 8d if it had to be turned into butter or
cheese locally. Selling it fresh improved cash flow.

Not everyone was pleased. In several places, such as Broad Clyst, near Exeter, there
were protest meetings about the scarcity and high price of milk following the opening of
the local station, with virtually every farmer sending his supply to London for the high price
commanded there. In other areas there were similar complaints, and even riots, about the
shortages of meat, fish and other produce when they were switched to the capital's market
following the opening of the railway. Until the railway age, many farms remained profitable
within city boundaries. In 1850 Liverpool's dairy farmers could sell their milk at 1s–1s 4d a
gallon, compared with the general price of 8d–10d a gallon, because of the local shortage.
They complained bitterly when the railways introduced a mass importation of country milk
– and no doubt sold their land at premium prices for further building.

Landowners and farmers were usually among the most enthusiastic supporters of new
railway schemes. If a station opened within a few miles, up went the price of the milk and
other produce, and down went the cost of coal and fertilisers. The land itself could increase
in value by half. What did it matter if the few railway shares they had bought to set a good
example fell in price?

A large proportion of rural railways were built by small companies, often serving only
a dozen or so miles within a single valley. The usual pattern was for a mainline company
to encourage such local enterprise, perhaps with a nominal subscription of capital, advice,
and an offer to run the line, when opened, for part of the receipts. In numerous cases, this
ended with Goliath buying David a few decades later for, at most, half the sum invested.

From the 1940s creameries serving a large area began to collect milk by tanker, though
for local use milk churns held on longer. Every day the creameries sent their allocation of
railway milk tanks up the country. Special trains were run on a number of branch lines

as well as the mainlines. Until 1980 there were two daily milk trains passing through my home town of Newton Abbot on their way to London, this being the last route on which the remnants of the once ubiquitous business survived. Even in the early 1970s, the new M5 was given a hump to cross the then milk-traffic-only branch from Tiverton Junction to Hemyock. The hump remains for posterity, but the railway had been torn up before the motorway opened.

British Rail had ceased carrying milk anywhere. Eighty tank wagons – 'life expired' in the modern jargon – were mothballed. But with road transport problems during recent winters, a few milk trains again ran on a spasmodic basis, notably from Somerset and Essex.

For all intents and purposes, the era is over. The farmer's daughter attending a distant university may depend on trains with her student's railcard, but the railways have withdrawn from the farming scene they once dominated. Few revolutions have been so complete in the British countryside as the start and end of the railway age.

FOUR VERY DIFFERENT RAILWAYS

The series of books celebrating the first 150 years of the systems run by the four companies of the Grouping era (1923–47) were the joint work of myself and the late Patrick Whitehouse, the introductions being written by me. These introductions, here finishing somewhat arbitrarily, conjure up the totally different characters of the four systems of the Grouping era which persisted well into BR days and haven't totally disappeared today.

GREAT WESTERN RAILWAY

Few groups of initials have ever meant so much to so many people as GWR. In the minds of millions, they continue to spell romance, comfort, stability, good values that have been eroded, a spirit of adventure . . . and more specifically the days when the train journey was one of the best parts of a seaside or country holiday.

Many thoughts come to mind. The orderliness of Brunel's cathedral, Paddington, with pannier tanks bringing in empty coaches a good twenty minutes before departure time. The romance of the locomotives, basically the same design across half a century that encompassed two world wars and continual revolution in most other things mechanical. The world's fastest and the world's longest non-stop trains. The Great Western's peculiarities, such as Brunel's original broad gauge and the legacy of spaciousness it left; the automatic train control which made it not merely the world's safest railway, but probably the safest means of travel there

CHRISTMAS BONUS

With a big up-market clientele to serve, the GWR maintained a large fleet of first-class carriages, including, well into the post-1945, era many non-corridor ones. At busy times, such as Christmas, it gave third-class travellers the bonus of going first . . . such as on the third part of the 11.55am from Paddington non-stop Newport (133½ toiletless miles), the train consisting of ten non-corridor firsts and two vans.

Great Days of Express Trains, 1990

THIRD HYMN, SECOND LESSON

The first hymn was almost over and the ministers at the churches on either side of the mainline were just starting prayers when the 11.05am express to Paddington ran into Teignmouth, because of the shortness of the platform the locomotive stopping well forward, right between the churches. Occasionally it would stop on a dead, and the congregations could tell the pressure the driver must be under from the general hissing and puffing. Once one of the ministers even included him in the prayers . . . no doubt hoping he'd be on his way the sooner.

Then one Sunday the engine would not budge at all. Prayers, second hymn, first lesson, third hymn, second lesson . . . wasting steam was lifting the safety valve and making concentration difficult. And two enthusiastic members of the congregation could restrain their curiosity no longer, slipping out to see help coming in the form of a second loco.

The express incidentally ran *via* Bristol, and at Swindon stopped one side of the up island platform while on the other side was a York train with its LNER loco, at certain periods the only one in the week to work beyond Oxford.

Great Days of Express Trains, 1990

has ever been in the history of man; the lower quadrant signals; the unique publicity machine turning out books for 'boys of all ages', jigsaw puzzles and pioneer films.

A remarkable institution, almost a way of life, or a sovereign state strung out along hundreds of miles of route? The land on either side might be governed from Whitehall; the GWR was a world apart governed and governed very firmly from Paddington. The values and the practices were often dramatically different. The two worlds, for instance, had their separate telecommunication systems, and most railwaymen would have said that the Great Western's was better than the Post Office's. A plug bought in a local shop could not be pushed into a railway socket, for the GWR had its own different design of socket and plug, along with everything else electrical and much else besides including even gas meters.

The railway was just the starting point. The GWR had extensive shipping, bus and lorry, and even air services. It ran docks, restaurants and hotels, designed its own linen and

DOUBLE TELEGRAPH

These days we go to the station to catch a train. The time was when we also went there to buy our newspapers, the Great Western Magazine and Holiday Haunts, and to enjoy the general scene (even if we were not enthusiasts). The time was, indeed, when many people called on the stationmaster much as they paid their weekly respects to the parson or minister, and when the station was as likely a place to hear the latest news of the locality as anywhere else.

Ticket collectors were seldom without someone to talk to, and were a particularly useful source of information about who had gone where to do what … as the police frequently discovered. Booking clerk, stationmaster, porter, ticket collector might all recognise you and be

genuinely interested in your reason for patronising the company and be proud there was an appropriate service.

If you were up to no good that presented a great difficulty, for if you somehow got yourself to another station, trying to be incognito, and were seen perhaps by a friendly guard, the staff at the station you should have started from would quickly learn about it and be outraged. The GWR developed its own excellent telegraph and telephone systems backed by one of the world's most fearsome bush telegraphs.

The Great Days of the GWR, 1991

Unlike Plymouth Friary, the Southerns' Exeter Central was a busy place with trains for the further west over what was known as the 'withered arm' constantly being made up or divided, except on summer Saturdays this being as far west as restaurant cars went. Traffic included frequent lengthy trains from Exmouth which might disgorge over 200 office workers here and locals serving an amazing range of destinations, including Topsham, Exmouth, Budleigh Salterton, Broad Clyst, Sidmouth and Yeovil as well as further west.

SAVING WATER

When a pick-up scoop plunged through the water in a trough, the water level built up at the sides and was lowered in the middle. The result was spillage over the sides of the trough and reduced depth from which to collect. LMS engineers overcame the difficulty by designing a simple vane attachment which was lowered with the scoop. Two vertical vanes placed 1ft 4in in front of the scoop projected down into the water and were angled to throw water inwards so that it heaped up at the centre of the trough while the level at the sides was lowered. Not only did this type of deflector reduce wastage, but it increased the amount of water picked up. If the scoop was kept down for the whole length of the trough about 400 gallons of water was saved at each operation. It was estimated that fitting the deflector to all locomotives with pick-up scoops would reduce the quantity of water supplied to troughs by 20 per cent.

LMS 150, 1987

laundered it, published a magazine and had its own bands. In the restaurant car you read Great Western literature, drank Great Western whisky and ate Great Western biscuits with your cheese. Is it surprising that if you lived on Great Western territory you felt superior to those served by lesser railways? Part of the magic was anyway that the Great Western served much of the best-heeled and most scenic parts of Britain. But then another part of it was that the Great Western was so consciously different from other lines. It may have built the first Pacific locomotive in Britain, but it – *The Great Bear*, later converted to a Castle – was the only one it ever did build. Continuity played a key role in its character, it being the only major railway to maintain its identity in the 1923 Grouping, yet no business in the 1920s and 1930s was so fond of telling its shareholders and customers about its improvements and innovations.

LONDON, MIDLAND AND SCOTTISH RAILWAY

Operator of some of the world's most famous, fastest and certainly most comfortable express trains, of prestigious 'club trains' for the cream of Manchester's commuters, a miscellany of unconnected and different electric systems, each a pioneer effort, express goods trains (some carrying containers which marked the birth of what decades later has developed into the Freightliner business) making ever longer non-stop runs; but also of branch lines with a single daily service and whose last evening train completed its run only if sufficient passengers presented themselves (or enough fares were paid for), of a Highland line with so sparse a service that passengers were carried in goods guards' vans and of countless branches where time stood still it seemed throughout the Grouping years, commuter and excursion trains a few still using six-wheeled coaches whose interiors were so dirty that discriminating passengers sat on a cloth or newspaper, of London-bound

MIDLAND DINER

The Midland had not been able to beat the LNWR in speed between London and Manchester; but it wooed the public with excellent meals, a scenic route and a useful facility: seats in the dining cars, first and third, could be reserved the day before by telephoning the stationmaster's office at St Pancras or Manchester Central. No charge was made.

You could stay in your seat throughout the journey, consuming morning coffee, a solid five-course lunch, afternoon tea or dinner, or a combination of these delights. All credit to the LMS for retaining for a long time this splendid alternative to the Euston route, and even publicising it in a booklet *The Track of the Twenty-Fives*. The Manchester trains left St Pancras at two-hourly intervals virtually throughout the day, starting at 8.25am.

LMS 150, 1987

The Merchant Navy class was launched soon after the war (before any of the other railways introduced anything new) on the grounds that it was a mixed traffic machine, though in practice it scarcely ever headed a goods train. Like everything else Bulleid designed, they were controversial, especially with their streamlined casing. The luxury Devon Belle *never flourished like the 'portmanteau'* Atlantic Coast Express *serving numerous destinations, and was hampered by the Southerns' lack of water troughs. Though to add to its distinctiveness it didn't serve Salisbury, soon after passing through it, it stopped to change locomotives.*

coal trains that spent long times queuing in the permissive block sections; provider of Britain's most luxurious holidays but also of the greatest number of bargain excursions to the seaside and sporting events; technical innovator in many fields yet giving its signalmen at its headquarters station, London Euston, nothing more than a blackboard and piece of chalk to tell which platforms were occupied, empty stock being loose shunted; builder of the finest express locomotives and passenger coaches but retainer of many inherited oddities and much out-dated equipment; the country's largest employer after the Post Office, sufficiently interested in training to create the first college for railwaymen yet not able to key up its executives so well that they could prevent imports from another system eventually dominating theirs after nationalisation.

The Southerns' route to and system in the West had been part of the South Western Railway, ever in competition with the GWR who thoroughly liked it for allowing third-class passengers to travel on all its trains. Another of the Southerns' constituents had been the London, Brighton & South Coast Railway, whose Victoria station is seen in this early (1887) photograph before the first of the all-pervading electric trains was even thought about. The trains we see here must have been uncomfortable, possibly the worst of the trains south of the Thames where before electrification the rolling stock was deplorable.

The LMS. A system of enormous size and complexity – and everlasting paradoxes. The world's largest transport organisation, the Empire's largest commercial undertaking, it was not only by far the largest of Britain's four railways between 1923 and nationalisation at the end of 1947 but also the Empire's largest hotel chain, and had an involvement in every kind of industrial activity including of course land development and shipping, bus and air services.

The LMS was an essential part of Britain's fabric, the subject of music hall jokes and songs (especially about Crewe). Its traffic receipts were often regarded as the best yardstick of the state of the economy.

From Shoeburyness at the mouth of the Thames and Richmond higher up the river to Swansea and up many of the South Wales valleys, from the Midlands and through the industrial heartlands of the North including much of the West Riding to the slate villages and quarries of North Wales, from the industrial Cumberland coast and along the industrial and tourist Ayrshire coast to greater Glasgow and almost throughout the Lowlands, the LMS carried armies of people to and from their daily work. It is indeed always as a working and workmen's railway that the LMS will be chiefly remembered. Liverpool Street and Waterloo might be quoted as the stations with the largest morning inflows, but Fenchurch Street, Birmingham New Street, Manchester Victoria, and Glasgow Central were not merely taxed to the limit and beyond but exuded such crowds as to bring the streets outside to a virtual standstill – and moreover almost all with steam traction.

*Another constituent, the South East &
Chatham, scarcely dumped continental
passengers at a congenial Dover Harbour.*

GREAT EASTERN SOJOURN

To escape the rush-hour noise and hustle on the platforms of Liverpool Street and reach the Great Eastern Hotel through its back entrance was like changing worlds. The only hotel in the City, the Great Eastern somehow maintained its quality ambience even in adversity.

It was, of course, heavily booked, stays of more than a night sometimes involving changing rooms. Apologies, and of course the staff moved everything; no need to pack up. But the family's ancient hangers disappeared in the transfer, accounting for the writer's supply of LNER ones proffered in compensation. They must have been varnished along with the coaches and still have a century's worth of service left.

But ever back to the station, for tea and cake in the café on the wandering bridge linking the two 'sides' that has epitomised Liverpool Street, and always to watch the stock of the Hook Continental come in and diners immediately take their seats and equally immediately be served (which certainly was not a Great Western habit) so that they would be into their main course before departure.

LNER 150, 1989

Even the signalman takes in a good view. The LMS Coronation Scot of the years just before the Second World War. On the LNER's competition, The Flying Scotsman, you could even hire a stenographer or have your hair cut. Good meals could be assured, Christmas Day on the LMS once being photographed by The Times and remembered till this day, no week-long shut downs on those days.

LONDON AND NORTH EASTERN RAILWAY

Images: of boyhood, walking down the tree-lined avenue to the recently rebuilt Gidea Park, exuding good-quality neatness; and along the path overlooking the quadrupled tracks, expresses (famous names among them) now given a clear run, and more modernity in the Continental wagons running to London courtesy of the Harwich train ferry. Pride in 'our' station, teeming with passengers at rush hours, terminus for many of the frequent suburban trains with a grand new signalbox and extensive sidings. Vivid memories of the first-ever train journey, to Liverpool Street by what must have been one of the last rakes of four wheelers. It waddled in like a goods and was so full that no chance of a former second-class compartment so had to endure the real McCoy of Great Eastern economy, listening to the conversation on the benches beyond the half partition.

On later journeys, always travelling in the rear and seeing the front of the train round the curves through the dismal arches into Liverpool Street, perhaps running parallel with an articulated set. Nothing like that in the toy shops. Last off platform, train out, next in seconds later, frightened by release of Westinghouse brake . . . all so quick, dark.

Back home, Dad was undoubtedly right to have chosen GWR for Hornby layout in garage; LNER OK but everyday, even ordinary. Of course, could not know just what an achievement the everyday peak service was; heard later that if the GWR had anything half so difficult its managers would have had twins on the spot.

Then to Harpenden where the joys of the Midland could occasionally be forsaken for the LNER's single-line crossing station a long way off. How could it possibly be called Harpenden? Branch-line love at first sight. How orderly, quiet; but why did the signalman cause false hope of another train by failing to restore signals to danger for half an hour?

Kings Cross: not ordinary at all. Too late to see the like of *The Silver Jubilee* but an unforgettable head-on view of an A4 sweeping out of the tunnel depending heavily on

CHEAPER BY TRAIN
....

Belle Vue was one of the most popular destinations for winter evening excursions to big cities, using rolling stock that would otherwise have remained idle and allowing whole families to see new places at an extremely modest cost. In the winter of 1934–5, 781 trains ran to cities such as Manchester, Sheffield, Nottingham and Newcastle carrying 300,000 passengers.

In the early 1930s, the LNER ran an excursion from Lincoln to Belle Vue, Manchester and back for 2s 6d (12½p), a distance of almost 200 miles. Its driver, Herbert Harrison, who started on the GCR in 1903, took several of his family on the trip.

On arrival back at 2.00am, a fleet of Lincoln Corporation buses was awaiting, enhanced fares of 1s (5p) being charged because of the late hour.

The air went blue. Herbert Harrison roared: 'I've just taken this lot over the Pennines to Manchester for 1s 3d and you lot want 1s for a mile-and-a-half down Monks Road.'

LNER 150, 1989

last-minute application of brakes, and northbound expresses starting off for really interesting places with deservable commotion.

Immediately after the war, Nottingham Victoria, vast endless trains but hardly any of them going anywhere special or carrying many people, though endless goods snaking through. Aboard for Sheffield Victoria, all stations; how sensible those island platforms seemed, but so slow – and dirty. Back by express, job to find standing room between soldiers and kit bags in corridor, equally dirty and forever slowing (probably for mining subsidence). But a compartment to self from the platform-next-the-wall at Manchester London Road to Sheffield, still in steam days, guard checking all windows closed before going under Pennines. We passed a long goods, mainly coal, immediately before and after going through one of the twin single bores.

SOUTHERN

Until you consider it in detail, the statement may sound bland, but it is full of great meaning: the Southern Railway was one of the most sensible large transport organisations the world has ever seen. It had a touch of magic, and among those who really knew it, its achievements were wondered at, its demise on nationalisation bitterly regretted.

Among the Big Four, it was not the largest (it was in fact by far the smallest) nor the grandest, and despite the fact that Southern Electric became a household name neither it

North British Railways' signals for testing drivers' sight north of Blyth, Northumberland.

DISAPPEARED INTO THE NIGHT

It must have happened often but without the same consequences.

The signalman at Swanage tucked the locomotive of the day's last train into the depot, shut off the lights and locked up without giving 'train out of section' to his opposite number at Corfe Castle with whom, at the best of times, relationships were strained.

Instead of telephoning a few minutes after the train should have reached journey's end, when Swanage signalbox would still have been open, the Corfe man waited (earning overtime) until his call was ignored – and then called Control.

Control's first reaction was that had anything been wrong someone would have heard about it by now, but on reflection felt that referral to higher authority could not be ignored. So the Police were called out.

They first went to the station which they found in darkness and then woke the stationmaster who went with them to the signalman who by this time was fast asleep.

Only when the signalman was dragged back to his box was the Corfe man's overtime terminated. Next day the whole branch and most people in Swanage and Corfe Castle were expressing their views on the incident.

The Great Days of the Southern Railway, 1992

nor its services were best known, at home or among the many thousands living elsewhere in the world who then took a keen interest in Britain and her railways and played a major part in determining 'popularity'. Railway modellers, for example, were naturally more attracted to anything but the Southern, for the other three all had more glamorous trains and locomotives passing through more dramatic scenery. Very few of the best-known stations, those large cathedrals of steam, were on the Southern, and the same went for Britain's famous industries.

Yet the Southern went about the business of steadily improving the scope and quality of what it did with masterly determination. Its policy, based on common sense rather than dogma, was pursued consistently and therefore economically; but it was not too proud to admit mistakes and to change when need be. Its management atmosphere was that of a large, reasonably happy family. Above all, it controlled its finances wisely. Save in one locomotive matter right at the end of its life, it virtually made no investment

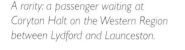

A rarity: a passenger waiting at Coryton Halt on the Western Region between Lydford and Launceston.

that it regretted. It certainly never threw anything away – locomotive, train or piece of equipment – that could continue to be used usefully or incorporated into something else.

Before the air age, the Southern was Britain's front door, at least three quarters of all visiting royalty and political and other famous people first glimpsing our countryside through its windows. In the days that Gatwick airport was a grass field and London's airport was at Croydon, all the world of politics and fashion was to be seen at Victoria before the departure of the *Golden Arrow*. One of its main successes was in the development of Southampton, often described as the jewel in its crown, attracting the Cunard liners which had previously used Liverpool. It had unrivalled experience in carrying great crowds, going to the seaside, on day trips, and later on for longer holidays, visiting the numerous racecourses on its territory, and so on. This proved invaluable in the various wartime evacuations of London and especially in the brilliantly executed operation of dispersing the nearly a third of a million soldiers brought back from the beaches of Dunkirk.

Yet it was essentially an everyday railway, carrying workers and crops. It had no special sophistication, but a great aptitude for getting the detail right. Not merely did it develop the world's largest electrified suburban system, but it made it work with much precision. Indeed, throughout the system there was a smartness of operation that was the envy of other railways. Fifteen seconds was all that trains were normally allocated for station stops, a few more at junctions. Different portions of trains were joined and separated in two or three minutes, at dozens of locations and at many of them hour by hour. Were the arrival at the terminal late, electric train motormen would often be seen running the whole length of their train to ensure a punctual departure.

PHOTOGRAPHY BY JOHN EDINGTON

John Edington's photographs brilliantly record the last decades of steam and show what the railway was really like.

ABOVE *The North Eastern Railway trans-Pennine line from Barnard Castle to Kirkby Stephen, Penrith and Tebay was notable for two viaducts, Deepdale and Belah, designed by Sir Thomas Bouch. LMS design class 2MT 2-6-0 No. 46472 is crossing Belah viaduct hauling the 10.30 Penrith–Darlington on Tuesday 7 August 1951. The line closed to passengers on 22 January 1962.*

LEFT *The line from Wenford Bridge to Wadebridge was very popular with enthusiasts being worked by one of three LSW 2-4-0WTs – of the other two, one was the Wadebridge pilot and the other was spare. No. 30585 is on the outward journey (10.03 ex-Wadebridge) taking water in Pencarrow Wood on 5 May 1959.*

RIGHT *The 'Patriot' Class 4-6-0s were not well represented on the Midland Division of the LMR but No. 45506 The Royal Pioneer Corps was one of the few. It is seen leaving Bromsgrove with a Bournemouth–Manchester train on 6 August 1960 banked by two GW 0-6-0PTs.*

BELOW *On Easter Sunday, 2 April 1961, ex-LNER Class B1 4-6-0 No. 61006 Blackbuck passes Dudley East with a return excursion to Lincoln. The GWR half of the station is behind the train in the middle distance. Dudley Zoo was a popular destination for excursions, especially from the East Midlands.*

LEFT *Cadbury Bros at Bournville near Birmingham owned a number of coke-fired shunting locomotives (coke-fired to avoid contamination of the chocolate during manufacture!). On 4 March 0-4-0T No. 1, built by the Avonside Engine Company of Bristol in 1925, Works No. 1977, was at work.*

BELOW *The RCTS ran many special trains in the 1960s. On Saturday 31 March 1962 one covered many lines in East Anglia. The NRM's Class J17 0-6-0 No. 65567 has just brought the train into Thetford, ex-Great Eastern Railway, from Swaffham and No. 70003 John Bunyan is backing on to the train for the return journey to Liverpool Street.*

RIGHT *The 3ft gauge Manx Electric Railway (Douglas to Ramsey) connects at Laxey with the 3ft 6in gauge line to the summit of Snaefell, the highest point on the island. On 27 June 1963 Manx Electric Railway Car No. 6 and a 'toast rack' trailer are heading for Douglas. Two Snaefell cars (Nos 5 and 6) are awaiting departure for the summit.*

BELOW *Even in 1964 the Western Region was still very much the Great Western Railway perpetuating all the latter's differences from the rest of BR. At Hatton between, Leamington and Birmingham, on 25 July Modified Hall Class 4-6-0 No. 7927 Willington Hall is passing through the station on a down empty coaching stock train.*

One of the Welsh narrow gauge railways
– the Fairbourne on 5 June 1965. Still in
its 1ft 3in gauge guise – it was converted
to 12¼in gauge in winter 1985–6. 2-4-2
Sian is leaving Fairbourne station for
Barmouth Ferry. Sian was built by Guest
Engineering Works, Stourbridge, in 1963.

On 15 August 1963 at Wroxall, Isle of Wight, ex-LSWR Class O2 0-4-4T No. 29 Alverstone is about to depart on the 12.42 Ryde Pier Head to Ventnor.

CHAPTER 10
THE SEASIDE RAILWAY

SCENE ONE

THE evening crowds of Glaswegians at St Enoch station are similar to those of wartime evacuation scares, but the atmosphere couldn't be more different. No tension now, but excitement, laughter, expectation especially at St Enoch and Central among those going on holiday further afield than ever before. An occasional impromptu station announcement and friendly comment from ticket inspectors at the platforms' entrance add to the sense of occasion at the start of Glasgow Fair holidays in the mid-1950s.

The range of attractions offered didn't suffice to keep Meyrick Park Halt open as a study of old Bradshaws reveals.

MEYRICK PARK HALT
FOR
GOLF LINKS CRICKET GROUND
TALBOT WOODS & WINTON

Families have come well prepared with food and drink. We can only guess how much or little sleep they will have tonight. There (in old pm time) goes the 5.28 to Paignton, a relief to the 5.30 to Plymouth which is a summer Friday extension of a train that usually only runs to Carlisle. A Class 5 and a Royal Scot are at the 5.30, double-headed for the climb from Barrhead, while we hear that the relief is taking the easier but longer route by Paisley and Dalry.

The 5.58 Arran boat train is running in duplicate to Ardrossan Winton Pier (passengers will arrive at Brodick on Arran late but with luck should still have some sleep in a bed) but those for Dublin on the 7.55 to Greenock Pier will mainly spend the night sitting up. The Pickergill 3P hauling this is only one of many former Caledonian machines we'll see this evening. There's even a through train to Dover for those Glaswegians daring to cross the Channel.

Introduced two years ago to combat road competition, the Starlight Specials are proving popular. No fewer than nine trains this evening are all fully booked (so the thousands of passengers will have to sit, no room to loll). They are scheduled to leave at 3.40, 6.30, 7.10, 7.45, 8.15, 8.35, 9.23, 9.48 and 10.20, the last two going to Euston rather than the traditional St Enoch route to St Pancras. The Glasgow & South Western route is still a serious rival to the Caledonian's out of Central. Indeed, we pop into both station's fine hotels, and also the North British at Queen Street. The rival railways had hotel committees that toured the great hotels of Europe to ensure they built the best.

We walk along an unusually busy street to reach Glasgow's No. 1 station by its back entrance under a bridge and make our way to the large concourse which all the time we're there is filled with eager holidaymakers, mainly in family groups. Hundreds are looking at the long display of departure boards, two men constantly replacing those of trains that have left with new ones, a few for tonight's record number of trains with hastily prepared chalked ones. Fascinating as that is, we opt to walk down to the platform's end to watch what is happening at the station's complicated throat, out over the Clyde. Coronation and Royal Scots, Jubilees, Clan and Standard Class 5s and many other tender and tank engine classes offer a great variety of motive power, each train's departure generating two light-engine movements which must put heavy strain on the signalmen. The movement of points and their locking bars and of semaphore signals being raised and dropped is like a background orchestra, only totally drowned with accelerating departures, often two or three together.

More trains are leaving for London than we've seen before, two sleeping-car-only reliefs formed entirely of the older third-class couchette-like compartments, not offering the most assured rest. Though pre-Grouping practice still generally reigns, we notice that while two departures from St Enoch were tonight for Euston, unusually Central has a couple for St Pancras. The number of holidaymakers on the move tonight will be in tens of thousands. It is mind boggling thinking of all the thinking taking place as they try and grab some shut-eye.

We can't keep up with all the trains, but from one of the short platforms near where we are standing, suburban services drawn by tanks include the occasional one for the Cathcart Circle, which has inspired one of the most romantic railway novels (*Tammay of the Cathcart Circle*). A five-coach train for the separate route to Paisley Canal is especially well filled, as are some of the boat trains leaving from the three highest-numbered platforms at the far part of the station (looking out across the bridge) to our right.

LEFT *The short-lived Lynton & Barnstaple Railway still had nine years of life left when H.C. Casserley photographed two of the narrow-gauge locomotives at Pilton Shed, Barnstaple.*

BELOW *Who needs a steam engine? In 1900, passengers line up at the North British Railways Port Carlisle station to join the Dandy Car.*

Not only are the usual and the advertised Fridays-only trains running in duplicate or three sections, but the Isle of Man Steamship Company, getting the most sea miles out of its fleet, has duplicated its summer-Friday evening service to Ardrossan. Again, many thousands will be wondering what their voyages will be like: crowded for sure. Accommodating the extra traffic at the Clyde's terminals will be difficult – especially Wemyss Bay, where we hear there are four extras for the Rothesay and Millport sailings. There is already talk about the possibility of reducing the four tracks to Paisley's main station to a single pair, but they'll all be fully used tonight and no doubt for the continuing rush tomorrow.

So to Queen Street, with its short platform and steep climb through the tunnel just beyond the station's throat. Again it is busy, with some long-distance relief trains using the smoke-filled Lower Level platforms, and we hear half a dozen engines at the top of Cowlais incline lined up for their turn to descend to take away their departing trains.

Despite the great exodus we've seen, and it will reach its peak tomorrow, Saturday, many thousands will spend the Fair staying at home. A huge excursion programme, 'dune the watter' (*Jennie Deans* round the Isle of Bute for 59p in new money) and to many Scottish destinations such as Fort William, has been planned.

Glasgow's fourth terminus, the Highland's inconveniently situated Buchanan Street, will no doubt also be busier than usual, but that's not saying much and there will be more pleasure than sorrow when services are transferred to Queen Street.

Looking back, Glasgow wasn't the only city then with four stations where holiday-makers joined with pleasurable holiday expectations. The list of those which have lost one or more seems endless. Remember Liverpool Exchange (also with its railway hotel), Manchester Central, and oddities such as Leicester Belgrave Road, the Great Northern outpost, which at one time allowed a faster journey to Edinburgh than the Midland *via* York. The list includes many minor termini such as Perth and Salisbury and perhaps especially the one-platform Norwich City.

Belgrave Road never changed in its lifetime and had more platforms than Monday–Friday trains until, after they were withdrawn, only summer Saturday and excursion traffic remained. Serving many resorts, including popular Mablethorpe, miraculously these lasted until 1962, though at the end 'expresses' were limited to 25mph because of the poor state of the track on the Leicester branch. Somehow Belgrave Road maintained its reputation as a friendly station, loved by those going away on holiday and day trippers.

We must sometimes wonder why, when our railways now carry record numbers of passengers, such generous arrangements were needed even in the 1950s and 1960s. The answer lies in the nature of the traffic. Peaks were much sharper, which certainly counted in Leicester Belgrave Road's case. Trains served many more destinations (often splitting en route) and were steam-hauled, necessitating more movements. Platforms were also congested with luggage and trolleys, and far more people seeing off friends. Even the porters of yesteryear added to the crush. And although there are more main-line trains, excursions in several parts are a thing of the past.

Not that the modern railway is always unfriendly. Staff still occasionally wish passengers a happy holiday over the tannoy, and I recall a driver at Manchester Piccadilly, taking a Newquay-bound service on the first part of its journey, actually coming through the train to do so.

SCENE TWO

ON one of the last Saturdays in July in the early 1950s, the day's last long-distance train draws to a halt nearly two hours late at one of Newquay's long platforms. For a few enthusiasts, the last part of the journey over the steeply graded, curving branch from Par has been exhilarating, especially so the climb up Luxulyan Bank with two tender engines (one a Castle) at the front and a banker at the rear. For most, however, it has been an irritatingly slow end to a tiring day.

The really anxious folk are the hoteliers waiting to serve makeshift dinners to overdue guests – held up by delays on the roads, especially the notorious Exeter bypass, as well as by train. They know that some of the passengers who have just arrived will be further delayed since each of the available taxis will have to make several journeys to clear the queue – and a few may have been stupid enough not to have reserved a bed.

Newquay is on the crest of a wave, its popularity growing more rapidly than that of any other resort. There was already a queue of those looking for accommodation when the information bureau next door to the station opened early this morning. With not a bed to be had in Newquay, all day its staff have been sending the overflow visitors to anywhere they can between Saltash on the Tamar and St Just in Penwith near Land's End. As for the local hoteliers, the price of such pressure has resulted in nearly half of them being on tranquillisers.

The astonishing success of Newquay, exploiting its unique cliff-top position and many sandy beaches, is down to close co-operation between the go-ahead, publicity-minded Town Council and the railways. Though the branch line, partly modernised by the Great Western in the 1930s, is expensive to operate, the number of passengers making long journeys from Paddington, the Midlands and North makes it very worthwhile. Today, well over 6,000 have arrived from at least as far away as Bristol.

To help the expresses get through, on summer Saturdays scarcely any trains stop at the intermediate stations in the china clay district, but during the coming fortnight those at places

Lustleigh on the Moretonhampstead branch was an attractive station in a pretty village, many people using it for an afternoon tea though in later years an auto-car sufficed.

such as Bugle and Roche will be unusually busy, since, extraordinary though it seems, they have their own substantial holiday trade. Overflow visitors, first directed here in an emergency a couple of years ago, so enjoyed being part of village life in an utterly different environment that they have chosen to return. One of the joys is that they can hop on a weekday local for Newquay and easily spend a long day there or at many other Cornish resorts.

As Holiday Correspondent of the regional morning paper and also on radio, I highlighted Newquay's success and was said to be partly responsible for an increase in property prices in the town as newly retired people, some of whom had holidayed there, chose it as a safe place to run a bed and breakfast in semi-retirement.

The railways' share of the holiday traffic declined sharply after 1958. But though they have long ceased running on any other Cornish branch, even today summer Saturdays bring through trains from Paddington and by cross-country from the Midlands and North. However, as the season has lengthened, the peak has become far less pronounced and 'Vacancy' boards can be seen at almost any time. Deprived of fresh overflow visitors, Bugle and Roche steadily lost their holiday trade and have again become insular in china-clay landscape.

SCENE THREE

ON Scotland's longest platform, at Nairn, the signalman is cycling between the signal cabins at either end and his block post in the booking office. A small knot of passengers, some heavily laden with luggage, has formed to join one of two summer Saturday trains that technically originate from here, though the stock comes through from Inverness. Both are Edinburgh-bound, one for Princes Street, the other Waverley.

Soon, many lines, including that to Banff, which had a through train to Glasgow at the end of its Fair, and the summer Saturdays branch to Heads of Ayr taking people to and from the Butlins camp, along with many more will soon be removed from the map.

Again no passengers – but an overpowering smell of pigs. Calling points, such as Whitehall Halt on the GWR's Hemyock branch were, as rural as you could get.

Scottish traditional tourism is in sharp decline. The Scots head south, increasingly to Spain, while the English no longer come to spend August on the Moray Firth as Ludovic Kennedy did as a child to the house next door to ours, where in the past the owners moved out for the peak summer month to make useful cash and the visitors brought just about everything bar the kitchen sink with them.

Today's English visitors mainly head for the West Coast and, since the cessation of Motorail, drive the whole way to enjoy grand scenery but be pestered by midges. Though still advertising itself as the Brighton of the North with a pleasant mini-climate on the Moray Firth, Nairn generates negligible holiday traffic by rail. The usual tenants of our holiday cottage are Scots from the Central Belt and Aberdeen who actually head north for the sunnier climes of the Moray Firth and the town's holiday amenities. Nowadays the only rail journey they might make is along the fabled Kyle of Lochalsh line.

SCENE FOUR

CROWDS of Wakes Week departing visitors from one Lancashire town are taking their seats on one train while those from another are arriving at a nearby platform. Unable to walk down the platform (because only those with Regulation tickets for the appropriate train are allowed past the barrier), a group of train lovers content themselves with the general organisation, comparing how things are going at Blackpool North's 15 platforms and Central's 14. At the peak of the season any time between the wars or until the 1950s, it might be described as organised chaos.

Named after a peat-coloured pool slightly inland, the sleepy village of Blackpool took time to take root as a holiday resort, but thanks to the railway grew rapidly into the nation's largest, and is now an institution with 7 miles of promenade and unequalled man-made facilities. Two pence on the rates for publicity to encourage visitors has greatly helped.

Well over 100,000 staying visitors will arrive by different routes to three stations today. We can tell from the accents that nearly all are north country people, most indeed Lancashire – and that the railways are under great strain. Whistles blow interminably as drivers, guards and station inspectors glance at their watches. Bringing empty trains in on time from the miles of sidings is difficult enough, though disposing of incoming rolling stock as the day wears on will be even harder.

How the Lancashire folk love their sea. Children come to life from the moment they can first run free on the sands. And how the railways struggle to make it all possible, handling burgeoning excursion traffic every day of the week except Saturday mornings and afternoons when there's no room for them.

Our enthusiasts change train stations again, but after a hasty sandwich wander inland to watch trains approaching and departing from the resort with its three routes and stations. There are vantage points well known to those who frequent the area but are too baffling for the newcomer to discover. Baffling sums up the whole Blackpool railway scene. Where else would you find the slip coach that once arrived before the train it was shed from – or a famous Club Car train for well-heeled commuters?

While Blackpool was slow to develop, for the railways, decline set in early. New horizons were opening in the 1950s and they were far south of Lancashire – at first largely in the South West whose tourism fleetingly seemed to have a bright future as it attracted the

Auto-train LB & SCR style.

'more adventurous', the very ones who later increasingly became Mediterranean sun worshippers. Many who had seen Blackpool's direct mainline built specially for the Saturday traffic lived to see it close. Central station followed.

Some who have mellowed with age fondly recall those baffling, chaotic peak weekends when stress levels were high and they realise that since Blackpool still largely serves the North, the millions who still visit it can conveniently drive or take a short coach trip. Only for the illuminations are people from all parts of Britain now well represented on the promenade, and few of them come by train. Conference business remains important, but the long absence of through trains from London hasn't helped and has produced many caustic comments from politicians.

Yet it seems so recently that it was different, when you could sit in a through train from Glasgow going through Preston non-stop in one direction only to pass through it soon after again in the other, this saving scarce platform and track capacity but making some passengers wonder if they or the railways had lost their wits.

SCENE FIVE

THERE is a high decibel rate as we're with a mass of young chatterboxes on a train of old rolling stock hired for a journey of not much more than 15 miles from a small town to a coastal resort at the end of one of the numerous short branch lines reaching the East Anglian coast.

The hirers are a group of rival churches who annually club together to give their youngsters a treat: a Sunday School Outing of the kind that, so far as the railways are concerned, largely died before the end of the 1950s.

Excitement is of a level that reminds us that until car ownership becomes more common, many children even living within a dozen miles of it seldom see the sea. But also that many more people did so enthusiastically at the beginning of the Railway Age. Before then, it was not unusual even for adults living within a good horse-ride's distance of the sea never to see it in their whole lifetime. Horses and horse-driven vehicles were for the wealthy. Cheap tickets opened up many opportunities. On summer Sundays, to cite an example from another part of the country, 6,000 tickets were once sold at Exeter's suburban station of St Thomas just to Dawlish Warren, between which there were special relief services, one timetabled to run whatever the summer weather.

However, for many cheap tickets are still too expensive, or arrangements too inflexible. For some of the kids on our Sunday School Outing, this will be the sole opportunity of the year to romp across the sands, being without parents adding zest.

Across Britain, railwaymen realise that the youngsters on Sunday School Outings are noisy but well behaved. On this, as on most such trains, the adults shepherding the children of different churches talk together wholeheartedly aiming to give pleasure: freedom, good eats, an occasion to remember. If there is competition it is to conduct the best-behaved group, formed in orderly lines, to leave the station and walk to the beach before letting go. Mind you, arriving back at the home station in the evening, parents waiting, keeping strict discipline will be altogether harder.

Few tank engines displayed names as prominent as this LBSC No. 469 seen here on the turntable at Eastbourne.

SCENE SIX

WE'RE on the Highland Chieftain in GNER days, joining at York just two hours after its departure from King's Cross. Many southerners feel that York is in the far north, but we've still just over six hours to go. Having had a sandwich in the former railway hotel at York, we forgo the last sitting of lunch and snooze till we squeak round the curve over the bridge leading to Newcastle where, sure enough, the Inverness crew who will serve us dinner soon after Perth are waiting and wave at us. The food for dinner will not be loaded until Edinburgh. The Great North & Eastern Railway is perhaps the best of all the franchises under privatisation, offering excellent restaurant cars on nearly all trains and providing an outstanding at-seat service in first class. As yet there is no hint of problems.

Many regular passengers wake up around this point, for soon after Newcastle, departing over another bridge with one of the world's best urban views, things get interesting, especially for lovers of the coast. At first the sea is elusive, and we half wonder if we caught a glimpse of Amble-by-the-Sea, on this late spring afternoon at the little resort of Alnmouth, still with a station. Then we spot the course of the long-abandoned branch to Seahouses. Soon Budle Bay, and Bamburgh with its ancient castle and the Farne Islands beloved of monks and now birdlovers. As we race along the near-straight track, next to command attention is Holy Island or Lindisfarne with its old castle and famous church where, under pressure from day trippers, the priest once told me he thanked God for the tide and the peace it brought. The tide is coming in. The cars driving across the causeway will be the last until morning.

Edging closer to the sea, we look down on Tweedsmouth, now with no station though there used to be a junction one, and then slow down to cross the Royal Border Bridge with its bird's-eye view of Berwick-upon-Tweed, once neither England nor Scotland but a separate entity.

Today's border is further on – when we are actually on the cliff top, watching fishing boats plying their trade in the foreground and coasters heading north and south on the horizon. We have to keep a sharp eye out for the point where the branch left for Eyemouth and to catch a fleeting glimpse of the fishing port familiar with tragedy in the unpredictable North Sea but surprisingly successful if attracting few visitors. There's been tragedy on the railway, too, notably when a rock fall buried workers in a tunnel – their bodies were never recovered – and a diversion had to be made slightly inland.

Then a wandering diversion inland until we come back to the sea and a racing ground to Dunbar with its single platform served by occasional expresses in both directions. Most of the day, GNER offers a half-hourly service to Edinburgh, a far cry from the era of the *Flying Scotsman* (the train, not the preserved locomotive) when only a handful of daily expresses reached the Scottish capital. Somehow that train, though slow and dirty by today's standard, still evokes great nostalgia, and GNER's legend 'The Route of the Flying Scotsman' incorporated in its distinctive dark livery has gone down a treat.

Now we are a little inland, noting the junction with the busy branch to the resort of North Berwick and, as we're possibly a minute or two early, could be slowed by one of its frequent electric services calling at the mainline's local station running ahead of us.

For passengers going on to Aberdeen, there is much more great coastal scenery to come, with many glimpses looking down to coves and gullies . . . not to mention first the crossing of the Forth Bridge. But we've Highland scenery and dinner to look forward to though our spirits have once more been refreshed by our exhilarating run along the North Sea.

SCENE SEVEN

THE train crowded with holidaymakers has almost been brought to a signal stop at Dawlish Warren, giving ample time to read 'The End of the World is Nigh', the message of a sandwich-board man tilted toward us. Most passengers have their eyes glued to the window, some with their heads stuck out and, as we reach the open sea and many adults as well as children catch their first-ever sight of the waves, there is a deafening thrill of joy.

Welcome to the era of holidays-with-pay. In the early post-war years, Saturdays at the end of July and beginning of August bring new records of those going west on holiday. The Great Western substantially invested to carry the increasing traffic of the 1930s, their separate summer Saturday tables still making fascinating reading today. They coped with the profitable traffic then, but with ever more passengers it is much harder for the nationalised railway to do so now.

The train we're on has old rolling stock and there are far more passengers than can be seated. Luggage is everywhere. For a full fifteen bogies, the train is somewhat underpowered, recovery slow from signal checks, not that that seems to matter much for, as we crawl through Dawlish we see the train ahead of us also crawling. We're already nearly an hour late, and will be much later before even reaching Newton Abbot, where probably we'll lose more time. No matter, as we saw in Scene One excitement is a feature of trains like ours in the early post-war years. We may be an island nation but, amazingly, till now many have always stayed inland, among the masses of industrial cities generally only soldiers having been abroad.

Out of the last and longest tunnel, by the Parson & Clerk rocks, we're on the Sea Wall proper, where many visitors and train-loving locals are walking the pedestrian way that Teignmouth demanded be given to the townspeople in exchange for Brunel's right to take his broad-gauge tracks between cliffs and sea.

Now let us skip Saturdays and, between the frequent passage of trains, join those enjoying the cliffs and rabbits scampering up them and the waves and the people on the beaches at low tide. There's a special crowd at the Teignmouth end, where the railway turns inland and we can spot the end of the down platform. Whenever a long train stops here, there's a porter who checks that the tail-lamp is correct and telephones the signalbox so that 'Train out of section' (two bells one) can be given to Parson's Tunnel signalbox.

Including the slotted distant of Teignmouth Old Quay, we can see the signals of three boxes, and a total of seven signal arms: on the down, Parson Tunnel's starter, Teignmouth's distant, home (with Old Quay's slotted distant), and on the up Teignmouth's advance starter, Parson Tunnel's distant and home.

Especially on the down, it is block-to-block working most of the time. Because of a sharp curve at the approach to Teignmouth, drivers, cautioned by the distant still being horizontal, have to crawl until seeing Teignmouth's home. And on the up, similarly to its advance starter. Though they always checked for themselves, sometimes they welcomed help from an onlooker giving a professional 'right away'. Especially after Parson Tunnel's signalbox has been switched out at the end of its single-shift working, it is possible to talk with drivers held at Teignmouth's advance starter, and hear their experiences. It was when one driver said that his empty stock had come all the way from Newquay that, when I checked on Monday, I discovered it had been forced to continue to Severn Tunnel Junction to rest its wheels.

The post-war Pullman-car the Devon Belle *didn't live up to expectations, and the days it operated and the stations it served were rapidly cut back.*

Not only could one tell when trains had been signalled (being able to see the rear as well as front of semaphores), but in those days, even under clear signals, expresses did not pass along the Sea Wall as rapidly as today and had windows easier to see into. Much of the fun was being able to look through the windows, passengers perhaps having the simplified summer Saturday restaurant car fare (cold salad, dessert and coffee) and wave or even exchange a greeting with those leaning out of compartment windows.

Though goods traffic was halted for most of the busiest Saturdays, there were still parcels and perishable trains, and milk trains and, as road congestion worsened from the 1950s, Motorail trains usually with every last space occupied on the string of open flats behind the sitting coaches for drivers and, their passengers, sometimes with restaurant car.

Altogether summer Saturdays are great sporting occasions, and among many I enjoy a picnic lunch at Spray Point, the mid-way point along the Sea Wall where the land had been artificially extended seaward. There was once a café here but, with no running water, it can't meet new hygiene rules.

Many enthusiasts know the significance of the numbers on the front of locomotives, put there to help signalmen identify trains. We can thus tell how late trains are, and whether they are running in their proper order. Sure enough, one we hadn't marked off turns up seven trains later than it should have. Why we'll never know.

The Sea Wall has always been the best known place where trains run feet from the

So popular, with its through coaches serving dozens of destinations, at busy times the ACE, as it was nicknamed, ran in many separate parts.

waves at high tide and are frequently engulfed by them. The washing away of ballast has always been a problem and, since the down line is the more vulnerable, the up is now signalled for two-way working. Not only is the location fantastic, but between Taunton and Newton Abbot a single pair of tracks carries trains from both the Paddington and Bristol routes going to both Torbay and Plymouth. Added to that, especially in the days we are talking of, many trains stopped at Dawlish and Teignmouth, then relatively busier resorts.

At best it was always a case of squeezing a quart into a pint pot. Many trains were up to fifteen coaches. And when there was no chance of adding further capacity in the middle of the day, an increasing number of trains ran both in the small hours and well into the evening. The whole day's performance might depend on how late the early morning arrivals were, delays of over two hours resulting in the reverse working not being able to start on time. On Torquay station the first arrivals, especially from Wales, before any café opened, stayed on the platform and passed the time singing songs. When they did open, cafés served hundreds of breakfasts.

A particular bottleneck on the Torbay branch was Paignton's single down platform. A queue of trains waiting to use it could back up at every possible signal to the Sea Wall. That meant that Plymouth and Cornwall services were also caught up.

The railway between Exeter and Newton Abbot, especially the Sea Wall, is unquestionably unique. Busy and readily accessible, among other things it began as very Brunel:

broad-gauge and daring atmospheric power. Even the natural history of the cliffs is exciting, with rabbits and other small mammals, birds of prey, and two colours of mesembryanthemums which, knocked back in a hard winter but steadily spread back in good seasons, cover large areas of the cliffs.

However, the coastline can still be viewed from many more parts than those already mentioned. In the far south-west, on the way to Penzance, you glimpse the north coast before running along the south while, if you change at St Erth, you look down on the small harbour of Hayle, handmaiden to the Cornish mining industry and then, from the cliffs, the pure white sand of beaches including that right below today's simplified dead-end single platform at the terminus. Once the *Cornish Riviera* was diverted here on summer Saturdays.

Almost as far away as possible on our mainland, the Far North line runs only a few feet above high water along what might be described as an everyday piece of coast between Golspie and Helmsdale. Here passengers are few and sightseers rare.

The North Wales mainline keeps near to the coast for many miles, with stretches of good scenery, though it is somewhat industrial at the eastern end, where you can spot planes landing and taking off at Liverpool's John Lennon airport, and a big outbreak of caravans around run-down Rhyl. A more exposed section of the line was seriously damaged by a rough high tide some years ago, which has also happened periodically along the west-facing Cambrian Coast. A severe case in the 1930s was repaired by the GWR at incredible speed.

Some of the scenery on this section is spectacular. All the way from Dovey Junction to Pwllheli, salt water is seldom out of mind, if not actually in sight, though one does not run beside the sea proper until after Aberdyfi. There are also glimpses of several of the Little Trains of North Wales, including the Fairbourne miniature railway going off along the sea bank as we veer slightly inland before crossing Barmouth Bridge, over which you really need to walk to make the most of the great scenery including Cadair Idris.

This section has always been difficult and expensive to run. In the 1930s, near Fairbourne, where the railway climbs one of the outliers of the Cadair range, a mail train to Barmouth ran into a landslide. The line is built deep into a cliff, and at 200ft above sea level a section of artificial support for the main road above had given way. The 0-6-0 (one of the last locomotives built for the Cambrian) overturned and fell 80ft onto the rocks below, engine, frame, wheels and tender parting company and the two enginemen being killed. A similar accident had happened here at the beginning of 1883.

I love the section just before Harlech, and the run along the beach at Criccieth, and into Pwllheli itself. You breathe the very spirit of Wales on this trip though, alas, today you can only do it by unit train without the front and rear views from the early Diesel cars. As on so many seaside lines serving resorts, since so many people now take holidays abroad, traffic has greatly declined. Once lengthy trains from both the Welshpool and Ruabon routes, joining at Barmouth Junction, disgorged crowds at Barmouth, and in summer both Porthmadog and Pwllheli enjoyed a daily through service from Paddington and Euston. Yet better any train than none, and staying at Portmeirion there is still fascination in seeing the two cars heading north-east across the very tidal Glaslyn on their roundabout route before, out of sight, they turn sharply west just before Porthmadog.

Until the great simplification of services in recent times, timekeeping was notoriously poor, former writers complaining that nowhere else had they experienced such routine expectation that even expresses from Paddington would be late. I myself recall an unusual lack of *esprit-de-corps* among the staff, for example signalmen not hurrying a token to a train after a delayed crossing and the fireman making no effort to help. A crossing station with only one platform didn't help.

A higher proportion of the Welsh coast is followed by trains than that of either England or Scotland. Waves can be seen from several points along the South Wales main-line, notably around Llanelli, and there is fascinating cliff-top running near Tenby on the Pembroke Dock line.

But for sections of intimacy with the coast, the long loop from Carnforth *via* Barrow-in-Furness and Workington on the periphery of the Lake District takes real beating. For many miles the train is closer to the coast than any road. There is a delightful short section around Grange-over-Sands with its own sea wall and gardens, and beyond Barrow-in-Furness long stretches where the railway hugs the coast, including breathtaking cliff-top sections between Whitehaven, Workington and Maryport, interesting even in their industrial decline.

And so the list goes on, for example with sections of the line from Hull to Scarborough, Hartlepool to Sunderland, the line into Cleethorpes, and on the North Kent line from Whitstable, from Hastings toward Eastbourne to Margate and, above all, under the White Cliffs of Dover between Folkestone and Dover.

Second only in fame to the Sea Wall at Dawlish, the latter shares with it occasional talk of closure because of rising sea levels, weather damage and expensive upkeep, not to mention forced closures in winter storms and cliff falls.

Ireland's best-known section of coastal railway is from Bray to Greystones, now incorporated into the electrified DART (Dublin Area Rapid Transit). Daringly built on, and at one point through the cliffs, it has been nicknamed Brunel's Folly, since a cliff slippage meant it had to be resited slightly further inland and through a new tunnel.

The broad estuaries of the Severn and Humber also offer good views from trains, but except from a rare special, the full glory of the lake-like, tree-lined Fowey estuary can now only be enjoyed by those on china clay trains.

I've no idea how this postcard joined my collection. It was sent by one driver to another: 'Ernest: She ran very well, so fast it was hard to believe the flanges could keep us on the track. I was glad when we got onto the long straight section between Pluckley and Tonbridge. Managed to keep the bowler on all the way. See you down at the sheds.'

What is remarkable is that the vast majority of sea-hugging routes have survived. They were generally well-built early in railway history, while the short branch lines serving resorts came later and have gone. No major well-balanced resort has developed since 1860, Bournemouth being the last to do so. Along the coast as elsewhere, most trends took root early in the Railway Age when among other things it was affordable to build grand hotels whose presence today seems to help beyond the number of guests actually staying in them.

Long lines of stations on routes happening to be by the sea and the short branches to the seaside shared common characteristics. Their traffics were exceptionally seasonal. Staff were used to handling PLA (passenger luggage in advance) and, because coastal communities tend to be spread out, many passengers transferred to or from connecting bus services and taxis. They also nearly all carried Sunday School outings similar to that in my Scene Five earlier in this chapter.

While seaside lines might have shared such characteristics, their characters varied greatly – and especially so among the dead-end branches serving East Anglian resorts. Thus Hunstanton developed as an up-market resort and didn't welcome excursions in its early years, though later the traders protested when the railway itself threatened to withdraw them. Hunstanton still seriously misses its railway, which should possibly not have been closed.

Liverpool Street served great variations for London people going to or staying at the sea . . . from the one-time pair of daily non-stop Pullmans to Lowestoft to camp specials, and (including a change) 'refined' Aldborough and queues of through Bank Holiday excursions to 'vulgar' Southend-on-Sea.

Nor should one forget the contrasts between yesteryear's cross-country lines of the Grouping Era, such as between the Somerset & Dorset Joint which (though Burnham-on-Sea once had many local excursions), wholeheartedly concentrated its long-distance holiday traffic on Bournemouth, and the equally colourful Midland & Great Northern Joint straying into Great Eastern territory to become important though distinctly second best at Cromer and Yarmouth with only a few resorts including Caister-on-Sea to itself.

Some resorts were kick-started by the railways themselves, a good example being the Furness Railway's investment in Grange-over-Sands where a large hotel was built and a large area of land reclaimed from Morecambe Bay to lay out the gardens still much-enjoyed today, though few people perhaps realise their origins. How would planners view such schemes now?

The long branch through thinly populated countryside to Wells-next-the-Sea never had a good service or well-used trains. Only served by occasional all-stations trains, the 43-mile journey was among the least attractive options for Norwich folk to visit the sea. But traffic was still very seasonal and included occasional Sunday School outings and carried fish. Works specials from Norwich and further afield naturally went to Yarmouth. As things developed, successful resorts with good services continually benefited at the cost of places such as Mundesley-on-Sea with its four platforms once served by two separate services from North Walsham but now trainless.

Before its centralisation at a few large ports, fish was carried, if only for a few miles inland adding a welcome addition to the diet for many of the better off. Sending it by passenger train wasn't cheap and shops tended to under-order.

Almost everywhere where there was a harbour, rails were extended to it. Even Wells-next-the-Sea had a branch curving from the goods yard round the town to the harbour.

To cite West Country examples, Teignmouth Old Quay signalbox, already mentioned, opened for a single turn a day, to allow a morning shunt into and alongside quayside tracks. At other times, an ungainly road vehicle nicknamed The Elephant pushed them around. In the age when it was gross revenue that mattered and accountants didn't analyse costs in detail, it is doubtful how profitable much quayside traffic was. Many journeys from port were surprisingly short, in Teignmouth's case some coal literally only a few hundred yards to the local gas works which could only receive by rail. Coal to Dawlish wouldn't have been a great money maker either. And exported ball clay from Teigngrace also had a short and complicated journey.

Little of the china clay exported through Par and (for ocean-going ships) Fowey came far, and the steeply graded Fowey line included Cornwall's longest tunnel with a signalbox at its entrance. Torbay's gas works were rail-served, the coal coming into Kingswear, another steeply graded line and a busy one. Sometimes a coal train crossed a passenger one at Churston which waited to cross the following one, the coal train being quickly parked at Gas House siding.

Rail offered such an advance over horse haulage that such arrangements were entrenched and not questioned, staff and their managers viewing road as evil competition that would lead to job losses. That is until losses were so great that it was panic stations. Beginning in the 1950s, there was a massive withdrawal from quaysides – aided by the fact that many small harbours were losing all or much of their trade. The legacy is sections of track in harbours that put together would stretch many miles. There's even a surviving piece of broad-gauge track beside Plymouth's Sutton Harbour, though the most unusual coastal survivor is a series of isolated pieces of track at angles to today's ever-moving thin spit of land down to Spurn Head, Yorkshire's 'teardrop' hanging at the entrance to the Humber.

The story of old ports is just as interesting as that of their railways. Gentrification has frequently followed waterside trade, such as at Watchet, where the unique West Somerset Mineral Railway (whose 2-mile inclined plane and engine house to work the ropes can still be seen), once brought huge quantities of ore and, later, esparto grass was imported for a local paper-mill. Porthleven, served by pioneer railways, now also has luxury housing lining its quaysides.

That is a reminder that in most areas the earliest railways to reach the coast were short isolated concerns, mainly built by mine and quarry owners. The standard gauge of 4ft 8½in followed coal-carrying lines in Northumberland.

It is only when we see the abandoned railway routes to harbours, often lengthy spurs from the passenger line, and again spot the isolated sections of quayside track that nobody has bothered to reclaim, that the full extent of the seaside railway's goods business is remembered. In most cases, seaside branches ended their lives serving passengers only . . . as do nearly all the surviving lines.

Fish from ports on the Buchan system north-east of Aberdeen was big business. Aberdeen itself was a major fish port, but to see the greatest extent of rail's fall you need to go south, to Hull, where harboursides served by rival routes have again been gentrified with the decorative streetlights that go along with that, or Grimsby where miles of quays themselves have been abandoned, to cite two east coast examples. Grimsby tells an especially sad story, for the port and its fish trade were basically railway inventions run with great skill. Deep sea trawlers mainly bringing in cod often congested the port, whose history is told in its admirable fishing museum.

To consider what fish meant to the railway, let us consider one area in greater detail: the far South West. It shows that Cornish fishing was a poorly organised, purely local industry until 1859 when the Tamar was crossed and fishermen could suddenly command higher

THE
Forth Bridge Railway Company.

The Ceremony of Opening the Bridge will be performed by **H.R.H. The Prince of Wales**, and the Special Train conveying the Party who will accompany His Royal Highness and the Directors, will leave the Waverley Station for North Queensferry at 10.45 o'clock, on the morning of

Tuesday, 4th March 1890, arriving at the Forth Bridge Station at 11.15. The Train will then cross the Bridge, going by Inverkeithing to North Queensferry, whence the party will take boat, in order to view the Bridge from the River.

In the course of the return journey by Train from North Queensferry to the Forth Bridge Station, His Royal Highness, on arrival at the centre of the North Span, will affix the last rivet, and on the South Cantilever End Pier will declare the Bridge open.

Luncheon will be served in the Bridge Model Room at 2 o'clock.

The return Train will leave the Forth Bridge Station for Edinburgh about 4 o'clock afternoon.

Acceptance or otherwise of the Invitation to be present should be addressed as early as possible to the undersigned

G. B. Wieland,

4 Princes Street, Edinburgh.

Morning Dress.

THE FORTH BRIDGE AND RAILWAY.

Total Length of Bridge, including approach Viaducts, 1 mile 1005 yds.

2 Spans,	each 1710 feet
2 ,,	,, 680 ,,
Depth of Main Girders at Piers,	330 ,,
,, ,, at centre,	50 ,,
Width of Bridge at Piers,	120 ,,
,, ,, at centre,	31.5 ,,
Clear Headway for Navigation at High Water,	150 ,,
Deepest Foundation below High Water,	91 ,,
Highest part of Bridge above High Water,	361 ,,
Depth of Water in centre of Channel,	210 ,,
Weight of Steel used in construction,	51.000 tons.

This Card will admit to the Special Train, to and from Edinburgh and North Queensferry Pier, and to the Steamer "John Stirling," and must be presented in order to obtain entrance to the Luncheon Room.

prices. One of the first results of the opening of the Cornwall Railway was riots as fish and meat prices shot up, but things were quickly changed as east coast fleets joined the expanded local ones, especially operating out of Newlyn, near Penzance. By April 1868, _The West Briton_ reported that:

> All day long the fish were being rapidly carted from Newlyn to Penzance and kept the roads, streets and the railway station very busy. The total catch brought in and

despatched was about 115 tons. No less than five thousand baskets of fish were rapidly despatched by three specials and the main train on Friday; and mackerel which that morning swam in shoals 7 or 8 miles south-west of the dreaded Wolf Rock were sold in Billingsgate early on Sunday morning. On the same day 20 tons were sent from Hayle, making the total about 325,000 fish for the night's catch.

By then transhipment from standard to broad-gauge at Truro had become unnecessary since a broad gauge rail had been added. The West Cornwall Railway, including the first part of the Paddington–Penzance route to be built, was originally standard gauge only.

A few years later the Cornish invested in their first steam trawler, and by May 1879 *The West Briton* recorded that not only had the West Cornwall Steamship Company boats expanded trade and brought costs down,

> . . . but the railways pay more attention than ever to the swifter and cheaper conveyance of the mackerel. Never have train arrangements been so good. The price per ton, once over £7.10s is reduced to £4.10s and telegraphic word from Scilly puts Mr J.G. Bone, the alert Station Master, and Mr Ivy, the local head of the locomotive department, on the alert, so that special train after special train may hurry the fish away.

Up to 80 tons of fish had been sent away in a week.

The year before that was written, special cheap fares to the International Fishing Exhibition in London were issued to 'authenticated Cornish fishermen and fisherwomen and curers of fish'. Newlyn has been an exception, never directly rail-connected and still busy.

It was the railway which made fish available throughout the British Isles and steadily made it more affordable. Indeed it could be said that it was the railway that encouraged over-fishing leading to today's declining stocks.

A nightmare to operate, the short-lived Ramsgate Harbour station was popular with those who had the shortest of walks to the beach with its busy kiosks.

For fish or other specialist or general cargoes, the greater the expansion, the greater the retrenchment. The PLA (Port of London Authority) wasn't the only one to own its own locomotives serving an extensive system. Abandoned, what were massive docks are now towered over by the Canary Wharf skyscraper. Dublin's Docklands may be the name of a new commuter station but one can now only imagine the freight traffic handled on miles of sidings. Belfast tells a similar story. Britain's west coast has a tale of many contrasts, from minor ports such as Dinorwic exporting slate brought down by a miscellany of Welsh narrow-gauge and little passenger terminals such as Fairlie Pier off the Largs branch, to the one-time giant passenger terminal and commercial docks of Liverpool, now a shadow of its former self. A determining moment was when Cunard switched from Liverpool to Southampton, where special trains occasionally still reach the waterside.

All three rival railways serving Glasgow had their separate ports and services to the islands, but with Craigendoran and Greenock long gone, Gourock, Wemyss Bay for Rothesay, Ardrossan for Arran and Mallaig for southern Skye remain the only waterside terminals for passenger trains. These days most approach ferries by road and trucks carry the goods straight to the islands. Loads being transferred to Clyde Puffers is a romantic memory immortalised in fiction.

Brighton station and its fine roof with LBSC 0-4-2 B1 No. 172 in September 1919.

Glasgow has many miles of abandoned waterside routes, serving shipbuilding (which long ago virtually ceased) and other industries, particularly at Clyde Bank.

So the list could go on, but pause for a moment to consider the hopes and fears, the rise and decline of employment and general relevance to commercial life with very different traditions and atmospheres that the waterside tracks and the quays they served have experienced over boom times and bust, not to mention war and peace. There is endless fascination behind each terminal, great and small, even comparing how laboriously loads used to be transferred between truck and ship and vice versa by an army of dock labourers whose going on strike would soon bring whole industries to a standstill, and today's container terminal, especially Felixstowe, where few workers are needed to load and unload.

Container trains, those from Felixstowe helped by the lowering of the track through the tunnel at Ipswich and some extended electrification, are the new blood of the railway's specialised port services. After yeoman fights to improve and cheapen services, fish and also cattle and meat business was lost, but container trains are here to stay along with those carrying imported coal while the remains of the great coal export ports of South Wales (once enormously profitable for the GWR) continue to rot or wait for their turn for gentrification. Who in the 1930s could have guessed that Britain would become an importer rather than an exporter of coal?

A memory of a different kind. I was spending the night at Hartlepool and in the evening decided to take a trip along the coast north. Never had I seen such a sight as around and beyond Cemetery North Junction signalbox: overhead cableways, abandoned pits with their own systems and a drunken signal tipped to all clear, trees casting shadows on the cliffs in the setting sun, rough mainline track, still an occasional coal train and a ship leaving harbour, chemical works which had also seen better days, a few remaining visitors in a less than happily placed holiday camp. From on high I looked down on a valley at an oblique angle, to allotments looking more like building sites with their multitude of assorted huts and, more happily, a lone man playing with a dog in a playground at the valley bottom. What a mixture as industry and the railway it served were retreating, the whole area depressed.

The timetable showed that I had to change at a small intermediate station short of Seaham for my last service back, but the signalman (the only person on duty) said he couldn't close the level-crossing gates as my return train had already been signalled. 'You'll not be able to catch it and it's the last one that stops here.' Taxi? Not here! So I prepared to jump onto the track and, when the train stopped, managed to climb up with the help of a rear buffer to join it unseen, once more to witness what I had just come through, but now closer to the viaduct's northern edge, looking down in the twilight on the coal industry's own twilight and waving to the signalman at Cemetery North Junction soon to become redundant along with his box.

I was staying at what had once been a fine railway hotel but, like many in smaller places, was no longer State owned. Mind you, if its industrial eyesores near to the sea that grab you, there are still ample choices in the North East.

So far as the line north of Hartlepool is concerned, you can now enjoy what has become Durham's Heritage Coast – everywhere tourism seems to follow industrial decline – from comfortable through trains to London operated by the Grand Central open-access franchise.

There's a new spirit of enterprise here I could have scarcely imagined on my evening trip. Despite any gloomy forecasts, even manufacturing is fighting back. And that reminds one that much of the seaside railway remains alive, traffic guaranteed by the renaissance of some resorts such as Scarborough and Morecambe where, if nothing like as important as in the 'great days', it still plays a serious role

CHAPTER 11
RAILWAYMEN AND THEIR EMPLOYERS

THIS IS A SAD TALE. While running the extremely pushy joint businesses of David & Charles Publishers and Readers Union Book Clubs, I spent several years of holidays gradually writing an ambitious *Shell Book of Railways*. It was to be a two-part work, a series of general chapters followed by detailed gazetteers, one for each area of Britain divided as in the Regional Railway History series.

Following the buy-out of the shareholding of Hambros Bank, our management was simplified and steadily we created more bestsellers. A pioneer among these happened to be the '150 series' (see pages 158–69 for parts of the introductions of all four). It was good business and good fun, but meanwhile the two-thirds-written *Shell Book* silently rotted. It was a period of rapid change on the railways, and keeping the gazetteers up to date would have become almost as continuous as the legendary painting of the Forth Bridge.

For years, my only copy of the manuscript of pre-desktop computer days has been unseen. Recently I had an urge to reacquaint myself with it. The result is that I have selected this one chapter to see the light of day. I have deliberately resisted the temptation

Chaos at Folkestone Harbour with SE & C crane tank the centre of attention.

to bring it up to date. It rescues just a touch of the grand scheme that – like so many railway ones whose cutting the first sod was celebrated in style but of opening date there was none – ground to an ignoble halt.

*   *   *

THERE is a great respect for the railwayman of yesterday and his many different skills. Everyone remembers colourful characters, and many have stories – going back to broad-gauge days in the West Country – passed down from father to son, or uncle to nephew.

A lad in Newton Abbot locomotive works had his name called out by the visiting superintendent, the famous Churchward, to be congratulated (with a note from the general manager) for reporting track foundations washed away in a nocturnal flood.

Like that of the Methodist minister, the family of the up-and-coming stationmaster spent their lives on the move, a position here for three years, there for four, until maybe a large junction station fell into his lap. Wherever, he was an essential part of the local community; his descendants still display the testimonial he received along with twenty-five guineas on his retirement.

The poaching skills of the ganger were legendary. But what about the old man who broke down unable to stand the pace of his job as sack auditor, tracing the progress and charging for the use of sacks, discussing discrepancies with farmers and infestations of insects with grain merchants? For months he showed interest in the signalbox but did not speak. Eventually he sat with the signalman in his box and, when trust was established, blurted out in tears that he was the signalman responsible for Britain's worst railway accident, at Gretna Green.

The variety of jobs was endless, even within the locomotive sphere. There was the steam raiser (who lit the fire ready for the driver to take the locomotive out hours later), the shed turner (who was authorised to move locomotives from road to road), the fire dropper (who performed his menial task to allow the more expensive fireman to get on his way), the ash loader (who shovelled it into trucks for disposal), the coalman (who manually in smaller depots and with various mechanical aids in larger ones repleted the locomotive's tender or bunker), the sand furnace attendant (who saw all the sand used to help on slippery rails purified through the furnace), the roster clerk (on whose quality of decision depended the wellbeing of all the locomotive men and their families, but who frequently arranged for men to be kept on standby for dreary nocturnal hours before a wheel was turned), and the running shed foreman (sometimes hated or despised, frequently feared, occasionally revered, ever making adjustments to arrangements to keep the show on the road).

Even at a medium-sized country station employing only a dozen men, nearly everyone had his independent life to lead. The hours of the two signalmen might be extended by a four-hour turn put in by a signalman-porter in later years. To begin with, the two signalmen would have kept their box open around the clock without relief, and when the ten-hour day became the rule, a fifth signalman allotted between two boxes would work four hours in one and be allowed two hours to walk to the next before doing four hours there.

The senior porter laboured over the written work in the parcels office and was on hand when the station truck on the local goods stopped outside, usually in mid-morning. The junior porter trimmed and refilled the signal lamps each day, and swept the platforms clean.

As a special privilege he might be allowed to release the daily cage of pigeons in training. The two booking clerks met the passengers and took their money, but spent most of their time doing paperwork. They also handled the parcels traffic when the porters were off duty in the evening and on Sundays.

The stationmaster disciplined the staff and allocated their holidays, canvassed for traffic until this task was specialised in later years, canvassed for advertisements in the railway's tourist guide, and distributed magazines, timetables and traffic announcements, ensured there were adequate wagons on hand for regular and special traffic such as that generated by a cattle fair, paid a daily visit to the station signalbox and to any other between stations that came under his jurisdiction, also visited the goods depot, watched the daily shunt in the goods yard and ensured that visiting locomotive men did not do anything improper on his territory, balanced the books and sent the cash off to the district office in the pre-scribed pouch by the same daily train, ensured that passengers boarded their trains safely, that doors were closed and departures as punctual as possible, and met the visiting officials including inspectors, auditors and vermin controllers.

The goods office was usually 'down the yard', a less glamorous but equally hard-working establishment again with masses of paperwork and anxious moments balancing

SE & C 4-4-0 No. 728 'D' Class heads an express on the trestles under the White Cliffs of Dover.

the books at each month's end. Receipts here probably exceeded those at the booking office, even small stations frequently being the source of quarry or some specialist horticultural, agricultural or manufacturing line. A month's takings would greatly exceed any working man's life's savings. The physical loading and unloading onto the wooden platform in the goods shed was done by the two goods porters, who also got the road delivery vehicles under way.

In later days the lorries probably came from the nearest large town, where vehicle servicing facilities were concentrated long before parcels and goods traffic was itself. The senior of the goods porters also did the coupling and uncoupling in the daily goods shunt, probably early in the morning so that traders could receive their goods from 8.30, having to adjust to the ways of different drivers and guards perhaps every week of the year.

Finally, lengthmen used to walk every mile of track each day, though in later times they'd walk the section on either side on alternate days, riding it on a motorised trolley the other.

Even at a well-regulated station there would be terse moments. The different grades usually kept to themselves. For instance, the goods clerk was less likely to visit the signalbox in twenty or thirty years of service than a visitor spending a weekend in the town. All visitors, including enginemen, guards, track gangs, signalling maintenance gangs, and especially personages from district offices, were regarded with some suspicion and heartily disliked if they messed up the lavatory. Even telegraph and later telephone messages from the district office set stationmasters and clerks in a flutter.

The stationmaster calling up HQ for twenty cattle wagons for Thursday's fair would have no other occasion to use the railway's telephone in the signalbox. If he were allocated a typewriter, it would be a strange instrument outside his experience. He had to use it himself, and the quality of his letters did little to improve his employer's image. His courtesy and friendliness did and, though he might be best pleased when the engine crew were off his beat, he nonetheless enquired after the health of a driver's wife and perhaps commented on some shared gardening or sporting interest. The signalman might ask the driver to carry a newspaper to his colleague at the next box and, if offered hospitality while his goods train was overtaken by a passenger one, the driver might drop a piece of locomotive coal to help the signalman's meagre official allocation.

In all this the staff would be conscious of the social function they were performing. The station was perhaps the town's most important trading establishment. Until the rise of road transport, it was used by all people and goods travelling any distance. It remained the pulse of the local economy for many years longer, at least until the end of the 1940s. The work was hard physically, often mind boggling for poorly educated staff trying to balance the books. Hours were long, and by the 1930s the pay was not keeping pace with what the rest of the world was earning. But all staff could see the purpose of what they were doing and felt valued.

The least fortunate were those working in factory-like conditions at major stations and workshops. They lacked variety of work – and even fresh air. The only advantage they retained over workers at any industrial or commercial establishment was the better guarantee of continued employment and more generous fringe benefits, especially free travel. Their superannuation may seem laughably inadequate by today's standards, but their friends in other industries had none. Their housing was probably better.

Railwaymen were once the elite of industrial society, but their relative position began to decline much earlier than most people realise – well before the end of the nineteenth

LBSC 0-4-2 No. 218 Beaconsfield BI Class at St Leonards.

century. For over a hundred years their loyalty, and the respect in which they were held, had grown ever weaker, though for many there has remained a unique commitment to the interest of the job, if not to the employer. 'Morale is lower than ever before' is thus a statement that could truthfully be made – and often has been – at almost any time from the 1880s to the 1980s. Yet the starting point could hardly have been brighter for, as well as including the best paid workers, railwaymen were the first to experience a whole range of new practices and benefits.

The analysis of what went wrong perhaps reveals the very reason why Britain as a whole has slipped down the league table of industrial nations. It is not a happy story.

The great period of railway expansion came in the aftermath of the Napoleonic Wars and the Reform Act. The age was ripe for innovation. There were also the Enclosure Acts and the New Poor Law of 1834, not to mention the rapidly increasing population, that made labour abundantly available. Across the Irish Sea famine made hundreds of thousands willing to go anywhere to eke out a modest survival, but even within England many went long distances in search of railway work. It was also an age in which the establishment held the military in high esteem and in which revolution and lawlessness that might lead to riots were feared. Thus the directors of the Liverpool & Manchester naturally asked the Duke of Wellington (a great public figure but totally unsympathetic to the social change the railway would unleash) to open the world's first inter-city line. In booking offices up and down the land, the sergeant of police worked alongside the clerk. The constables often came direct from the Army or Navy. Their duties included the first signalling: to this day signalmen are sometimes called 'bobbies'. Down to the 'duty band' above the left wrist, uniforms for the early Great Western staff were based on those of the Metropolitan Police.

Railwaymen were the first civilians to wear uniform at work. The rule books ordered that the uniform be kept clean and neat, and a hundred and one dos and don'ts, with military-like precision. Dismissal for betting or smoking on duty was common, as were fines

South Eastern Railways 'club train' (regular commuters enjoying each other's company) passing Tonbridge.

amounting to a quarter or more of the week's wages for minor misdemeanours. Many railway directors thought about their men in the same kind of way as commanders in the field thought about troops, and indeed the sheer numbers of railwaymen (64,000 in 1851: 100,000 in 1856) in part justified the comparison. The men were cogs in a machine, to do as told, kept under stiff discipline at work and controlled to some extent (certainly as regards drinking) even out of hours.

Even Brunel said he would not pay sixpence in hiring an engineman because of his education. 'It is impossible that a man that indulges in reading should make a good engine driver; it requires a *species of machine*, an intelligent man, a sober man, a steady man, but I would rather not have a thinking man.'

Brunel was wrong, for many enginemen and other railwaymen quickly became the most thinking, the most serious-minded and committed of workers, the proudest of their job and all that was attached to it. Riding on their machines that first carried men faster than the speed of an animal, the drivers in particular enjoyed the full glamour of the new railway, and earned substantially more than they could possibly have expected to do from most local employment. To begin with, drivers were exempt from uniform, and usually wore white fustian, and hats rather than caps. Some were employed on a contract basis, buying their own stores, or gaining bonuses from fuel economy. They were among the first to take advantage of free or cheap travel for themselves and their families – many went to the Great Exhibition of 1851 – and to join friendly societies and other services the paternalistic employers provided.

The Great Western introduced the first railway provident society in 1838, and by 1870 there were fifty, along with temperance societies, sporting societies, musical and arts societies, and numerous facilities for further education. Enginemen were also among the first to benefit from railway housing, provided more liberally and to a better standard than in most industries. Enginemen had to live near their work and theoretically were always on call, there being no neat shift system. Much of the work was physically hard, but the combination of responsibility, interest, good wages and other benefits attracted successive generations of men to follow in each others' footsteps.

Unless he fell foul of the disciplinary machine, it was unheard of for an engine driver to quit for another job. Many of them dreaded retirement. They knew they were lucky and, by historical standards, they were. Drivers of the stage coaches had mainly come from the middle classes and were far better educated, but enginemen were mainly working-class people, many displaced by rapid changes in the pattern of rural life. Never before had nobodies so quickly become eminent somebodies. The value of practical experience was emphasised by the fact that many companies started by importing a nucleus of enginemen from the North East. This also explains why, when everything had to be learnt from scratch, the traditions of enginemen were somehow founded almost on day one.

In an era that anyway encouraged it, there was much desire for self-improvement. 'It would have astonished anyone to have seen, as I did, the material from which engine drivers spring,' said a writer in 1845. Formal training was mixed in quality, but seldom great. Said another: 'It is simply marvellous that, with such a training, we have at the present day such an immense number of worthy men as engine drivers. During my railway career I never recollect an unkind word or act from an engine driver and I contend they are marvels of manufacture.'

In truth they were more marvels of self-discipline and improvement with, for example, a frequent resource to the printed word for information. Something of the same can be said of railwaymen as a whole. From the 1830s, schools were an integral part of every railway settlement – decades before compulsory education. Down to the 1950s, 'railway children' were expected to progress faster at school with better motivation from home.

If enginemen were the kings of the working railwaymen, others still shared in substantial benefits. Again if they did not fall foul of the disciplinary machine, at least those with a skill could expect a job for life, rare in Victorian Britain. In the 1840s an engine driver made between 33s and 45s a week, his fireman from 18s to 33s, porters an average of about 18s 6d, pointsmen rather more, and booking clerks from £50 to £150 annually according to their responsibility. Against this a skilled engineer in Manchester could command only 26s to 33s a week, while farm labourers earned as little as 8s 5d in the south, though rather more in the north. Added to all that, while other available jobs might have remained at the same rate until retirement, the railways offered regular promotion prospects.

Competition for almost all railway jobs was keen, far more lads wanting to become humble porters and gangers than could be accommodated even on a rapidly growing system. 'Your petitioner is anxious to obtain employment as a Porter on your line of Railway,' stated a testimonial from a group of people recommending someone to the GWR. 'We the undersigned inhabitants of the said Parish recommend him as being a sober, honest, industrious person as a candidate for that office; he therefore solicits the kind approval of your honourable company hoping they will be pleased to grant him an early appointment and should he be the object of your choice will no doubt to the utmost of his abilities merit your confidence and approbation in discharging the duties committed to his care.'

In the early 1960s there used
to be a single sleeping car from
Manchester to Plymouth. Though
never greatly used, it was useful
for those with a late-night
appointment returning from the
North to the West. Sometimes,
perhaps after a signing session, I
caught the train from Manchester
itself: electric to Crewe, steam
to Bristol and then Diesel. Other
times, arriving from further north,
I'd wait well past midnight to join
it at Crewe.

It was typical of sleepers
attached to ordinary trains,
carrying mail as well as seated
passengers, in the days before
services speeded up and a night
in bed and early start made them
redundant.

It is worth saying again: many of the first stationmasters and clerks were military men, who had seen service in the Napoleonic Wars. But in addition to employing the first civilians in the countryside to wear uniform, the railways soon broke from tradition in employing almost wholly *working* men, and promoting entirely from within the ranks. 'I wrote to London to learn what situations a Railway afforded for *Gentlemen* to fill,' said a promoter of a West Country branch anxious that his son took up a career; he would have received a disappointing answer, if one at all. Branwell Brontë's famous appointment as assistant clerk at Sowerby Bridge was seen as letting the family down.

Promotion from the ranks was great for those who benefited by it, but it had its cost. For one thing, nearly all grades of railwaymen *struggled* to get on top of their job. Taking heavier trains faster and faster taxed ingenuity as well as physical strength. Coordinating staff hundreds of miles apart has never been perfected. And even the most menial clerical jobs were infernally complicated. 'It was like an immense schoolroom, only the boys had whiskers and most of them were out at elbows and all looked miserably thin', wrote Ernest J. Simmons in his life of a stationmaster on the accounting offices. 'Moreover they were all standing to write, and the bundles of paper before each were enough to turn each poor fellow's heart.'

The red tape even from the earliest days of railways was endless. Why was that truck routed such-and-such a way? But market tickets are not available on Tuesdays. Does consolidation apply? Balancing the accounts, even getting the petty cash right before the next inspection, involved headaches and midnight oil. You did not necessarily have to be on the fiddle to fail to satisfy the auditors. Promoted stationmaster in 1879 in place of a man who could not balance his books, Simmons looked back on a long railway career. He gives us an interesting glimpse of what promotion from within was doing to the railways:

> With all due respect to stationmasters of the present day, I beg to say that a stationmaster at a small station was then a personage of much greater importance in the estimation of the public than he is now. It was a new thing, and clerks and stationmasters were for the most part supplied from the middle class of society, and able to hold their own in a gentlemanly way; whereas, at the present day, they are, for the most part, descendants of the porters and policemen, who, having been educated at the British and Free Schools, have been drafted into the Telegraph Office, and thence to the clerks' appointments. There is nothing sharpens the wits of a lad like a telegraph office, but it cannot be expected that the associations of their homes will make them conversant with the habits and manners of gentlemen. Consequently when these young men become stationmasters they also become 'Jacks in Office', and have seriously injured the old friendly feeling which existed between the public and the officials.

The stationmaster could not hold his own socially or academically with the schoolmaster and parson. Having battled up the promotion scale the slow and hard way, he was unlikely to help younger men of quality take short cuts. Often ill at ease, he was apt to take refuge in red tape. It was perhaps the strict adherence to promotion through the ranks – broken only marginally by the North Eastern Railway and the LNER before management trainees became the vogue after nationalisation – that led to the railways being inward looking. Even most senior officers had joined immediately after leaving an ordinary school, and spent years doing mundane jobs that would have been unbearable to anyone of wider horizons.

Southampton Town with the LSWR's large hotel which still stands but has long been offices and includes the BBC's studios.

The railway and its rules and regulations were people's total lives – and the railway meant just that, one's own line, others being seen as inferior. Except after amalgamation, and in a few cases following disputes, rarely did staff move from one line to another. Companies suffered from a chronic inability to adopt the best parts of each other's policies and practices. Common sense, and looking after the customer, often gave way to ensuring that rules were obeyed to the letter . . . so that if a piece of machinery were loaded at the wrong end of a train, the stationmaster would delight in refusing to allow it off at his station. Throughout the country, every moment of the day, railwaymen were preaching rules – and economy – to one another. Check that there are no partridge nests before setting fire to grass. Cover ink bottles when not in use. Use both sides of blotting paper. Turn out half the lights when the moon shines: route traffic this way. Charge for it on that basis. Ensure there is an adequate minimum load.

Yet if anyone wanted practical advice about a new or unusual problem, he would be hard put to find it. For it was management by precedent, and inspiration was as threatening to those who had been promoted by the system as the literate engine driver had been to Brunel.

Isolationism went even further. Different kinds of railwaymen largely kept themselves to themselves in their own private worlds. Especially private was the world of the signalman, notably in cabins remote from pedestrian movement even on the lines leading out of big city stations.

Nothing sums up the ritualistic side of the railway better than the scene of an engine driver with oil-stained overalls and boots covered in coal dust knocking on the signalbox door, waiting patiently for an invitation inside and then apologetically hopping across the polished floor, perhaps handing the signalman a clean rag by way of peace offering. The

Signals as they used to be even on busy routes near to London.

rules said he had to make the visit, but the two men were as ill at ease as had they come from different continents. Even their lingo was different.

There were of course many fine men in senior positions as well as engine drivers, guards and signalmen, but they knew their place, and excellent work though they might do within it, they were usually unable to use initiative to break through the ritual and secure a better overall deal for staff or customers. The traffic manager, engineer, solicitor, accountant, they each kept to their own, and on most companies all were remote from the directors. The board of course consisted of gentlemen, appointed in most cases as part of a portfolio of experience and service to the community, military men and those from finance always prominent.

The system grew and became more complicated. Procedures grew and became more complicated, too. The number of staff also rose so that the railways became the nation's second largest employer (in 1913 there were roughly a million coal miners and three quarters of a million railwaymen) yet there were always more people wanting to join the service than could be accommodated.

Though on some lines 'memorials' from the staff were heeded, on others anyone complaining, about wages or anything else, was invited to hand in his notice. The law of supply and demand being allowed to operate without effective union intervention, the wages of the 1870s were still very much as they had been in the 1840s. Conditions as a whole had worsened. Once the system stabilised in size, promotion became slower. Traffic grew but, especially after the depression of the 1860s, a stronger case had to be made for an extra pair of hands. The average railwayman was thus much busier and without the excitement attached to his earlier status. Pettymindedness was also more common, again those who had come up the hard way not naturally wanting to give an easier life to successors. Having had time to catch their breath, the employers sought greater productivity wherever they could. Fewer firemen were promoted to drivers, but at busy times had to drive on firemen's wages. At many stations clerks routinely worked sixty hours a week. Signalmen more frequently found themselves without a relief at the end of their turn of duty and had to soldier on a further ten or twelve hours. 'Railway sheds now resemble contract premises,' wrote a railway blacksmith at Swindon. 'Piece-work rates are cut to the lowest possible point, it is all push, drive and hustle.'

To be sure, worse examples of exploitation could be found in most other Victorian trades, and on the credit side the railways continued to pioneer 'fringe benefits' for their loyal staff. They encouraged attendance at Mechanics Institutes and with the men contributed to retirement, accident and widows funds, making it even less likely that men would quit the railways, except for those who took their skills with them to start new lives overseas.

In the North West, by 1850, many railwaymen were regular visitors to Blackpool and Southport. In 1870, still before the first official Bank Holiday, the Great Northern Railway gave a week's holiday a year, unheard of for most working men. Other railways followed, also increasing privilege tickets for employees and families. Soon Swindon and other works towns emptied for a week each year when emigrés from all parts of the system renewed contact with home. Many works also had their annual outings as another means of encouraging staff loyalty. A flag-bedecked train, taking the men and their families to a supposedly secret destination, left at crack of dawn. A wicker basket full of goodies, covered with a white cloth, was in the crook of mother's arm. Children could scarcely repress their excitement, and dads showed off their knowledge. Workers from other industries looked on jealously.

There was much to be said for being a railwayman, but even things like improved housing could not hold back a growing discontent about work and wages. The public steadily became aware that railwaymen were frequently being overworked, and that safety sometimes suffered as a result. 'Eight hours of continuous duty at very busy signal cabins and twelve hours in any signal cabin, are sufficient; but periods of eighteen, twenty-five and even thirty-seven hours, for which men have been known regularly or periodically employed, principally during exchange of duty, once in two, seven or thirteen weeks, are inexcusable,' said an 1871 official report to the Board of Trade on accidents. Reports of the Board's railway inspectorate, written with what the railway historian Jack Simmons delightfully describes as 'an Olympian candour, sparing neither the shortcomings of the men nor, on occasion, the harshness of their employers' increasingly showed that all was not well.

It was all this coupled with low wages that really hurt. Wages had been behind all but one of the ten short, local strikes that took place between 1830 and 1870, the first involving drivers on the Liverpool & Manchester shortly after its opening and quickly squashed. Early attempts to unionise met great opposition. In 1866 a newly formed Engine Drivers & Firemen's United Society, demanded a ten-hour day, payment for overtime and time-and-a-half for Sunday work. Five of the larger companies agreed, but the London, Brighton & South Coast and the North Eastern would not. Strikes took place. Several men went to prison. The North Eastern sacked all 1,000 plus striking drivers and firemen and replaced them permanently.

Unionisation was hampered both by sectionalism within the industry, which even in our own day can cause problems, and by the belief that essential services should be immune from strike action. 'You might as well have trade unionism in Her Majesty's Army as have it in the railway service. The thing is totally incompatible,' was a typical director's view. Considerably later, G.J. Churchward, the GWR's revered locomotive superintendent, wrote to the secretary of a sectional board: 'If you and those you represent are not satisfied with the conditions in my department, I shall be pleased to receive your notices.' Bosses intended to remain bosses. Firing employees continued on some lines well into the twentieth century.

Unsuccessful in direct approach, railwaymen thus concentrated their attack on public opinion and Parliament. Here they were luckier. As early as 1871 *The Times* pointed out that, while it was not among those who normally supported combination or strikes, 'we confess that a great part of the excessive labour exacted from railway servants might have been avoided or mitigated if railway servants, like other skilled workmen, had known how to combine for the purpose of bargaining with their employers'.

Talk about combination was increasingly in the air, but depended on public opinion to progress. The employers argued that profits were declining, and stiffened their attitude further after 1888 when the Government began to control freight rates. The Board of Trade encouraged the railways to discuss working conditions more openly with their employees, but to little avail. Grievances were increasingly aired in the Press and in Parliament, but even when proved wrong or ridiculed, the management held firm, dismissing any who dared to step out of line. It was this extreme opposition that led naturally moderate men (including many non-conformists) toward socialism. Two events involving the Amalgamated Society of Railway Servants (ASRS) gave particular impetus.

The ASRS, with a strong non-conformist membership in the lower-middle-class self-improvement ethic, was mainly concerned about things like sickness, unemployment and death, declaring itself opposed to strikes. But its demand for a ten-hour day inevitably took it to conflict. In 1890 it had a quick, successful local strike against the prosperous coal-carrying Taff Vale Railway in South Wales. Afterwards, relationships between union and railway were good until a new general manager, Ammon Beasley, appeared on the scene. He wanted to maintain the Taff as one of Britain's most profitable railways, and overworking the men led to a series of strikes, ending in a complete shut down in August 1900. Though the men were forced back to work on the same terms and conditions as before the strike, Beasley agreed to the establishment of a conciliation board and dropped the case against some of the strikers for picketing offences.

On the last day of the strike, however, a judge gave an injunction against the union's leaders which threw doubt on the legality of picketing, generally accepted since an Act of 1875. The Court of Appeal reversed the decision, but the House of Lords upheld it. Beasley sued for damages and was awarded £42,000 against the union. The strike weapon was defused, temporarily, but the Taff Vale Judgement roused public opinion. The Liberals, with prompting from the growing newly named Labour Party, reversed it by the Trade Disputes Act of 1906, giving unions legal immunity in all civil cases.

Barnstaple Junction in LSWR days.

In 1909, a porter who was a member of the Walthamstow Liberal Association succeeded in obtaining a judgement named after him, the Osborne Judgement, preventing the ASRS using its funds for political purposes. But again it backfired, the Trade Union Act of 1913 allowing unions to set up a political fund with the famous right to 'contract out'. Meantime the inevitable conflict had happened. After a threat in 1907, the first national railway strike took place in 1911. It was a bloody affair – literally since two Welsh protestors were killed by troops, damaging the reputation of Winston Churchill (then Home Secretary) for the rest of his life. The railways still refused to recognise or meet the unions until forced to do so; and when the unions said they wished to discuss certain points arising from a Royal Commission's report, the railway again refused. Public opinion was now very largely behind the men, and ultimate settlement was grudgingly reached and even more grudgingly implemented.

Things were never going to be quite the same. By now there were 600,000 railwaymen, and improved organisation clearly meant that the balance of power had changed. Trade Union membership grew rapidly.

A national strike threatened for late 1914 was only averted by war, when railwaymen patriotically gave their best. Nearly a third of the labour force went to the front, and those who stayed behind handled unprecedented workloads. Every effort was made to maintain schedules and smartness until the latter days of the war, when just keeping the wheels turning was challenge enough. The hours worked were often beyond human endurance, particularly on lines such as the Highland Railway, where there was an especially sharp increase in the wartime traffic. Men sometimes worked around the clock, their tiredness endangering life and limb. There were inevitably many breakdowns, human and mechanical, but (apart from the terrible crash at Gretna Green) serious crises were avoided, and everyone agreed it was a magnificent effort. Railwaymen were temporarily restored to a high position in the public's esteem.

It did not, however, stop the demand for better pay and conditions. The eight-hour day was granted before the end of the war, to take effect afterwards. The second national strike occurred in September 1919, less than a year after the end of hostilities, and from the railwaymen's point of view was highly satisfactory. It was detonated by the enginemen, but they then solidly lent their support to railwaymen as a whole. For the only effective time in the whole of railway history, there was unity based on class lines, fired by a common sense desire for fairness. The strike resulted in an entirely new outlook, the companies no longer being able to ignore the unions.

Yet it was too late. The great railway age was already over. The age of the problem railway had begun, with a low level of economic activity, and the growing competitiveness of road transport as many returning soldiers had nothing better to do with their gratuities than buy a lorry or bus. Nationalisation was on the cards; Churchill said he was in favour in a pre-election speech. Instead, the railways were 'grouped' into the big four, creating in the LMS the largest commercial organisation in the world.

Ilfracombe station high above the resort it served.

Now the price had to be paid for past neglect. With imagination and less red tape, the railways should have entered the era of road competition leaner and more virile. But initiative of all kinds had been killed, and thousands of jobs that it would have made sense to mechanise, had labour commanded decent wages throughout, were still there to be done manually – by men who now worked only a third of the clock. The rigid hierarchical structure had sadly eliminated flexibility and common sense in many important areas of operation, and the insistence of maintaining their tight individuality in virtually everything that could be made or conducted differently eroded the benefits of Grouping. A surprising degree of loyalty to the old railways – to the railway as a railway, not so much to it as business or employer – was still retained. It was inevitably largely killed as the old liveries of over 100 companies disappeared and instructions began arriving from high places in distant parts – from England for the first time in the case of all Scottish and some Welsh lines.

Rapid change inevitably brought visible waste and that, combined with an enforced wage cut, brought morale tumbling down, never totally to be restored. From now on many railwaymen abandoned any expectation of enlightened management and conditions, though in many cases remaining committed to the interest and responsibility of their job. The engine driver saw himself working for society, enjoying the responsibility of taking 500 tons at speed through the night, and was proud if he made up lost time. He distinctly did not do it for his employers as such. The exception was the Great Western, the only one of the four 1923–47 companies substantially to be made up of a previous entity with continuous management, and always in the forefront of social development.

Things were made a great deal worse by the 1926 General Strike (two years after a damaging locomotive men's dispute called by ASLEF). The employers saw it as a quite unnecessary act of disloyalty. The men were less clear in their ideas than in 1919 and ended poorer instead of better off as they had been then. The public at large was no longer behind them, the middle classes going to tremendous efforts to demonstrate that the nation was indeed no longer so dependent on rail. In 1911 and 1919 many men, notably of more senior ranks like chief clerks and stationmasters, had stayed at their jobs and afterwards strikers and non-strikers had regained harmonious working relations. Companies like the GWR sent cards bearing the general manager's signature by way of thanks for such loyalty, and did so again in 1926.

They were not so treasured; everything had turned sour. While the companies marked the cards of those who had 'remained loyal' the unions never forgave 'blacklegs' some of whom were ostracised for the rest of their working lives, in some cases, such as at Neasden, until well into the 1950s. The stigma was especially painful in those tight-knit railway communities serving isolated junctions or works in small towns.

Though generally railwaymen became readier to use negotiating machinery, in some places men were also set against men by the Railway Vigilance Movement of 1934. With evangelical zeal, the Vigilantes protected the rights of the men, starting with engine cleaners, against the petty despots in charge of depots who tried to save money by eroding agreements (and who were congratulated by the higher management if successful). In some depots, knowing your rights became more important than knowing the road.

Slow promotion, lack of appointments for apprentices completing workshop training, short-time working, especially in the works producing locomotives and rolling stock, make do and mend, branch lines opened for shorter hours and some closing entirely, and redundancies for around 100,000 workers: that was the mixture for much of the 1920s and 1930s.

In truth, there should have been many more redundancies, since the best hope of long-term prosperity lay in greater productivity through mechanisation. Even with technology as it then existed, perhaps a quarter of a million workers could have been laid off with scant loss of traffic in the two decades.

In many people's minds the definition of a railway remained 'source of employment', and harsh though many economies were at the local level, the boards of directors would have thought it outrageous to set such a pace. They were, after all, committed to buying British even if it did not make selfish economic sense. So large-scale Dieselisation, using imported fuel, was out of the question even when the USA was showing what economies could be made. The Southern, however, made good progress with electrification.

It was a conservative period, change feared rather than accepted, the Government theoretically supporting the railways against competition, though in practice much traffic was lost. So most branch lines continued to operate with exactly the same arrangements as though the parallel buses had not drawn off many of their passengers. 'Mechanical horses' were grudgingly accepted as better than animals in making deliveries outside city centres (where many real horses continued to be employed until the 1950s). Little was done to rationalise the bulk-carrying role of the railway and the use of road transport where it would have been more effective. The railway was legally common carrier, and throughout the land staff were busily engaged carrying things at a loss that could perfectly well have been sent by other means, or discouraged by charging a true price. The railway was still essentially Victorian.

To be sure some changes were made. Bigger engines to carry heavier loads at higher speeds over longer distances were the greatest manifestation. While Stanier was introducing the use of pre-fabricated parts at Crewe and Derby, most of these locomotives – certainly the LNER's streamliners – were entirely hand made. They represented the very best of British, and for the chosen few drivers renewed pride in the job. They were forever in the public eye, for the publicity departments were coming into their own. Never before or since have the railways been so well publicised as they were in the 1930s. It was mainly varnish, for under the surface the cracks were beginning to show. The low state of morale on lines that had been absorbed into the new giants could be gauged by the growing griminess of the locomotives. In independent days the Highland's engines had always been kept immaculately smart, but in their new unwelcome liveries were now allowed to collect dirt. Restaurant car stewards who had once almost grovelled canvassing trains to ensure an adequate level of business could no longer be relied upon not to take an off-hand attitude.

And so back into war, a surprisingly railway war, largely because of the scarcity of imported fuel for road vehicles. Strategically Britain had been right not to Dieselise but the system was already suffering from a backlog of maintenance (though there had been some slight catching up with a higher level of activity and some Government loans especially for electrification in the 1930s). Morale was at best mixed. Again railwaymen grasped the challenge, performing many noble deeds. This time they were often in the front line, and very much part of the successful evacuation from Dunkirk and the landings in Normandy.

The blackout increased accidents, great and small. Civil engineering staff were perpetually on call to replace bomb damage. Many Home Guard units were raised specifically for railway purposes. The expertise of railway staff in ambulance work and first aid was also of great importance.

Shunting operations in confined yards in the pitch dark were especially hazardous, though nobody welcomed skies lit up by incendiaries and their fires, and moonlight

A reminder of the in-fighting there was between the rival railways packed onto the Isle of Wight.

increased the chances of attack. Touch and sound, already highly developed among foot-platemen, gangers and shunters, became an alternative to sight on the long foggy night of duty all over industrial Britain. Glamour quickly went out of the passenger side, the fewer trains being excessively long and often late after delays and diversions. They were worked by engines that had to be flogged mercilessly and fired with poor to indifferent coal by crews who lived in constant danger. Guards and ticket collectors did their best to climb over recumbent forms, extract tickets and excess fares by dim blue lamplight and cope with frequent emergencies. Railwomen undertook a greater range of tasks, such as cleaning firetubes and signalling, than in 1914–18, and this time many stayed on, though some areas such as signalboxes returned to being male preserves when peace returned.

Again railwaymen went up in the public's esteem, and remained popular, thanks to things like the role they played in keeping fuel supplies going in the cruel winter of 1947, when East Coast storms on top of basic coal shortages produced emergency conditions. The number of wagons cleared on special weekend openings of freight yards merited news bulletin coverage.

A new era was enthusiastically ushered in with the sounding of every whistle and hooter with enough steam to blow it on 1 January 1948. Nationalisation, considered by Gladstone, and actually legislated in 1844, had become a reality. Expectations were genuinely high. Disappointment followed. Then despair. Change once more took its toll as loyalties were broken without anything immediately to take their place, other than a vague delight in public ownership. Unfortunately the change continued, since the nation failed to discover how best to operate the system and chopped and changed the governing bodies and regional boundaries. Yet the underlying conservatism remained.

British Railways inherited 640,000 staff, only 15 per cent fewer than at Grouping in 1923, demonstrating how much the system was still being operated in the Victorian manner. Despite streamlining, suburban electrification and some colour-light signalling, a few more marshalling yards and some new rolling stock, most signalmen worked manual boxes and most trains were of geriatric stock, hauled by steam locomotives manned by driver and fireman. Shunting was still largely a manual operation, dependent on the skill of a man with a long pole who linked wagons together with a deft flick. The ubiquitous little steam shunter was only slowly being replaced by single-manned Diesels. Goods trains were largely loose-coupled, slow and ponderous in operation, needing to stop to pin brakes down by hand before descending an incline, and requiring frequent sorting as they meandered across country. Damage to goods was frequent. Wheeltappers at major junctions were essential to see that wagons and carriages were fit to continue their journey. Much track maintenance was also manual, crowbars, sledgehammers and callipers plus many pairs of strong arms being the main equipment.

The steam railway, with over 20,000 iron horses and still many flesh-and-blood ones too, was a labour-intensive system which even at peak traffic was scarcely capable of breaking even. The jobs to be done were usually dirty, often undertaken in appalling conditions. In the post-war boom years go-ahead youths naturally looked elsewhere. For the first time in peace, there were staff shortages. Even the security that railway employment had traditionally given counted for little. The shortages were reflected in the dirty engines, stations and carriages. And while freight yards remained choked with traffic waiting to move, it was already clear that much of the better-class business was being lost to road.

Modernisation did not begin in earnest until 1954, and was too late and too badly ordered (especially with the railways remaining a political football with numerous changes of policy and management structure) to do much for general morale. Certain groups, such as drivers of the electrics out of Euston, could take renewed pride in their job. Certain elite groups, notably the accountants and the signal engineers, flourished, the latter apparently immune from the normal commercial pressures applied by the former as they installed unnecessarily elaborate systems for traffic densities of their imagination. University graduates enjoyed playing a role for the first time, under the management trainee scheme already mentioned.

Most railwaymen now enjoyed an improved standard of living with pay rises well above inflation and, in an age of labour shortage, massive overtime was worked. But this did not prevent a further drop in morale on the job and growing anxiety about the future. It was clear that labour-saving schemes that had been shelved for years would now have to be implemented, and such were the mounting losses that numerous branch lines were closed, freight services rationalised and steam power replaced by Diesel. So much curtailment of the labour force within so short a period was bound to cause pain and grief, but most railwaymen would say there has also been considerable unnecessary agony – caused by changes of policy, management by people who did not really understand their jobs or who were more intent on courting favour than acting professionally, and by the increasing anti-railway lobby.

The decline has been uneven, less rapid in the big cities but more so in rural areas where a railway career had been especially respected, and promotion prospects have always been bleaker. Tens of thousands of families whose men went to work for the railway, generation by generation, now found themselves many miles from the nearest station or depot. Closures affected the quality of life for countless retired railwaymen, unable to meet socially, see the latest in locomotives or rolling stock pass through their own town, or take advantage of free travel.

Morale became lower than ever, though since 1926 the strike record has been surprisingly good. Lack of confidence, investment, sparkle . . . whatever the reason, the outlook for railwaymen was not good until privatisation coincided with growing passenger traffic compensating for the loss of most freight. Today things are different, many drivers for example doing a stretch of railway work in a mixed career. But the elite of express drivers still take great pride in their work. And the railway is still a railway; that is to say it goes from place to place with its own specialist track, along which there is a unique comradeship and a great sense of history and purpose.

No group of workers talks more about the past than do railwaymen, an increasing minority of whom are railway enthusiasts themselves. Some youngsters only offer their services on that premise, combining hobby and career, even if realising they could earn more money elsewhere. A special greeting to those railwaymen, especially those who are reading and even bought this book.

An 1880s view of Yeovil Town, a joint station at the end of a short LSWR branch from Yeovil Junction and intermediate stations on the GWR's Taunton–Yeovil Pen Mill branch.

PHOTOGRAPHY BY BERNARD MILLS

Bernard Mills is a West Country photographer I've known since he was in his young teens. He has the railway bug badly, and spends all his holidays 'chasing' trains, while he devotes many evenings to giving slide shows and with a locally legendary Christmas one – or to improving old photographs digitally. Here is a selection of some of his favourites, including of many things that have long disappeared. Incidentally, he has been personally most helpful over the years, for example supplying the last picture of a quarry line, on page 139.

BELOW *The sun has just come out, the steam engine is heading north, and is on the last lap towards the summit cutting at Shap. Black 5 44920 is working hard with the morning parcels from Crewe to Carlisle on 22 July 1967. He says: 'To me, this is the sheer beauty of Shap, lonely, remote and what a location to see and photograph steam at work. Those of us who had the privilege of walking the paths of the green fields of Shap in search of steam were indeed fortunate. Within six months steam would be a just memory, within a decade the line electrified and the M6 motorway constructed, changing the scene forever.'*

RIGHT *Carlisle Citadel in December 1967, just two weeks before steam ceased serving the border city. Black 5 44910 is simmering away under the South footbridge, which linked the Maryport and Carlisle bays. 'There seems to be steam coming out from the engine everywhere it should and shouldn't.'*

BELOW *The country railway, where time stood still, is recalled in this picture of a Diesel unit on its way from Bere Alston to Callington crossing the road at Latchley with the Upper Tamar Valley as a backdrop. No yellow lines, no barriers, a red telephone box. A fortnight later the Gunnislake–Callington section of the Light Railway closed (October 1966).*

ABOVE *It is hard to believe that Newton Abbot once looked like this: D1012 Western Firebrand heads west with the 2.30pm Paddington to Penzance on 28 April 1971. D1012 and its train occupy what is now only one of the three remaining running lines here. The other two which remain are either side of the train. The power station in the background closed not long after, the shed and carriage sidings would be gone by the 1980s and the track severely rationalised and manual signalling abolished in 1987. Once Newton Abbot had four signalboxes. What remains is now controlled from Exeter. The signal gantry is that by the offices of David & Charles. See Chapter 7 for more of Newton Abbot.*

LEFT *Before Sprinters took over, type 2s held the sway, on the scenic line to Kyle of Lochalsh and trains were very traditional, in summer one having an ex-Devon Belle observation car. On 25 September 1982, 2602 crosses Loch a Chuilinn with the 11.10am Kyle of Lochalsh to Inverness as the autumn colours manifest themselves.*

ABOVE *On St Valentine's Day 2001, a combination of a beautiful spring day, hardly any wind and a high tide came together for Bernard for this shot of 153 370 heading over the Tamar with the 10.20am Gunnislake to Plymouth.*

RIGHT *On 27 March 2007 as part of a series of 'Branch Line Week' steam hauled specials, this was the first time in forty-two years that a steam-hauled train ran on the former Southern mainline between St Budeaux. The spring morning sunshine lit up the incoming tide, and with hardly a whiff of wind the still water. Says Bernard: 'Not long after Black 5 returned from Bere Alston to provide a gem of a photo without getting stuck in a Scottish bog, or climbing a remote hill in Yorkshire, but just down the road from home.' No. 45407 is crossing Tamerton Lake Viaduct with 9.05am Bere Alston–Plymouth Friary Special on 27 March 2007.*

Mountain, moor and loch come together at Loch Dubh. The literal translation from Gaelic is The Black Loch. No. 76001 puts on a dramatic show with a photo charter on 9 October 2008. Such trains provide an opportunity to reach places on this line either inaccessible or a long walk over boggy ground from a nearby road. Careful planning has brought the photographers and the train here at 8.40am, at the right time of day for the sun which duly obliged.

*Dutch elm disease in Spring 2010
caused wholesale tree cutting by the
Forestry Commission in the Glynn Valley.
Locations were opened up which had
not been available for over forty years,
making possible this view of Largin
Viaduct, seen with 66 612 with the
6C59 11.00 Burngullow–Hackney Sand,
a train usually running once or twice
a week. The train actually runs in two
parts, this being the first. On arrival at
Hackney yard at Newton Abbot, the
engine deposits its train and returns
Light Engine to pick up the second part,
due to leave Burngullow at 5.45pm.
Weight limits on the Royal Albert Bridge
and the steepest gradients now behind,
the combined train heads on to London.*

LEFT *Happy outcome from a photo charter on the Isle of Wight on 16 November 2010, with the newly overhauled last remaining 02 W24 Calbourne. On a misty morning, Bernard waited at Ashey Crossing for the sun to rise, and conditions were perfect. The train, so typical of the line since the 02s first arrived on the island almost eighty years ago, the right line, the right engine, the right stock and for a moment, an instance of pure magic. Says Bernard: 'Such luck doesn't happen often.'*

RIGHT *A 'King' on its way to Plymouth, 6024 in full flight at Ufton Crossing with the Flying Dutchman Rail Tour 08.15 Paddington to Plymouth, 9 November 1996.*

BELOW *The Great Western country branch line scene does not really get any better than this view of the South Devon Railway. At one of my favourite locations, 1369 ambles beside the River Dart at Dartington Hall with the 15.45 Buckfastleigh–Totnes on 11 March 2012.*

OVERLEAF *Early on an Autumn morning, a stunning view of the newly restored GWR Rail Motor No. 93 pulling away from Terras Crossing towards Looe with 2Z20 08.30 Liskeard–Looe.*

CHAPTER 12
65 YEARS OF RAILWAY WRITING
(3: 1984–2011)

THREE 1950S JOURNEYS

From The Great Days of the Southern Railway, *1992.*

EXMOUTH–BOURNEMOUTH

A steady trickle of travellers arrive at Exmouth's red-brick 1920s station, a handsome Southern rebuilding, and all four platforms are in use. The 9.42 and 9.49 arrivals from Tipton St John and Exeter Central have disgorged shoppers and day trippers, we are due away at 9.52 and four minutes later there is a departure for Central. We had been tempted to take the latter to enjoy the run along the Exe and it actually gives the shorter time to up-country, but we settle for the daily Waterloo through coach. The scene is dominated by those ex-LBSC tanks whose shrill whistles frighten passengers at Exeter St David's and still feel out of place in this part of the world.

Ours is a standard Maunsell coach, half full; the two ex-LSWR coaches only have a couple of passengers between them. Though this is the only through train to anywhere except on summer Saturdays, there is no departure ceremony, but the tank engine works

Climbing from King Tor Halt to the highest point on the GWR at Princetown.

hard crossing the long red-brick viaduct and climbs until we are almost on the cliffs at Littleham. The long rake of the summer Saturdays Exmouth–Cleethorpes service rests in the refuge siding.

Climbing again on one of the last pieces of railway to be built in Devon, we reach the summit and drop through a deep cutting into Budleigh Salterton, where we cross a down train and where the Mogul of the daily goods is shunting. Rush hour! Two very Budleigh Salterton ladies claim their reserved seats, talking plummily without acknowledging our existence. Over a tall viaduct and we are in the Otter Valley, the next station being East Budleigh though it is actually Otterton. The LSWR had too many stations beginning OTT, so it was said, but caused total confusion by first calling this Budleigh and naming Budleigh Salterton just Salterton.

Four minutes smart running brings us to Newton Poppleford, served by all ten daily stoppers each way but missed by occasional summer Saturday extras, including a Waterloo service that starts at Littleham for the campers. Now Tipton St John and a daily ritual that is always enjoyable. Normally the Exmouth train goes into the yard so the locomotive can run round free of the running lines, but our engine leaves us in the up platform. We look out and see the Sidmouth train descending almost mountain-rail style before we are pulled back the way we came. The Sidmouth train takes our place. The engine we have just given up shunts our coach to the other London-bound Maunsell coach and sets back the other two coaches into the down platform to form a local to Sidmouth.

Ottery St Mary, whose locals have a choice of two through coaches to Waterloo, is our only stop before we abandon the Otter for a run across the fields to Sidmouth Junction (now Feniton), arrive 10.45, 16¼ miles so far.

Thoughts have already been given to the origins of the train we are about to be joined to. It should have left Central 10.30, a few minutes after the arrival of the Exmouth train that left after us, and have through coaches from Torrington and Ilfracombe (joined at Barnstaple Junction) and Plymouth, its refreshment car – we fear it will be a Bulleid Tavern job you cannot see out of – added as the Plymouth and North Devon sections were put together at Central with precision timing. The service offers a huge range of journey options. Torrington and Ilfracombe coaches both started at 8.10, a Bude–Okehampton connection into the Plymouth section will have started, almost before we were up, at 7.58; a third 8.10 departure was the single coach Launceston–Halwill connection into this – while the Plymouth section set off from Friary only five minutes later at 8.15. And running ahead of us up the mainline to Templecombe and serving all but one of the intermediate stations will be the 9.33 stopper from Central carrying the through carriage from Seaton we will eventually pick up. It all runs like clockwork daily, an intricate system of through coaches and locals, every one of which has to perform to avoid delaying the vital London service. Only on summer Saturdays do things sometimes go awry.

A Merchant Navy pulls short into the up platform punctually at 10.48. It is allowed five minutes to pull forward, cross the down main to pick us up in the bay and take us over to be the first two coaches of a lengthy train. It is done smartly but unfussily, and people from all over the West Country who have endured frequent stops and shunts relax in the knowledge that smooth high-speed travel is about to begin – seven minutes before the *Atlantic Coast Express* that detaches the Sidmouth and Exmouth daily through coaches leaves Waterloo: we imagine the scene. There is great contrast between locals that utterly reflect the deep countryside they serve and carry far more short than long-distance passengers and the great expresses that hurtle through the land filled with a fascinating collection of minorities skilfully brought together.

We have three minutes less than an hour for our next 63 miles. The route is far from level, or straight, but it is well laid out and we have the power we need – though our Merchant Navy slips as we get started – and the second steward visits the extended front of the train inviting us to coffee and proffering luncheon tickets. We decide to miss that and the Tavern car with its mock brick and sit back. Through Honiton and its tunnel and down its bank at 85mph, through the centre road at a deserted Seaton Junction, and on we go . . . Axminster, Yeovil Junction where a handful of people are on the down platform waiting for the arrival of the day's first express from Waterloo, and then up and down beautiful, unspoilt landscape. We are now going through but are scarcely of the countryside and, after we brake sharply down downhill and come to a standstill at Templecombe; the stop is all about connections and not the local life.

We alight, see the Seaton coach added, and reflect that the Lyme Regis and Yeovil Town ones are on a following train that will call here in an hour or so, to be added at Salisbury to the up *Atlantic Coast Express* which will itself dash through on a non-stop run from Sidmouth Junction (with Sidmouth and Exmouth connections but not through coaches) to Salisbury. Though our journey is well into nationalisation, the routine has changed little over the years: there were wartime curtailments and shavings while Bulleid's Pacifics enable heavier loads to be carried at slightly higher speeds than during the 1930s. Oh, and there is now a 6.30 as well as 7.30am express from Exeter Central to Waterloo. More people seem to go on day trips to London and start earlier.

Fifty or so passengers who have arrived on the Somerset & Dorset Highbridge, Bristol and Sturminster Newton trains (the latter giving a connection off the *Pines Express* from Bournemouth) join the Waterloo-bound train, but of the similar number getting off, three quarters are young lads going to report for national service at Blandford. Since the Bristol–Bournemouth left ten minutes ago (connections from the West to Bournemouth are traditionally bad), we have to wait for 12.32 all stations except Corfe Mullen Halt to Bournemouth West, first seeing off the noon to Bristol headed by one of those famous S & D 2-8-0 freight engines that often fill in time on gentler duties and the 12.01 to Yeovil Town hauled by a Mogul.

We of course back out, a 4-4-0 at each end and reverse before going south. We have a Southern coach and generally this southern part of the route has become Southernised but (the train almost empty after losing the conscripts who alight with their noise at Blandford Forum) we do not regain pure SR metals until Broadstone. High tide makes it an enjoyable ride onto Poole, picking up three mothers with prams at Creekmoor Halt, and then we pass a succession of expresses and locals through Bournemouth's rich western suburbs before bearing right and dropping into Bournemouth West. Four hours thirteen minutes, everything on time, great contrasts of scenery, trains and speed. Our final thought is why Bournemouth has such a ramshackle terminus, making Exmouth's feel very civilised?

PLYMOUTH–GUNNISLAKE

The 'withered arm' they may call it, but there are excellent journeys to be savoured on the Southern in the West. Over the gradients to Mortehoe and down the curves with excellent views of the Atlantic to Ilfracombe's high-above-the-town terminus; along the Torridge past the Southern's own busy port of Fremington to Bideford; along the Camel into Padstow, if

One of three Adam's 4-4-2 radial
tanks that provided all power for the
Lyme Regis branch, the first to serve
a string of branch line coastal towns
down the coast to Exmouth, all having
a daily through coach from Waterloo.

you are lucky behind a T9 which always seems at home here and makes a magnificent spectacle when being turned in the evening sunlight. [The Torridge and Camel lines have been restored as excellent walks still with some railway hardware.] Then there is the grandly named North Devon & Cornwall Junction Light Railway where you will probably enjoy the very rural ride in solitary state as passengers at least south of Petrockstow are rare.

But for sheer idiosyncrasy take the 5.00pm from Plymouth Friary to Gunnislake. In 1 hour 21 minutes you will traverse 18¼ miles and apparently travel in equal amounts heading east, north, south and west. And [this is in the 1950s] you still do in a pair of LSWR auto cars with open platforms protected by wrought iron gates.

Friary is already on the way out. The Turnchapel branch has been closed and no longer does the railway make any pretence of carrying suburban traffic. We leave as almost the only passengers. There is the usual queue through Mutley and as usual we are late into North Road, and glad to be off the Western at Devonport Junction. Passenger numbers double at Devonport King's Road, the original LSWR Plymouth terminus; more at Ford. The train's purpose is now clear. It carries dockyard workers home. No business at St Budeaux and we miss Tamerton Foliot, but after we cross the Tavy estuary and enjoy the last of many glimpses of the Royal Albert Bridge we do brisk business at Bere Ferrers – where in the First World War dozens of young New Zealand soldiers lost their lives as a down express mowed into them. (They had been told they would be fed at the first stop out of Plymouth but that at Bere Ferrers was by signal and they got out on the wrong side.) And at Bere Alston business positively booms, as it does a few minutes later when the following Tavistock-bound train arrives. Geography protects the railway. Even the Brighton–Plymouth stops here and we pick up a few who have transferred from it as well as some dozens from the Tavistock-bound service which gives a faster connection from Plymouth to Gunnislake than our one daily through service. Indeed for the second time in this chapter we learn that through trains may be convenient but are not necessarily the fastest. Our engine has meanwhile run round for these ancient LSWR auto cars are no longer used for push and pull.

We zig-zag down the bends that heavy trains carrying the Tamar Valley's strawberries struggle even double headed coming up, and then have a magnificent view of the Tamar going into its gorge as we cross Calstock viaduct. We squeal into Calstock station, cramped and amazingly busy, and then get down to hard work. It is less than 3 miles to Gunnislake but the slog and the whistling at the open level crossings (for this is a Light Railway) takes all of the fourteen minutes allowed. As we climb the view it becomes even wider, but for the one daily train terminating at Gunnislake – the rest go over the moor to Callington – it seems positively wasteful to have to go high up above the town when most of the thirty or forty passengers immediately walk off down to it.

The tank engine leaves its auto cars in the siding and goes to the shed only it occupies. As we stand on the island platform we recall the great mineral wealth of the Tamar valley and the collapse of mining and the emigration that led to Cunard maintaining an office in Gunnislake. The newly opened railway was a godsend, and since Devonport Dockyard did not yet have electricity the times of trains changed weekly in spring and autumn to maximise daylight working hours. [Even today, dockyard workers struggle up the hill to catch the morning train, Plymouth–Gunnislake surviving as single-line branch with reversal at Bere Alston because the Tavy and Tamar bridges gave the railway a much shorter route than the road.]

FOLKESTONE–CHARING CROSS

In the early 1950s, the Kent Coast still feels a long way from London, especially on Sunday, even in summer, when there are huge gaps in the through service and only one express in the whole day offers refreshments. But this is still the era of solid Saturday-to-Saturday bookings, and Folkestone (still largely a holiday town) is obviously choc-a-bloc as we see from our taxi taking us to the Junction station [the one that survives today].

We catch the end of the symphony of a train heaving itself up the Harbour branch as we dash along one of the two island platforms: too late to identify the two tank engines in the front, but an R1 from the Canterbury & Whitstable section, an 0-6-0 with a cut-down cab and boiler mountings, and to a Western enthusiast a bit of a museum piece, is at the back. [Pannier tanks were just about to be brought in for the Harbour branch but this was not known and had it been would have caused considerable surprise for in the early 1950s the former Big Four still kept themselves very much to themselves.]

Then we have to buy singles to Sandling Junction, so to the booking office and back to find much activity, most of it purely local. Trains on the opposite island include a well filled excursion. Our 2.36 from Margate arrives a few minutes late, just after 4.15; we are alarmed by the number of passengers on board, but most again on local journeys alight, and we leave the Kent Coast only moderately full, though a full five hours have elapsed since the previous Charing Cross service, the one with refreshments.

Coming from the Western, again we are not over the moon about having only a 4-4-0 to take us all the way to London. The squat-looking School looks a bit like a compressed

Lord Nelson, but we have heard the class is not only powerful but that the power is flexibly available and often gives fine performances over the switch-back route to the capital. We certainly make a brisk start, and though we are all stations to Ashford do not hang about. Our coaches, by the way, are a mixture of Maunsell and Bulleid, more Maunsell and since Dad's work has gone well we are in its first-class version with a splendid distance between the seats. There is, of course, the ever-pervading special Southern smell; they must use oceans of their disinfectant or whatever it is.

Through the tunnel and first stop at the curved platform of Sandling Junction where we alighted on the down journey. The word 'junction' brings pangs of regret. We see that the track of the Hythe branch has already been removed. While most pre-war holidays were at Hythe, Dad always switched us to the private bus that took you to any part of town, no doubt a lot more efficient than being dumped up the hill where the branch train terminated. We used to watch the progress of its steam and smoke from the seafront. The closer attraction of Romney, Hythe & Dymchurch station always beat a determination to walk up that hill one day. But mother remembered how the guard of the businessmen's morning departure would tick off his regulars to make sure they were all present. Even when an inspector ordered him to start, he refused to do so until the last of the bunch dashed in a minute late.

A rural ride to Ashford, always a highlight. In pre-war days as now there were lines of ancient tenders and locomotives some presumably waiting for the next world. Today's bunch includes numerous SE & C 4-4-0s plus a couple of H class 0-4-4 tanks. But then the engines of the other trains we have seen or passed are nearly all pre-Southern and, while Bulleid's Pacifics dominate Exeter Central, they are conspicuous by their absence in Kent this summer Sunday. There are some ancient coaches of six wheels waiting their valhalla at Ashford, too. But we always dash past the works too quickly and come to what one friend called a 'stopping

Isle of Wight Central 2-2-2T on a Sandown–Newport train.

finish', i.e. brakes on hard, at Ashford station, a busy and welcoming junction affair. Though we are much closer to London than where we live, it still seems a different world.

The disappointment of this route is always that the dead straight section from Ashford to Tonbridge is not the racing ground the map suggests. It is a fascinating piece, up hill and down, in cuttings and on embankments, truly through the Garden of England, many fields alive with Sunday workers, the hops beginning to swell, the oast houses plonked neatly into the scene as though by design; but the miles pass slowly. Smart station work (amazing how the Southern manages that even on Sundays) means we left sharp at 4.47, but are allowed until 5.50 for the 26½ miles . . . and that's in theory.

It soon becomes clear that our ten coaches are quite a challenge for our School going up hill, speed varying sharply according to the grade. 'Bad coal,' Dad remarks; there is indeed a filthy exhaust when we climb, making the game of counting the oast houses quite difficult. We are twelve minutes late into Tonbridge, where many more passengers join but a malaise sets in, even the station work being a touch slapdash. Now our School finds the climbing really hard going. No longer on that dead straight route (on whose continuation by cross-country trains to Reading pre-war progress was also disappointingly slow, if compensated for by the complexity of through-coach and connection arrangements) we head north polluting the landscape and raising an ineffective noise. We pant with occasional slipping (there is now light rain) until peering out of the window we can see the signals against us for our journey through Sevenoaks Tunnel. Immediately they show clear, but the slightest touch on the brakes brings us to a stop at the starting signal, just short of the tunnel entrance. The driver alights with oil can, the fireman climbs his coal heap no doubt in search of more combustible material.

Silence. A few passengers poke their head out of the window but return to snooze or read the *Sunday Times* in which 'Spectator' is no doubt warning of the dangers of war with Russia. This post-war land is not all we had expected it to be.

Another School flashes past us on the down line, followed a few minutes later by a King Arthur in full splendour with as long a train as we have seen on this route. Only a gentle hiss from our School . . . but eventually the safety valve blows off, the signalman who returned the starter to danger after our halt again lowers it, and we are off . . . uncertainly at first, but then surely, if forty or so minutes late. The guard walks quickly along the corridor checking that all windows have been re-closed. Enough sulphur comes into our compartment even so. We seem to be underground for ever, though the lights that only feebly flickered at first steadily make it possible to read again.

Thank goodness for that; we are out in daylight, albeit gloomy daylight, and we cut quite a dash through Sevenoaks where the platform is crowded with people no doubt returning to London after the weekend . . . as many of our passengers are. 'Sorry about that,' says the ticket collector, accepting personal responsibility for the delay. 'Coal isn't what it used to be, and instead of running an extra train they will give us two bogies too many.'

Now we are in those approaches to London where you always see trains, electric and steam, passing, crossing, starting and stopping, like a huge but somehow uninteresting model railway system. We reflect how we wait for hours to see two trains cross at a characterful passing station on the 'withered arm' yet here, where there are trains, trains and more trains, there is such lack of our understanding as to what it all means and how it fits together, that we merely gape. Yet every mile has its intricacies, and certainly the driver cannot rush ahead mindless of the numerous curves and junctions. It is a challenging but not a comfy way to approach London. Much of the surroundings are positively hideous.

Many passengers get off (and more surprisingly quite a few join us; how long have they been waiting?) at the grand muddle of London Bridge and at the less glamorous part of Waterloo. We start crossing the Thames about thirty-five minutes late, noticing the abandoned Festival of Britain site and after a minor check take our place at number five platform. Charing Cross has been familiar since early childhood, and unlike its approaches it is fully understandable: one of London's smallest but by no means quietest termini, where when things go well, which means normally, the platforms are seldom empty more than a couple of minutes and drivers and guards of steam and electrics alike seem to play a game with just as much intensity as teams in the Cup Final.

Though we are in the front part of the train, we are not surprised that our School is already unhooked and the fireman combing through his coal again as we pass. Dad and the driver exchange wry glances such as to say better coal will surely be available one day, and if not, God help us. The rest of the family want to push straight ahead through the crowd to start queuing for a taxi, but the writer is anxious to take the scene in. Platforms 5 and 6 spelt many early holidays on that very different railway, the Southern, where they did so much with precision, where there seemed to be such goodwill and common sense, yet such backwardness . . . and again slowness just where you'd expect to move fastest. And there, as always, people are having to queue until the last moment (or so it seems) before being allowed to join one of the Kent Coast trains at platform 5 or 6. Somehow the more trains, the less significant. You never felt special getting on at Charing Cross like you did at Paddington or a wayside branch line station or even at one of those great northern cathedrals of steam. We didn't mind the lack of a refreshment car today since most Southern cars, even when the staff wore Pullman uniform and the sugar lumps were Pullman wrapped, offered pretty ordinary fare with service that was polite but no more.

Yet even on Sunday, the number of people, the number of trains coming and going, make Charing Cross feel the centre of the universe. The taxi queue stretches half way round the station square overlooked by that most glamorous of Southern institutions, the Charing Cross Hotel, even if its roof had once fallen in (obviously not built by Brunel). So ten minutes' freedom are allowed for a further look round. Astonishingly, the train we had only just seemed to get off has finished loading passengers and the ticket collector has closed the gate . . . that beastly gate that prevents you from getting on early or at the last minute and which the ticket collector seems positively to enjoy using as a weapon. Perhaps necessary here but shocking; the Southern does the same thing at Exmouth. Yet how would the Great Western cope with Charing Cross with only two thirds of platforms of Newton Abbot?

SCOTLAND THE DIFFERENT

This is an extract from the introduction to The Romance of Scotland's Railways, *1993.*

WHY, when we so enjoyed them, did we not make more romantic dashes by train to and around Scotland? Was it that we so savoured the memory of the trips we had done, that magic of train and terrain everlastingly demanding our attention, that we were nervous to risk disappointment in returning . . . perhaps to discover that the grand continuity of yesteryear had finally crumbled? Or that we felt we had to follow the crowd to the sun? For many it was undoubtedly the arrival of children that made it impossibly complicated and expensive, necessary to use our own cars and only furtively follow the rails, making do with a snack at a deserted Crianlarich refreshment room between trains, and a quick walk around Edinburgh Waverley or Perth General before bed.

How we regret our caution. For those rail-based holidays north of the border were always the best, ceaselessly opening new horizons. They had many ingredients but it was the holistic relationship between train and landscape that was unforgettable. And indeed the rails *had* been placed there for our enjoyment of the mountain, loch and moor. As the two labouring locomotives of your West Highland train climbed a mountain ledge echoed through the empty land, you suddenly heard (and felt the coolness of) the water cascading down to track level, passing underneath and plunging again to the bottom. It was hard to keep your seat for long; but then you discovered that fellow travellers, even Scotland's own, were not indifferent to God's beauty either. Often they would alert you to the gorge coming up on the other side or some especially fine vista.

The people were indeed an important ingredient, as different as the countryside, and Scotland's own Lowlanders just as excited exploring the more romantic parts of their country . . . always warm, communicative, as interested in you as telling you about themselves. And you wondered at how predictably those prim and proper elder women got talking about that taboo English subject of money. The people of course included the railwaymen who, as is recorded in later pages, often went to great lengths to ensure your perfect enjoyment . . . though it has to be said they were increasingly bitter about what their bosses were doing to them. You now have to be pretty old to recall the days when railwaymen thought their lot was improving, though always new services were enthusiastically welcomed.

Well into BR days you found that the locomotives (many surprisingly clean) and rolling stock were often very different from those south of the border, much pre-1923 stock surviving the entire Grouping period. And into the 1960s, even if you reached the junction by train that was Diesel-hauled, you might find that across the platform was a tender locomotive (sometimes quite new, more likely exceedingly old) at the head of a branch train in which you were almost certain to have your own compartment.

Another ingredient was – and still is – the magnificence of the great stations and bridges. Who did not feel himself excited having explored Waverley to take a seat in a tea car for the passage over the Forth Bridge (whose everlasting painting cycle was taught at school) and the Tay Bridge (alongside the cut-down piers of the first one that tumbled with a train in its high girders on that famous stormy, winter's night we had so often been told about)? Who could not marvel at the East Coast mainline's daring cliff-top route north of Berwick and before Aberdeen, or the Highland's romantic passes protected by snow fences?

The railway simultaneously epitomised man's triumph (with hiccups) over the elements and unique relation of past and present in the Scottish landscape. Until the 1950s, for example, you could see the rotting remains of parts of the great Caledonian forest (sacrificed when sheep became supreme at the time of the Highland Clearances) from the Far North line, and there were everlasting castles, battlefields, harbours, canal swing bridges and other places of interest such as Gretna (railwaywise more notorious for Britain's worst-ever railway accident at nearby Quintinshill than its amorous blacksmith who once attracted many lovers by train). Even with its accidents, Scotland's railways did things the grand way.

LBSC London Bridge with much going on but a grander station than today. To which line did the distance signal only partially shown apply?

A train at my home station of Nairn over a century ago. Highland Railway 4-4-0 No. 13 Ben Alisky of the Small Ben class.

THE SCOTTISH COUNTRY RAILWAY

Another extract from The Romance of Scotland's Railways, *1993.*

LONG platforms and even longer loops, solid yet mellow stone buildings, well-kept signals and footbridges, often colourful gardens and arrays of posters, even more concentrated activity between longer lulls than was normal in England. The Scottish country station, built for posterity and managed as the most important trading post for miles around, has always been attractive. Many happily survive in good order still in business and others closed as interesting monuments of a different commercial age.

Like their southern counterparts, they reflected the character and trade of their patch, but the difference was of course in the size of that patch. While those congregating at most English stations came from a similar background, in remoter Scotland those from totally

---

MAGIC MOMENT
....

An especially memorable moment was coming off the Crieff branch after an interesting saunter through the Perthshire countryside on a four-wheeled railbus, alas devoid of other passengers though luggage loaded at Crieff (where we occupied perhaps one fiftieth of the platform length) spilled from the 'van' into much of the seating.

Just as we came round the curve, with a prolonged view at a changing angle, an A4 dashed toward Glasgow with one of the three-hour Aberdeen expresses, complete with restaurant car, a busy one at that. But it was the head-on and then steadily angled view of the A4's streamlining

enhanced by a compressed chime from the whistle of the racing locomotive that made it a moment that could simply never be forgotten.

Mind you, it was distressing that the branch train *could* have been provided with a well-timed connection for Glasgow. This was not the only Scottish junction one arrived at by branch line to see an express dash through . . . and had to wait an hour or more for a slower train for the continuing journey.

The Romance of Scotland's Railways, 1993

different geographies and ways of life jostled for the porter's attention or best seats. And with rapid changes in the terrain, often adjoining stations might well have been hundreds of miles apart for all their appearance and traffic had in common.

Whatever their role in life, most stations fitted well into their individual environment. The use of local stone helped, but geography often dictated a picturesque position in the glens or beside lochs. On a long journey, especially if you had travelled from England overnight, just momentarily to step on the platform surrounded by heather-clad hills and breathe the fresh air was to experience Scotland.

Most of the country lines fell into two distinct categories: they were very long, with varied claims to mainline status and through traffic, or very short . . . like apple trees prunes the old-fashioned way with well-spaced (but occasionally overlapping) branches and fruit-bearing spurs. The English naturally mainly experienced the first category and were struck by the sheer scale (311 rail miles from Stirling to Thurso) but sometimes had the doubtful pleasure of changing to a branch off the branch to reach places like Banff or Killin. Many junctions only existed as such, not serving worthwhile local communities; several such as Killin Junction were indeed strictly changing places with no public access. You had to leave by train.

For most of the year, the Scottish country railway ticked over like clockwork, but unusual not to mention disastrous occasions upset the pattern all too soon: bad weather (much publicised but actually infrequent), Glasgow Fair and other holidays (very disruptive but lucrative), derailments and breakdowns far from help, and umpteen local events that just occasionally brought the whole world and his wife to nearly every station in turn. Relief shunters and porters moved on from one over-taxed station to another, the local men (especially the stationmaster) enjoying temporary importance but being pleased when normal routine returned.

Yet most of the year the same trains approached either end of their appointed crossing loops within seconds of each other, the signalmen controlling the loops seldom having to fling their levers and rush round with the tokens to save precious seconds. Many loops were rarely used, and when they were it was generally for extra livestock or fish traffic.

When timings went seriously wrong, everyone north of the border assumed it would be the reflection of problems imported over it, or because a ferry was running late. Until the quality of coal and locomotives declined temporarily in both world wars and permanently from the mid-1950s, locally induced delays were genuinely unusual. The enginemen loved their jobs and worked themselves and machines hard when the need arose. Most station work was exemplary, and more than two minutes crossing usually meant the other train was late or the engine was taking water.

Generous layouts helped, setting back into refuge sidings because the loops were not long enough hardly ever happened in Scotland as it did in parts of England, and the Scot who was delayed on the Cambrian in Wales because both trains at a crossing loop had to use the same single platform could hardly believe his eyes. In Scotland both platforms had proper protection from the weather, and fires would be lit in both waiting rooms even though it might be five hours before the next train. Some thought it was a pity there were not more island platforms as on the West Highland or more stations signalled to allow up and down trains to us the main platform when there was no crossing.

Just as stations serving wide areas brought together farmers, fishermen and others from totally different cultures, so many branch trains had passengers making the kind of assortment of journeys you expect to find on a modern air service. The range of opportunities provided by connecting services was incredible. Those aboard slower trains had ample time to satisfy curiosity about each other, and many a farmer improved his technique reviewing the passing crops with someone from another district or experience. Looking round guard's vans or seeing pieces of new-fangled equipment being unloaded not only satisfied curiosity but also helped spread new techniques.

The termini of short branches had their own distinctive culture. The actual despatch of a train seemed an anti-climax after passengers had chatted in the booking hall and the enginemen and guard had put the world right in the signalbox. Most termini were naturally designed for the exceptional rather than everyday traffic, and so much income came from special occasions that it would have been unthinkable to turn business away. But economical curiosities like engines changing ends by the train being allowed to pass by gravity were there for the finding . . . and extravagant oddities, too, like the mile from Killin to Loch Tay surviving decades after the pier was closed solely to allow the tank engine to reach its shed at the dead end without any siding or point. Wherever there was an engine there were onlookers and, like more conveniently but less splendidly situated sheds, this was a very social coaling and watering place.

Let us home in on the North East, a region that provides almost all the ingredients one could desire for a gourmet lunch or dinner. The very name conjures up thoughts of Scottish salmon, Aberdeen Angus beef and Scotch seed potatoes, Baxter's luxury tinned foods, shortbread, oatcakes, not to mention whisky. In days gone by all these went to market by rail, even if a whole salmon tended to travel singly, enfolded in a matting carrier, with the guard. It was white fish that provided the major flows; cod, haddock, hake and herring. Whereas meat and potatoes were freight-rated and journeyed largely in express goods trains, most fish was passenger-rated and in special trains moved faster than many passengers themselves.

Fish from Aberdeen and the area beyond was once enormous business and even by the 1960s still big enough for railways – in contrast to other Scottish ports further south and in the west. But fortunes change, in fishing as in transport; a combination of overfishing in the North Sea, the Icelandic 'cod war', the decimation of the mighty herring and other factors have brought long rail-less Peterhead to the forefront as *the* white fish port, with a corresponding decline in the others.

Many ports are but a shadow of their former selves. The likes of Eyemouth, Pittenweem and Arbroath increasingly serve local and Scottish needs. Ullapool lives by the Russian and Polish factory ships. That has been bad news for railways, which thrived on the long and heavy trunk hauls rather than on the odd van swinging on the back of a passenger train. In 1964, with the aid of outside marketing experts backed by the first moves into traffic costing, BR declared the fish traffic uneconomic and it was abruptly terminated – to outraged howls from the fish merchants' associations.

It had all been different in the days of the herring. Some surprisingly heavy flows – seasonal, of course – originated in the smaller east coast ports and in Mallaig as the shoals migrated. The picture postcard harbours in the East Nuek of Fife, Crail, Anstruther, St Monan's, Pittenweem, Elie and the rest could be bustling centres which came near to swamping the single line from St Andrews to Thornton Junction. Anything up to six trains a day had to be sent south where odd vans or open fish trucks usually sufficed. Empty vans had to be moved in and Thornton shed combed for power.

Another view of Nairn with passengers on what is Scotland's longest platform (ground frame signalboxes at either end, block instruments in the booking office and a bike for the signalman who will be busy dashing to and fro crossing trains on the Inverness–Aberdeen line).

Meat provided a much steadier flow. Aberdeen and the Buchan area is a volume producer of high quality beef with a special emphasis on the London market and the south of England. It was carried, hanging, mainly as full sides weighing over 700lb dressed, though with some half sides, and it was fresh, not frozen, ideally kept at about 38°F.

To deal with this flow Aberdeen ran a fast daily meat train to King's Cross Goods at 10.05. It was a solid load of BM containers, loaded at abattoirs in the city and surrounding countryside, travelling on conflats. From midnight the containers were craned onto lorries at King's Cross for the short haul to Smithfield market. Alas, from the 1950s it was neither profitable nor did it give real customer satisfaction against burgeoning lorry competition.

The lorries would load to capacity, then draw forward and stop suddenly; the carcasses closed up on the hanging rails and thus left space for another couple of sides to join them. Various moves to improve rail profitability led to train timings that were less than ideal for Smithfield's selling schedule. Rail transport of meat died before the Aberdeen freightliner terminal closed in 1987.

ON BOARD

This and the following piece are from The Trains We Loved, *1994.*

MERCIFULLY it is generally the things most enjoyed that are best remembered. So childhood train journeys, and those our fathers and uncles told us about, always seem to have

The photo that nearly got left out because I don't know the precise location. But it is so interesting that here it is. It's obviously on a route from London to the South Coast with a Bulleid hauling an express while to the right there's fascinating trackwork and a shunting movement.

gone smoothly in considerable comfort and nearly always with the sun shining. Not surprisingly, each age has loved the memories of its own trains: of the powerful locomotives of their day knitting the country closer together, new standards of comfort and on-board service and the element of exploration. Many journeys were memorable simply because they were novel, perhaps taking us to places (or for reasons) that our parents and grandparents would not have believed possible. The point has often been made that the great expresses of yesteryear displaying their destination boards had as little relevance to the population of the countryside through which they passed as today's hardware orbiting overhead in space. They were just better seen.

Many people thought the Great Days ended with the outbreak of war in 1914. Nothing like pre-war normality had been restored before Grouping in 1923 robbed every large railway (except the Great Western and a few joint lines) of its independence and character. Those who remembered the rich arrays of trains of the pre-Grouping companies always swore that travel (and particularly visits to those stations where routinely half-a-dozen or more different liveries were on display) were never again as interesting.

Helped by more powerful locomotives and more comfortable carriages, however, many new standards were set between the wars. The LNER's *Silver Jubilee*, *Coronation* or *West Riding Limited* and the LMS's *Coronation Scot* represented the best of that era, with aspects of caring for their passengers that have not returned since. Yet even routine travel on the expresses of the 1930s was truly lovable. Each train was its own individual entity, not part of a regular pattern, and had its staff and passengers to match. Graciousness and spaciousness were what we most remember. They had much to do with over-provision, the generous treatment of such few passengers as there were, few indeed compared with today. Not having a compartment to yourself on many services was a positive hardship. When the author's father arrived at Paddington on a summer Saturday for a train to Minehead, he was as amazed as he was upset that not even window seats were available for himself and his new bride. Of course he could have reserved space; there just did not seem any point in doing so. He had been a regular traveller on the former Midland route out of St Pancras, where feather-light trains of five to seven carriages including a restaurant car still had vacant compartments on almost every run. No wonder the dining car steward almost implored passengers to take a ticket from him after tempting them with the menu and a description of alternative sauces the chef would be delighted to prepare.

After the Second World War normality was far from being restored when again everything was changed, this time by nationalisation. Not merely was the post-war austerity deeper and longer but, with political change and workers less willing to be subservient, there were real doubts as to whether even 1930s standards would ever be attained again. That substantially they were, and in some cases exceeded, came as a pleasant surprise and is one of the reasons why so many of us think of the golden days of train travel as being as recently as the 1950s and early 1960s, and on some lines into the 1970s. The best on the routes were undoubtedly the trains we loved. We loved them at the time, soaking up every aspect of a highly satisfactory total experience, and we have loved them ever since and been upset by many recent developments.

Just what did the magic consist of? The list of ingredients is surprisingly long.

Accommodation was generous, geared more to peaks than troughs. On most long-distance expresses, including all named ones, it was extremely unusual not to find a comfortable seat except at peak times, such as immediately before or after a major holiday. Mid-week, probably over three quarters of those travelling by themselves enjoyed a corner seat in a traditional compartment, even in third class. Space per seat was as generous as it has ever been, much of the post-war stock having armrests between the three seats each side. Even in the limited 'open' stock around, windows and seating bays invariably matched. The seats were comfortable, finished in the contemporary moquette. The most common BR design had decorations akin to maps of minor railways, the largest of which from memory had sixteen 'termini'. Natural wood finishes were distinctly un-Victorian yet traditional, and the discreet notice identifying the wood used (there was considerable variety) added to travelling pleasure. The disappearance of the once-standard photographs of places on each railway's system was regretted, only a BR map facing a mirror now being provided.

Third- (later second- and then standard-) class compartments were so gracious that passengers were constantly checking that they had not accidentally trespassed into first class. Those who paid 50 per cent more for the ultimate luxury suffered just one drawback: the space between the facing seats was so great that only the tallest people wanting to put their feet up could bridge it. Greatly appreciated by the tall and large, it was said that the huge seats of the first-class compartments had been designed for the typical over-sized BR career chap. Small women sometimes complained they could not sit back in them at all, their backs being poised awkwardly in mid-air if their feet touched the floor.

Traditional Pullmans, including many with third-class accommodation especially on King's Cross services, were still in evidence adding further luxury; this was the age when the *Brighton Belle*'s breakfast kippers were much appreciated. Restaurant cars were a motley bunch but generally comfortable.

The first train from the resort is about to leave Swanage with a line up of staff that reminds one that one definition of a railway used to be a source of employment. The date is 30 May 1885. Once Swanage had through carriages off many Waterloo–Weymouth trains.

Cleanliness was good, and lavatories were never cleaner, at least on the top expresses where a cleaning woman was employed to walk up and down the train ensuring that all was in order, just one of the touches unique to this period. Another joy for passengers starting from London was that trains were ready for loading well in advance, usually at least fifteen minutes, sometimes thirty.

In these pre-motorway and air-shuttle days, the railway had no competition for speed and the fact that services on many routes were sparse was not much of a deterrent. On the contrary, once you were on board your chosen train you had the joy of much longer non-stop runs than can be found today. Indeed, one of the key ingredients of an enjoyable railway journey was the comfortable assurance that you would not be disturbed by the arrival of other passengers for three or four hours and could sit back and relax to the rhythm, enjoying the moist steam-heat and fresh air through the window. Though speeds were steadily creeping upward, few trains travelled for prolonged periods at more than around 80mph, at which point noise increases dramatically. Remember those top lights above the large picture windows with an arrow indicating the limits beyond which they should not be opened to avoid draught? Yet even now some double glazing was being introduced. Sealed windows and air conditioning were a by-product of faster Diesel and electric speed and, though now taken for granted, were never popular in themselves. Even few business travellers of the day saw much point in faster speed, reliability being regarded as the key issue.

ANOTHER ROUTE

ONE of the great joys of exploring Britain by train was that without extra cost your return journey could be by a different and much longer route. Even today there are plenty of opportunities for stretching a bargain, like going from the West Country to Paddington the direct way and stopping off at Swindon or Bristol on the return. But it is absolutely nothing

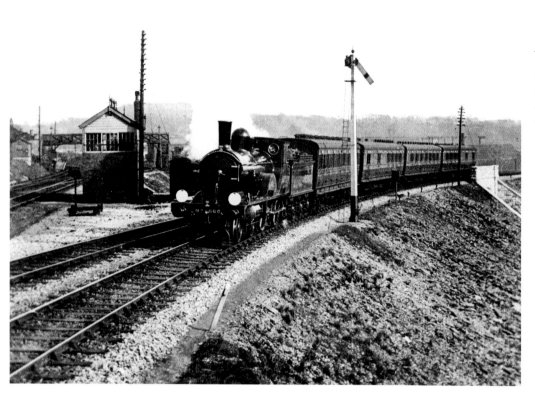

In 1908 an up London & South Western express is about to join the GWR's down line at Lipson Junction. Today no passenger trains use the curve but varied have been its uses over the years by Western and Southern services – especially in the days that Plymouth boasted nearly fifty suburban stations.

like it used to be. With few exceptions, today there is a definite route and anything else is at least out of the ordinary and much slower. Many of the trains we loved ran on parallel routes for hundreds of miles, or even took journeys that criss-crossed each other, such as at Carlisle. Who among us went to Scotland and returned the same way?

Another route. Just say those two words and the brain automatically recalls the great alternatives of yesteryear and the fun we had deciding how to make the best of our opportunities. 'Another Route' was indeed a heading liberally used in what might be described as the lazy Londoner's *Bradshaw*, the monthly *ABC Alphabetical Railway Guide*. Only being of use for journeys to or from the capital, and thus for practical purposes only for Londoners, it nevertheless had a substantial circulation and generations of hotel porters and individual travellers consulted it as the easiest way of seeing what was available. For enthusiasts, it usefully cited the fares for each route, 'Fares as above' of course implying you could return by the longer way for the same money.

Undoubtedly the most fortunate were those going from London north to places like Manchester, Edinburgh and Glasgow. Not only was there diversity of route but of restaurant-car trains as different as Catholic, C of E and Methodist. And while in many cases one route was quicker, there was often not much in it and one might anyway run at less convenient times. Or did we kid ourselves that the route we wanted to use was the one whose train left just as we would be ready?

To cite a few examples, Birmingham did have two nearly equal services until the London Midland's was effectively withdrawn to make way for the West Coast mainline electrification, after which the Western was a very secondary alternative. Birmingham business folk swore allegiance to Paddington or Euston, and when two of different 'religion' wanted to travel together it was like deciding whether the Catholic would go to the Methodist harvest festival or vice versa. Only perhaps in the Glasgow area were feelings more entrenched

. . . and there it was as much about which way to take the daily train to work as making an occasional long-distance journey. If the North Eastern Railway showed what monopoly could achieve, then Glasgow suburban services epitomised the glory of competition.

If you had 'done' all three routes used by through trains, the London to Manchester journey was one that called for especial deliberation. Euston might have a grand entrance but before rebuilding was a pretty miserable station to depart from and, while the train itself would be fast and comfortable, the scenery was not in the top league. Marylebone was a fun place to leave from, and the fact there were fewer opportunities to take ex-Great Central rails had to be taken into account. The end of the journey was spectacular and, since the completion of the first mainline electrification in Britain, the journey through the long Pennine tunnel was no longer a pain; but having to share the exit from London *was*, and the number of through services was limited. Against that, they tended to be less crowded, but the coaches could be dirty. The restaurant car was not as good: it was here we had been put in our place. The LNER did not serve Yorkshire pudding *and* horseradish. St Pancras was ever delightful. The train would be comfortable and the restaurant car probably the best, but it would be a short train and might be crowded. Again the later part of the journey was better, the passage through the Peak District indeed being grander than anything else on any of the routes. The train made more stops, seldom if ever missing Leicester, but Derby always gave a warm glow. Now, which way would you go tomorrow if you had to make the journey and all three routes were operating? For the writer it would have to be St Pancras.

No parking notices were ignored even between the wars but pressure at Bognor Regis, still served by a generous service, has seldom been overwhelming.

For most railway lovers it would undoubtedly be St Pancras for Edinburgh or Glasgow, simply because that has been impossible for so many years. When everything was still open and running, the choice was not so obvious for, while you would never waste a passage of the Long Drag over the Settle & Carlisle with your eyes stuck into a book, the extra time was considerable. You could indeed only do the journey sensibly by the one daily through train each to Edinburgh (*The Waverley*) or Glasgow (*The Thames–Clyde Express*). But hold on, what is the hurry? Why not break the journey at Leeds . . . but then if you went from King's Cross you could do so at York, or if from Euston at Preston and take that promised visit to Blackpool. The choice was endless, and it came back to personal preference or your railway religion. We just count ourselves lucky we could take each route in turn, enjoying Shap and Beattock, the Pennines and the Long Drag, the cathedrals and East Coast.

There was nothing stopping you mixing and matching your own route. Glasgow St Enoch to Carlisle by the Glasgow & South Western line through some of Scotland's finest non-barren scenery, to be savoured on a summer's evening after the LMS twelve-wheeler tea car came on at ugly Kilmarnock, and then south by the West Coast mainline since it would be too dark to enjoy the Long Drag. But then through trains, especially sleepers serving Paisley, also performed that trick.

Cambridge was another place that had you alternate between routes, though generally the ambience of the buffet car expresses from King's Cross won. As for a journey between Cambridge and Oxford, the choice was between not doing it at all, finding an excuse to do it *via* London or somewhere else, or treat the wretched direct train as a joke. The Somerset & Dorset was altogether more businesslike than the link between the great seats of learning. Many S & D journeys could of course equally well be taken *via* Southampton, but we loved the Joint Line and revelled in the fact that if you bought a ticket from Bridgwater to Paddington you could return from Waterloo *via* Templecombe . . . and occasionally save a minute or two on Western timings.

Sometimes we went from Marylebone out of homage to those who had put their faith in the Great Central, for here was a railway that hardly provided any journeys that could not be done equally well by another line. Faith indeed. We wondered what the hotel was like across the street at Marylebone when it welcomed the first passengers at the turn of the century, and despised the fact that, badly run down, it was now BR's headquarters. 222 Marylebone Road (nicknamed The Kremlin) was a hateful address, for while much of BR was super, the overall policy was and became even less attractive, culminating in Beeching's wretched 1963 report. The enquiry before the report had but one touch of joy: branch line closures were halted while it leisurely took place.

The era of the trains we loved ended along with many of their routes, certainly 'Another Route', with Beeching – the Great Central of course being a main casualty.

Glasgow to Edinburgh, Manchester to Leeds, Cardiff to Birmingham, London to Canterbury: we were not short of journeys where the choice could be sensibly made either way. But in practical terms one of the biggest choices was slightly different: whether to go cross-country or *via* London. From the West to Scotland that might involve leaving only an hour earlier for the same arrival time, and exhilaration of a fast trip to and from the capital in exchange for the undoubted delights of a cross-country West to North service (still *via* Hereford and picturesque Ludlow of course) but the dubious pleasure of being shunted away from a platform during the Crewe stopover. If we were interested in locomotive performance, accelerations of the crack trains to the capital began to sway things, and soon the cross-countries were anyway a dying breed. You could no longer get from Devon to Folkestone with a single change at Reading (and that after arriving there by slip coach), and East Anglia lost most of its through services, including the restaurant car train that had taken the Joint Line to Yarmouth and the Edinburgh–Cambridge service.

Cross-country trains had their own aura. Few had the most recent rolling stock, and most stopped at all major traffic points where a considerable proportion of the passengers changed. It sometimes seemed that only you and the restaurant car crew remained the same. Many of these through trains had run at the same time for decades, crossing or being skilfully interwoven with services to or from London on successive routes to the capital.

But so had many branch line services, and we must not forget that some services might involve taking a succession of all-station locals. One difficulty was discovering whether a return ticket was valid by our chosen deviation, as from Bristol to Aberystwyth out *via* Brecon and back *via* Carmarthen. If we could not do it by Monthly Return, the standard one-and-a-third times single rate, then there was always the Circular Ticket. That meant going to the local booking office and asking for a bespoke tour, subject to an attractive discount. You had to give three days' notice. But then such journeys were usually planned over weeks if not months. The only problem was that if they were to happen near the beginning of the summer or winter timetable, you had no way of knowing whether traditional connections would continue to be maintained.

In Ireland they seemed to insist on selling you tickets by routes that proved impractical and you were forever having an argument with one of the ticket collectors who seemed to appear with great regularity out of the bogs.

One other aspect of another route needs to be mentioned: the railway hotels. Mainly adjuncts to larger stations, they were railway institutions in their own right, in the days we are talking about almost invariably the best (outside London). Arriving in Glasgow by three different routes from England meant you could savour the delights of the showpieces of three former railways without going into the street.

RAILWAY PUBLISHING

The last in a series on the subject published in Review: The Journal of the Friends of the National Railway Museum *was on David & Charles at the editors' request, 2011. This is an extract.*

RAILWAY publishing at David & Charles was driven by passion and meticulous attention to detail. As the company developed, in terms of the number of titles we produced (once six a week), railways became decreasingly important, but they were what we started with and for what we were always best known, aided and abetted by being an essential part of the railway scene in Newton Abbot.

The series of which we were proudest was the Regional History of the Railways of Great Britain, which began with my own volume on *The West Country*. Setting the railways against the economic and social background, it contained more about agriculture, tourism, industry and population changes than any other non-academic title then available. All opening and closing dates were carefully included.

In five hardback and three paperback editions, sales exceeded 40,000, an astonishing figure for so serious a work. It was so epoch-making that booksellers stocked it nationally, and it was included in the library of most serious-minded people in the West Country whether or not they had a special interest in railways.

You can almost hear and smell London Bridge in pre-Grouping days.

As the number of titles published in the UK grew rapidly, such success was unsustainable though the rest of the series did well enough, most volumes needing at least one reprint. The only effort there has been to tell the story of all railways area by area, rather than on a company or line basis, it took a generation (thirty years) to complete. It owed much to my co-editor Allan Patmore, and to the fact we had to cajole some authors to do more research and improve perspective.

But then cajoling authors was part of the David & Charles brand. Several times a week I'd write an encouraging letter pointing out what had been done well, followed by a paragraph beginning 'But . . . can you do this and that?'

Success was in the detail, while part of our passion was the belief that a good subject should never be spoilt by a bad title. So with a small army of enthusiastic sub-editors, the editorial overhead was unusually high. We also insisted on good maps and carefully chosen pictures from different eras, some showing people and traffic carried, engineering features and so on – ideally pictures which made several prints which could be referred to in decent captions. Bibliographies and indexes were of supreme importance.

That is why we had the field of full-length, serious railway history almost to ourselves.

CHAPTER 13
FAREWELL

WHAT MUST BE A QUARTER OF A CENTURY AGO, I shared a table in the restaurant car on an express from Devon to Paddington with someone considerably older, who by now has almost certainly died. He told me that, having lost his wife and feeling lonely, he was moving to New Zealand to be with his family. 'This is probably the last restaurant car meal I'll ever have. I must say I've always enjoyed them. Come to that, this could be my last train journey ever.'

He explained that he increasingly hated flying and, having settled in New Zealand, would probably never return to Britain. 'New Zealand trains, such as they are, aren't great.'

As I come to say my farewell, that is a reminder that in many ways the railways have taken leave of older people before we do of them. New Zealand once had a dense passenger network. Although there are still plenty of reminders, such as a South Island township named after a long-closed junction station, the remains of which were still visible when I last visited, now there is little more than a remote pub there. Today's passenger lines are few. Since I began exploring the country in the 1970s, well over half the passenger mileage I travelled has been closed. The grand station at the large city of Dunedin is now only used by scenic tourist trains. The nation's railway system has been renationalised following a commercial operator steadily transferring freight to road. There is still a nationwide freight system, much occasionally traversed by tourist trains.

In Britain, the restaurant cars have said farewell to us. True, you still get refreshments of a kind on many long-distance journeys, but the whole experience of the trip has become

The railways and their trains south of the Thames never equalled the trunk routes to the north, but at least this Brighton express on the LBSC looks the part.

far less enjoyable, as seating has steadily become more cramped and we have been robbed of the invitation: 'Please take your seats in the restaurant car.' Sitting in a more relaxed atmosphere, enjoying fine food and wine and the banter of the stewards and conversation with different and usually like-minded passengers, was always something to savour.

In the days I was running the publishers David & Charles, having to pay visits to London, I had at least three main meals on trains most weeks, and they were uniformly excellent. In addition those from the West Country to London, there were restaurant cars; to London *via* Bath, Swansea, the Midlands, North and Scotland and, from Exeter Central, to Waterloo and Brighton. More restaurant cars passed my office window in a day than ran in the whole of Italy.

Cars seating forty-eight passengers were once the norm, but then came the High Speed Train, originally designed with separate catering cars for first- and standard-class passengers, but mainly built with just one, and only serving full meals on routes to London. Even so, keen crews retained their pride, laying out tables in half of the first-class coach (always referred to as the 'top car') next to the catering vehicle. Only two daily trains retain full catering on the route from the South West, and none serves the Bristol–Paddington route. It is the same throughout the country.

In many other ways, the railways have said farewell to us. For example, excursion trains, once offering cheap travel to millions a year, have gone; there's no rolling stock for them anyway. Only a handful of sleeping cars survive.

How glad many of we older enthusiasts are that we lived when we did. The surprising but good thing is that almost as many people still find interest in railways today as did in previous generations. Interest is obviously bolstered by the increasing number of preserved railways and steam specials and even Pullman excursions with full-meal service. Welcome though these are, for me the leisure industry is ever self-conscious, and what I miss is the everyday experience of yesteryear when stations were gathering points with their own fine restaurants where people from different areas would hold business meetings, and mail and newspapers, PLA, ice cream and day-old chicks were loaded in the guard's van at a platform outside. There was so much more to stations than just getting on and off trains.

I am delighted that steam survives in a major way, but I am also passionate about the future success of High Speed 2, Crossrail and much more planned but unlikely to be ready for my travelling days.

So as I rehearse my farewell, what is it that I have found especially enjoyable and interesting?

Firstly, the way railways gave me purpose. I learnt early enthusiasm from my father. His extensive 0-gauge model railway being Great Western, that became my 'team', support for it being the nearest I came to sport. We were used to taking lunches at station restaurants and walking out to spot trains between main course and pudding, and began each morning with a 'GWR station of the day', no doubt boring the female members of the family. There were early memorable journeys, including an untypically crowded *Cornish Riviera* to Exeter during the Munich crisis.

During our own later evacuation to South Molton, where life was pretty grim, the station and signalbox down in the valley over a mile from the town was a lifesaver. Meanwhile most issues of the *Model Railway News* carried an ad with me standing by the model railway featuring me as a 'lucky boy'; others would have to wait till the return of more normal times.

At school, back in Teignmouth, I was singled out for my railway knowledge, among other things, giving a young trainee teacher hell as she began telling us about railway geography by saying that everyone knew you went to Euston for trains to Devon, and went on to worse. An English master, planning a trip to Exeter, said 'Thomas, you aren't the only one who knows how to use a timetable,' and told me to be quiet when a girl gave a time of a Saturdays-only train for our mid-week outing. 'So that's arranged.' I had to tell him some time, and in the corridor afterwards blurted out it was a Saturdays-only train, and watched the class embarrassingly being reassembled.

When I joined the staff of the West Country's provincial daily, *The Western Morning News*, railways gave me a natural subject: as far back as the age of sixteen, my freelance contributions had been welcome, indeed helping me gain a job as reporter in the days of scarce newsprint and small papers. Thanks to the special popularity of railways, what I wrote provoked more correspondence than the output of any other member of staff.

It wasn't that I was especially skilled. I just cared about my chosen subject. As I am sure will be the case for many readers, I deplore frequent railway inaccuracies on TV and in the Press. Railways are so finite that, whatever people say – 'amazing but true' – you know that they cannot have been diverted by a non-existent route. Exactitude is the name of the game, though perspective steadily produces much of the pleasure.

The standard advice to anyone thinking of developing a writing career is find a subject. Half a century after my first broadcast, I found that I was the only one among a gathering of retired BBC staff who still occasionally broadcast. 'You have a subject,' was the comment. It is not that I'm only interested in railways – music and gardening are strong contenders – but professionally they have been my anchor.

My father had also written widely on railways, and when David & Charles got underway it was natural to do a joint book, called *Double Headed*.

In addition to a vast amount of travel around the British Isles in the David & Charles days, we were for a time very much part of the railway community at Newton Abbot, once described as 'railway and market town'.

Autumn glory. A London & South Western train is banked up a steep incline past corn stacks

When our address was the Railway Station, routinely, morning and afternoon, we served coffee and tea to the ticket collector, never paid for a platform ticket and I was regularly televised on the platform without having to make the formal arrangements and facility fee now necessary. 'Do your best today. Mr St John Thomas is travelling,' I heard crew being told when joining a London train. I could see the semaphore signals from my office and arrived on the platform as a train I was meeting ran in. 'On time again,' a porter pointed out.

The staff were the salt of the earth, welcoming understanding as suddenly their's was not a job for life. The railways' Newton Abbot payroll dropped from 1,950 during the war to today's few dozen. Once, all day long, shunting engines were joining and splitting trains, those from 'up country' losing their Torbay line carriages for the steep climbs over the Dartmoor foothills to the west. We saw that practice cease. Complete trains became for one route or the other. The carriage and wagon repair depot (whose premises became our warehouse) closed along with the locomotive depot. The 'Works' where broad-gauge locomotives were built and even 'Kings' repaired, had already gone, Newton Abbot's four signalboxes and their semaphore signals, and most of the Hackney marshalling yard all disappeared.

Railway contacts however survived and greatly helped in my railway journalism and broadcasting, which persisted throughout the David & Charles years and beyond. Not least were the string of new railway titles and enjoyment of gratis copies of the public timetable and sometimes the working ones. Another thing: on my way home at the day's end, I quickly reviewed the lines of Brutes (luggage trolleys) on the up platform to tell me, before the figures came through, how good trading had been. Exclusively using trains we won the Booksellers Association's prize of the publisher most rapidly to fulfil orders. Waiting for his train, an Archbishop of Canterbury was among regular purchasers from our bookshop. The railway and we were one.

Footplate trips were also aided by close management contacts though, as the world's largest publisher of railway books, they were easily arranged on business trips to Europe, the United States, Kenya, South Africa, Australia and New Zealand. In the Canadian Rockies twice I filmed ospreys fly off their nests with fishbone hanging out. The nests had been built on telegraph poles where they knew they'd be safe from gunfire.

Travelling 'up front' is a quite different experience, and a very satisfying one, drivers not slow to point things out and compliment or complain about permanent way gangs. Though I now need a doctor's letter, I still enjoy footplate rides on preserved lines. Overseas, I've been entertained in the homes of railwaymen, and here former staff remain among friends . . . as do countless enthusiasts who email the latest news and pictures. There is great unity but virtually no class distinction among the railway fraternities of most countries.

Irish railways have proved a great joy, providing *very* Irish footplate experiences and a totally different aura on both the broad-gauge mainlines and the former narrow-gauge systems of which only a few remained in my time. The loss of most freight traffic and increase in passenger business over a smaller system is echoed across the Irish Sea, but you have to visit say Dublin's Heuston station to realise just how greatly passenger numbers have increased. This handsome termini's traditional three platforms, including the Military one, have been expanded in stages to today's dozen, including three used by the Luas suburban system. A great disappointment is that the Irish annual timetable which grew and grew into a welcome spiral-bound compendium can now only be obtained online. Studying timetables for pleasure – often sheer joy – is something else that has been made so hard that again railways seem to have said farewell to us.

My father, brought up in Leicester, remembered the building and opening of the last mainline into London, the Great Central, and waxed eloquent over pre-Grouping days. My memories are quite different, and so will the next generation's be. In my remaining days, I record the stations at home and overseas I've used each year, still have my *Railway Magazine* bound each year to add to the set that begins with its opening in 1897 (my father was given a copy of the first issue by his father) and the fortnightly *Rail* about the present and future scene. There is a growing sense of optimism.

Possibly the greatest days of the train – certainly the fastest – are still ahead. Meanwhile I thank railways for giving me my *raison d'être* and a satisfying career, and hope my readers will have enjoyed sharing my farewell tribute in words and pictures.

A warm thank you to all (alive and to the memories of those passed on) who have shaped my enthusiasm and helped make this book possible. They include many former authors and railwaymen of all ranks.

Finally, a different Paddington, on our '0' gauge railway.